ENERGY SCIENCE, ENGINEERING AND TECHNOLOGY

NUCLEAR WASTE: DISPOSAL AND LIABILITY ISSUES

ENERGY SCIENCE, ENGINEERING AND TECHNOLOGY

Additional books in this series can be found on Nova's website under the Series tab.

Additional E-books in this series can be found on Nova's website under the E-books tab.

ENERGY SCIENCE, ENGINEERING AND TECHNOLOGY

NUCLEAR WASTE: DISPOSAL AND LIABILITY ISSUES

YLENIA E. FARRUGIA
EDITOR

Nova Science Publishers, Inc.
New York

Copyright © 2011 by Nova Science Publishers, Inc.

All rights reserved. No part of this book may be reproduced, stored in a retrieval system or transmitted in any form or by any means: electronic, electrostatic, magnetic, tape, mechanical photocopying, recording or otherwise without the written permission of the Publisher.

For permission to use material from this book please contact us:
Telephone 631-231-7269; Fax 631-231-8175
Web Site: http://www.novapublishers.com

NOTICE TO THE READER

The Publisher has taken reasonable care in the preparation of this book, but makes no expressed or implied warranty of any kind and assumes no responsibility for any errors or omissions. No liability is assumed for incidental or consequential damages in connection with or arising out of information contained in this book. The Publisher shall not be liable for any special, consequential, or exemplary damages resulting, in whole or in part, from the readers' use of, or reliance upon, this material. Any parts of this book based on government reports are so indicated and copyright is claimed for those parts to the extent applicable to compilations of such works.

Independent verification should be sought for any data, advice or recommendations contained in this book. In addition, no responsibility is assumed by the publisher for any injury and/or damage to persons or property arising from any methods, products, instructions, ideas or otherwise contained in this publication.

This publication is designed to provide accurate and authoritative information with regard to the subject matter covered herein. It is sold with the clear understanding that the Publisher is not engaged in rendering legal or any other professional services. If legal or any other expert assistance is required, the services of a competent person should be sought. FROM A DECLARATION OF PARTICIPANTS JOINTLY ADOPTED BY A COMMITTEE OF THE AMERICAN BAR ASSOCIATION AND A COMMITTEE OF PUBLISHERS.

Additional color graphics may be available in the e-book version of this book.

LIBRARY OF CONGRESS CATALOGING-IN-PUBLICATION DATA
Nuclear waste : disposal and liability issues / editor, Ylenia E. Farrugia.
p. cm.
Includes index.
ISBN 978-1-61761-590-0 (hardcover)
1. Radioactive wastes--United States. 2. Radioactive waste
disposal--Government policy--United States. 3. Government liability--United
States. I. Farrugia, Ylenia E. II. Title.
TD898.118.N8284 2010
363.72'890973--dc22
2010034017

Published by Nova Science Publishers, Inc. † *New York*

CONTENTS

Preface		**vii**
Chapter 1	Civilian Nuclear Waste Disposal *Mark Holt*	**1**
Chapter 2	Nuclear Waste Management: Key Attributes, Challenges, and Costs for the Yucca Mountain Repository and Two Potential Alternatives *United States Government Accountability Office*	**25**
Chapter 3	Nuclear Waste Disposal: Alternatives to Yucca Mountain *Mark Holt*	**85**
Chapter 4	The Yucca Mountain Litigation: Liability under the Nuclear Waste Policy Act (NWPA) of 1982 *Todd Garvey*	**111**
Chapter 5	The Federal Government's Responsibilities and Liabilities under the Nuclear Waste Policy Act *Kim Gawley*	**137**
Index		**145**

PREFACE

Management of civilian radioactive waste has posed difficult issues for Congress since the beginning of the nuclear power industry in the 1950s. Federal policy is based on the premise that nuclear waste can be disposed of safely, but proposed storage and disposal facilities have frequently been challenged on safety, health, and environmental grounds. Although civilian radioactive waste encompasses a wide range of materials, most of the current debate focuses on highly radioactive spent fuel from nuclear power plants. The Nuclear Waste Policy Act of 1982 requires the DOE to dispose of the waste in a geologic repository at Yucca Mountain in Nevada. This book examines the key attributes, challenges, alternatives, and costs of the Yucca Mountain repository, and the liability issues of nuclear waste disposal.

The Administration has announced that it intends to terminate the Yucca Mountain project and explore other alternatives for disposing of nuclear waste. Despite that change in policy, however, the federal government remains responsible for permanently disposing of spent nuclear fuel generated by civilian facilities, which pay fees for that service. Regardless of how the government meets that responsibility, discharging those liabilities will require significant federal spending over many decades.

The Department of Energy (DOE) has not yet disposed of any civilian nuclear waste and currently has no identifiable plan for handling that responsibility. Nevertheless, the operators of nuclear utilities continue to pay fees—of about $750 million annually—to cover the costs of disposing of the nuclear waste they generate. Over the past 25 years, those firms have paid a total of $16.3 billion for waste disposal services that they have not yet begun to receive.

The federal government is more than 10 years behind schedule in its contractual obligations to remove and dispose of such waste, and the government has paid nuclear utilities $565 million in compensation for costs incurred because of its failure to meet that schedule. DOE currently estimates that liabilities to electric utilities for such damages will total more than $12 billion if the department begins to accept nuclear waste by 2020. How the Administration's decision to terminate the Yucca Mountain project will affect the federal government's liabilities is unclear, but the estimate will climb if the department's schedule slips beyond 2020. Regardless of whether or when the government opens a repository, such payments (which come from the Department of the Treasury's Judgment Fund) will probably continue for several decades.

The Nuclear Regulatory Commission (NRC) has now extended the operating licenses of more than half of the nation's nuclear power plants for another 20 years beyond the span of their initial operating licenses. Meanwhile, the amount of existing waste may already exceed the amount authorized to be disposed of at the repository envisioned under NWPA. Ultimately, a change in law will be required to authorize DOE to permanently dispose of all of the waste anticipated to be generated by existing nuclear power plants at a site other than Yucca Mountain. Without such a change and steps toward that end, taxpayers will continue to pay utilities—through settlements and claims awards—to keep storing substantial amounts of waste.

In: Nuclear Waste: Disposal and Liability Issues
Editor: Ylenia E. Farrugia

ISBN: 978-1-61761-590-0
© 2011 Nova Science Publishers, Inc.

Chapter 1

CIVILIAN NUCLEAR WASTE DISPOSAL[*]

Mark Holt

SUMMARY

Management of civilian radioactive waste has posed difficult issues for Congress since the beginning of the nuclear power industry in the 1950s. Federal policy is based on the premise that nuclear waste can be disposed of safely, but proposed storage and disposal facilities have frequently been challenged on safety, health, and environmental grounds. Although civilian radioactive waste encompasses a wide range of materials, most of the current debate focuses on highly radioactive spent fuel from nuclear power plants.

The Nuclear Waste Policy Act of 1982 (NWPA) calls for disposal of spent nuclear fuel in a deep geologic repository. NWPA established the Office of Civilian Radioactive Waste Management (OCRWM) in the Department of Energy (DOE) to develop such a repository and required the program's civilian costs to be covered by a fee on nuclear-generated electricity, paid into the Nuclear Waste Fund. Amendments to NWPA in 1987 restricted DOE's repository site studies to Yucca Mountain in Nevada.

DOE submitted a license application for the proposed Yucca Mountain repository to the Nuclear Regulatory Commission (NRC) on June 3, 2008, and NRC docketed the application September 8, 2008. The NRC license must be based on radiation exposure standards set by the Environmental Protection Agency (EPA), which issued revised standards September 30, 2008. The State of Nevada strongly opposes the Yucca Mountain project, disputing DOE's analysis that the repository would meet EPA's standards. Risks cited by repository opponents include excessive water infiltration, earthquakes, volcanoes, and human intrusion.

The Obama Administration "has determined that developing the Yucca Mountain repository is not a workable option and the Nation needs a different solution for nuclear waste disposal," according to the DOE FY2011 budget justification. As a result, no funding for Yucca Mountain or OCRWM is being requested for FY2011. DOE filed a motion with NRC

---

[*] This is an edited, reformatted and augmented edition of a United States Congressional Research Service publication, Report RL33461, dated April 9, 2010.

to withdraw the Yucca Mountain license application on March 3, 2010. DOE's withdrawal motion has drawn opposition from states that have defense-related and civilian waste awaiting permanent disposal. Further consideration of the withdrawal motion was suspended by NRC's licensing board April 6, 2010, pending a ruling on related federal court cases.

Alternatives to Yucca Mountain are to be evaluated by the Blue Ribbon Commission on America's Nuclear Future, which held its first meeting March 25-26, 2010. Congress provided $5 million for the Commission in the FY2010 Energy and Water Development Appropriations Act. The Commission is to study options for temporary storage, treatment, and permanent disposal of highly radioactive nuclear waste, along with an evaluation of nuclear waste research and development programs and the need for legislation. A draft report is to be issued within 18 months and a final report within two years.

DOE's Office of Nuclear Energy (NE) is to take over the remaining functions of OCRWM and "lead all future waste management activities," according to the FY2011 budget justification. Substantial funding has been requested for NE to conduct research on nuclear waste disposal technologies and options and to provide support for the Blue Ribbon Commission.

Congress provided $198.6 million to OCRWM for FY2010 to continue the Yucca Mountain licensing process but terminate all development activities related to the proposed repository. DOE plans to reprogram the FY2010 funding toward shutting down the program.

MOST RECENT DEVELOPMENTS

The Obama Administration has decided to "terminate the Yucca Mountain program while developing nuclear waste disposal alternatives," according to the Department of Energy (DOE) FY2010 budget justification, submitted to Congress May 7, 2009. Under the Nuclear Waste Policy Act, the Yucca Mountain site in Nevada is the only location under consideration by DOE for construction of a national high-level radioactive waste repository. DOE had submitted a license application for the Yucca Mountain repository to the Nuclear Regulatory Commission (NRC) on June 3, 2008.

The Administration's FY2010 budget request, approved by Congress October 15, 2009, called for a halt in design and development of the proposed Yucca Mountain repository while continuing the NRC licensing process "consistent with the provisions of the Nuclear Waste Policy Act." Also as requested, the approved DOE FY2010 budget included funding for a "blue ribbon" commission to recommend an alternative waste strategy.

However, the Administration's FY2011 budget request, submitted to Congress February 1, 2010, reversed the previous year's plan to continue licensing the repository and called for a complete halt in funding. DOE moved to implement the Administration's policy by filing a motion to withdraw the Yucca Mountain license application on March 3, 2010, "with prejudice," meaning the application could not be resubmitted to NRC in the future.[1]

DOE's motion to withdraw the Yucca Mountain license application, filed with NRC's Atomic Safety and Licensing Board, received strong support from the State of Nevada but drew opposition from states with defense-related and civilian radioactive waste that had been expected to go to Yucca Mountain. State utility regulators also filed a motion to intervene on March 15, 2010, contending that "dismissal of the Yucca Mountain application will significantly undermine the government's ability to fulfill its outstanding obligation to take possession and dispose of the nation's spent nuclear fuel and high level nuclear waste."[2]

The U.S. Court of Appeals for the District of Columbia Circuit is considering several petitions to block the Yucca Mountain license withdrawal on statutory grounds. The Atomic Safety and Licensing Board issued an order April 6, 2010, withholding its decision on DOE's license withdrawal motion until a ruling is issued by the Court of Appeals.

The Administration's Blue Ribbon Commission on America's Nuclear Future held its first meeting March 25-26, 2010. The Commission's charter, filed with Congress March 1, 2010, calls for a "comprehensive review of policies for managing the back end of the nuclear fuel cycle, including all alternatives for the storage, processing, and disposal of civilian and defense used nuclear fuel, high-level waste, and materials derived from nuclear activities."[3] The Commission is to submit its final report within two years.

INTRODUCTION

Nuclear waste has sometimes been called the Achilles' heel of the nuclear power industry; much of the controversy over nuclear power centers on the lack of a disposal system for the highly radioactive spent fuel that must be regularly removed from operating reactors. Low-level radioactive waste generated by nuclear power plants, industry, hospitals, and other activities is also a longstanding issue.

Spent Nuclear Fuel Program

The Nuclear Waste Policy Act of 1982 (NWPA), as amended in 1987, required the Department of Energy (DOE) to focus on Yucca Mountain, Nevada, to house a deep underground repository for spent nuclear fuel and other highly radioactive waste. The State of Nevada has strongly opposed DOE's efforts on the grounds that the site is unsafe, pointing to potential volcanic activity, earthquakes, water infiltration, underground flooding, nuclear chain reactions, and fossil fuel and mineral deposits that might encourage future human intrusion.

Under the George W. Bush Administration, DOE determined that Yucca Mountain was suitable for a repository and that licensing of the site by the Nuclear Regulatory Commission (NRC) should proceed. DOE submitted a license application for the repository to NRC on June 3, 2008, and projected that the repository could begin receiving waste in 2020, about 22 years later than the 1998 goal specified by NWPA.[4]

However, the Obama Administration decided that the Yucca Mountain repository should not be opened, although it requested FY2010 funding to continue the NRC licensing process. But the Administration's FY2011 budget request reversed the previous year's plan to continue licensing the repository and called for a complete halt in funding. In line with that policy, DOE filed a motion to withdraw the Yucca Mountain license application on March 3, 2010, "with prejudice," meaning the application could not be resubmitted to NRC in the future. To develop alternative waste disposal strategies, the Administration established the Blue Ribbon Commission on America's Nuclear Future, which held its first meeting on

March 25-26, 2010. (For a discussion of policy options, see CRS Report R40202, *Nuclear Waste Disposal: Alternatives to Yucca Mountain*, by Mark Holt.)

The safety of geologic disposal of spent nuclear fuel and high-level waste (HLW), as planned in the United States, depends largely on the characteristics of the rock formations from which a repository would be excavated. Because many geologic formations are believed to have remained undisturbed for millions of years, it appeared technically feasible to isolate radioactive materials from the environment until they decayed to safe levels. "There is strong worldwide consensus that the best, safest long-term option for dealing with HLW is geologic isolation," according to the National Research Council.[5]

But, as the Yucca Mountain controversy indicates, scientific confidence about the concept of deep geologic disposal has turned out to be difficult to apply to specific sites. Every high-level waste site that has been proposed by DOE and its predecessor agencies has faced allegations or discovery of unacceptable flaws, such as water intrusion or earthquake vulnerability, that could release radioactivity into the environment. Much of the problem results from the inherent uncertainty involved in predicting waste site performance for the one million years that nuclear waste is to be isolated.

President Obama's FY2011 budget calls for long-term research on a wide variety of technologies that could reduce the volume and toxicity of nuclear waste. The Bush Administration had proposed to demonstrate large-scale facilities to reprocess and recycle spent nuclear fuel by separating long-lived elements, such as plutonium, that could be made into new fuel and "transmuted" into shorter-lived radioactive isotopes. Spent fuel reprocessing, however, has long been controversial because of the potential weapons use of separated plutonium and cost concerns. The Obama Administration has refocused DOE's nuclear waste research toward fundamental science and away from the near-term design and development of reprocessing facilities.

President Bush had recommended the Yucca Mountain site to Congress on February 15, 2002, and Nevada Governor Guinn submitted a notice of disapproval, or "state veto," April 8, 2002, as allowed by NWPA. The state veto would have blocked further repository development at Yucca Mountain if a resolution approving the site had not been passed by Congress and signed into law within 90 days of continuous session. An approval resolution was signed by President Bush July 23, 2002 (P.L. 107-200).[6]

Other Programs

Other types of civilian radioactive waste have also generated public controversy, particularly low- level waste, which is produced by nuclear power plants, medical institutions, industrial operations, and research activities. Civilian low-level waste currently is disposed of in large trenches at sites in the states of South Carolina and Washington. However, the Washington facility does not accept waste from outside its region, and the South Carolina site is available only to the three members of the Atlantic disposal compact (Connecticut, New Jersey, and South Carolina) as of June 30, 2008. The lowest-concentration class of low-level radioactive waste (class A) is accepted from any waste generator by a Utah commercial disposal facility.

Threats by states to close their disposal facilities led to congressional authorization of regional compacts for low-level waste disposal in 1985. No new sites have been opened by any of the 10 approved disposal compacts, although a site in Texas received conditional approval in January 2009 and might open in 2010.

NUCLEAR WASTE LITIGATION

NWPA section 302 authorized DOE to enter into contracts with U.S. generators of spent nuclear fuel and other highly radioactive waste; under the contracts, DOE was to dispose of the waste in return for a fee on nuclear power generation. The act prohibited nuclear reactors from being licensed to operate without a nuclear waste disposal contract with DOE, and all reactor operators subsequently signed them.[7] As required by NWPA, the contracts specified that DOE would begin disposing of nuclear waste no later than January 31, 1998.

After DOE missed the contractual deadline, nuclear utilities began filing lawsuits to recover their additional storage costs—costs they would not have incurred had DOE begun accepting waste in 1998 as scheduled. DOE reached its first settlement with a nuclear utility, PECO Energy Company (now part of Exelon), on July 19, 2000. The agreement allowed PECO to keep up to $80 million in nuclear waste fee revenues during the subsequent 10 years. However, other utilities sued DOE to block the settlement, contending that nuclear waste fees may be used only for the DOE waste program and not as compensation for missing the disposal deadline. The U.S. Court of Appeals for the 11th Circuit agreed, ruling September 24, 2002, that any compensation would have to come from general revenues or other sources than the waste fund.

The Department of Justice has since negotiated 10 settlements of the 72 lawsuits filed against DOE through February 2010 for missing the waste disposal deadline.[8] Under the settlements, utilities submit annual reimbursement claims to DOE for any delay-related nuclear waste storage costs they incurred during that year. Any disagreements over reimbursable claims between DOE and a utility would go to arbitration. Through the end of calendar year 2008, $406 million had been paid under the settlements. The payments are made from the U.S. Treasury's Judgment Fund, a permanent account that is used to cover damage claims against the U.S. government.[9]

Other nuclear utilities have not reached settlements, but have continued pursuing their damage claims through the U.S. Court of Federal Claims. Unlike the settlements, which cover all past and future damages resulting from DOE's nuclear waste delays, awards by the Court of Claims can cover only damages that have already been incurred; therefore, utilities must continue filing claims as they accrue additional delay-related costs. About 20 cases involving initial damage claims have been tried in the Court of Claims so far, of which four have reached final judgment, and about 52 more are pending. In addition, about half a dozen second-round suits have been filed by utilities that had already filed initial claims. According to the Congressional Budget Office (CBO), the federal government's current liability for settlements, final judgments, and entered judgments under appeal stands at $1.3 billion.[10]

Future Liability Estimates

DOE estimates that its potential liabilities for waste program delays will total $11 billion through 2056 (in current dollars) if the Department is able to begin taking spent nuclear fuel from plant sites by 2020, which had been the Bush Administration's most recent goal. DOE's methodology for this estimate is shown in Figure 1. The yellow line shows DOE's estimate of how much spent fuel would have been removed from nuclear plant sites had shipments begun on the NWPA deadline of January 1998. The rate of waste acceptance under that scenario is 900 metric tons per year from 1998 through 2015 and 2,100 tons/year thereafter. That assumed acceptance rate was negotiated by DOE as part of the settlements discussed above. The annual costs reimbursed by DOE under the settlements cover utilities' expenses for storing waste that would have already been taken away under the assumed acceptance rate (the yellow line).

The green and red lines in Figure 1 show DOE's planned waste acceptance rate if waste shipments begin by 2017 or 2020. Under those scenarios, DOE would take away 400 metric tons the first year, 600 the second year, 1,200 the third year, 2,000 the fourth year, and 3,000 per year thereafter. This is the rate assumed by DOE's Total System Life Cycle Cost Report.[11] At that higher acceptance rate, DOE would be able to eventually catch up with the amount of waste that it was assumed to take under the settlements (the yellow line). If waste acceptance began by 2017 (the green line), the backlog would be eliminated by 2046, and if acceptance began by 2020 (the red line) the backlog would be gone by 2056. Under the settlements, therefore, there would be no further annual damage payments after those years, if DOE were able to achieve the 2017 or 2020 acceptance scenario.

DOE bases its estimate of the total damage payments that would be paid through 2046 or 2056 on the amounts paid to date under the settlement claims. If damage awards by the Court of Claims (currently involving about two-thirds of U.S. reactors) exceed those assumed levels, then future payments would be higher than the DOE estimate in Figure 1.

Further delays in the start of waste acceptance would delay the point at which DOE would catch up to the cumulative waste shipments assumed under the settlement scenario (yellow line) and would no longer have to make annual damage payments. DOE estimates that each year's delay in the startup date would increase the total eventual damage payments by as much as $500 million.

DOE filed a license application with the Nuclear Regulatory Commission (NRC) for the proposed Yucca Mountain repository in June 2008, and has estimated that annual program spending would have to increase to nearly $2 billion (from around $300 million in FY2009) to allow waste shipments to begin by 2020 if the license were approved. [12] However, President Obama's FY2011 budget request would eliminate Yucca Mountain funding, as noted above.

FY2010 funds for the nuclear waste program, already sharply reduced from the previous year, are being used to close down the Yucca Mountain project, so it appears unlikely that spent nuclear fuel shipments to Yucca Mountain could begin by 2020, even if full funding for the project were to be restored in the future. Waste acceptance by 2020 might be possible if Congress were to authorize one or more temporary storage sites within the next few years, although previous efforts to develop such facilities have been blocked by state and local opposition.

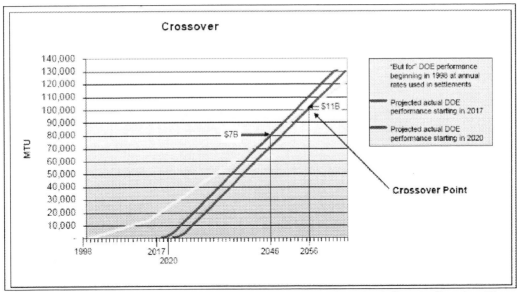

Source: Christopher A. Kouts, Principal Deputy Director, Office of Civilian Radioactive Waste Management, U.S. Department of Energy, "Yucca Mountain Program Status Update," July 22, 2008, p. 18.

Figure 1. DOE Estimate of Future Liabilities for Nuclear Waste Delays

Delays in the federal waste disposal program could also lead to future environmental enforcement action over DOE's own high-level waste and spent fuel, mostly resulting from defense and research activities. Some of the DOE-owned waste is currently being stored in non-compliance with state and federal environmental laws, making DOE potentially subject to fines and penalties if the waste is not removed according to previously negotiated compliance schedules.

The National Association of Regulatory Utility Commissioners (NARUC), representing state utility regulators, and the Nuclear Energy Institute, representing the nuclear industry, filed petitions with the U.S. Court of Appeals on April 2 and April 5, 2010, to halt the federal government's collection of fees on nuclear power under the NWPA contracts. The suits argue that the fees, totaling about $800 million per year, should not be collected while the federal government's nuclear waste disposal program has been halted.[13] DOE responded that the federal government still intends to dispose of the nation's nuclear waste and that the fees must continue to be collected to cover future disposal costs.[14]

License Withdrawal

DOE's motion to withdraw the Yucca Mountain license application "with prejudice," meaning that it could not be resubmitted in the future, was filed with NRC's Atomic Safety and Licensing Board on March 3, 2010. DOE's motion argued that the licensing process should be terminated because "the Secretary of Energy has decided that a geologic repository at Yucca Mountain is not a workable option" for long-term nuclear waste disposal. DOE contended that the license application should be withdrawn "with prejudice" because of the need to "provide finality in ending the Yucca Mountain project."[15]

The State of Nevada strongly endorsed DOE's motion to withdraw the license application with prejudice[16] and has moved to intervene in a court challenge to the license withdrawal.[17] Nevada has long contended that the geology of the site is unsuitable for long-term nuclear waste disposal.

However, DOE's withdrawal motion has drawn opposition from states and localities with defense-related and civilian nuclear waste that had been expected to go to Yucca Mountain. The State of South Carolina, which has large amounts of high-level radioactive waste at DOE's Savannah River Site, and the State of Washington, which hosts extensive nuclear waste storage facilities at DOE's Hanford Site, filed motions to intervene in the Yucca Mountain licensing proceeding to oppose the license application withdrawal.

NARUC also filed a motion to intervene in the Yucca Mountain licensing proceedings, contending that "dismissal of the Yucca Mountain application will significantly undermine the government's ability to fulfill its outstanding obligation to take possession and dispose of the nation's spent nuclear fuel and high level nuclear waste." NARUC's motion also contends that $17 billion collected from utility ratepayers for the nuclear waste program will be wasted if the Yucca Mountain license application is withdrawn.[18] Also seeking to intervene were Aiken County, SC, and the Prairie Island Indian Community in Minnesota.

South Carolina and Aiken County filed challenges to the Yucca Mountain license withdrawal in the U.S. Court of Appeals for the District of Columbia Circuit, contending that NWPA requires the licensing process to proceed. The NRC licensing board issued an order April 6, 2010, withholding its decision on the license withdrawal motion until a ruling is issued by the Court of Appeals. In the meantime, the licensing board noted that the NRC staff plans to continue its technical review of the Yucca Mountain license application as previously planned.[19]

(For more details about nuclear waste legal proceedings, see CRS Report R40996, *The Yucca Mountain Litigation: Liability Under the Nuclear Waste Policy Act (NWPA) of 1982*, by Todd Garvey.)

CONGRESSIONAL ACTION

President Obama's proposal to terminate the Yucca Mountain project and search for disposal alternatives has prompted substantial congressional debate and a number of legislative proposals.

Much of the debate in the second session of the 111th Congress has taken place in appropriations hearings on the FY2011 budget request. In a March 4 hearing by the Senate Appropriations Committee's Subcommittee on Energy and Water Development, Senator Murray sharply criticized DOE's proposal to eliminate funding for licensing the Yucca Mountain repository without an alternative disposal process in place.[20] Members of the House Energy and Water Development Subcommittee have expressed opposition to DOE's request to reprogram FY2010 funding provided for Yucca Mountain licensing toward termination of the licensing effort. Energy Secretary Steven Chu sent the House subcommittee a letter on

March 26, 2010, stating that the reprogramming would not require approval by the House and Senate Appropriations Committees.[21]

Senator Graham introduced a bill (S. 861) that would require the President to certify that the Yucca Mountain site continues to be the designated location for a nuclear waste repository under the Nuclear Waste Policy Act. If such a certification is not made within 30 days after enactment or is subsequently revoked, the Treasury is to refund all payments, plus interest, made by nuclear reactor owners to the Nuclear Waste Fund. DOE is to begin shipping defense-related high-level radioactive waste to Yucca Mountain by 2017 or pay $1 million per day to each state in which such waste is located.

Delays in nuclear waste disposal could affect the approximately 30 new U.S. reactors currently being proposed, because new reactors cannot be licensed without an NRC determination that sufficient waste disposal capacity will be available. Several bills have been introduced (see Legislation section) to prohibit NRC from denying a reactor license because of a lack of disposal capacity. Several recent bills would also encourage nuclear waste reprocessing and recycling, and would place the Nuclear Waste Fund "off budget" so that appropriations from the Waste Fund would no longer be subject to budget caps.

CHARACTERISTICS OF NUCLEAR WASTE

Radioactive waste is a term that encompasses a broad range of material with widely varying characteristics. Some waste has relatively slight radioactivity and is safe to handle in unshielded containers, while other types are intensely hot in both temperature and radioactivity. Some decays to safe levels of radioactivity in a matter of days or weeks, while other types will remain dangerous for thousands of years. Major types of radioactive waste are described below:[22]

Spent nuclear fuel. Fuel rods that have been permanently withdrawn from a nuclear reactor because they can no longer efficiently sustain a nuclear chain reaction (although they contain uranium and plutonium that could be extracted through reprocessing to make new fuel). By far the most radioactive type of civilian nuclear waste, spent fuel contains extremely hot but relatively short-lived fission products (fragments of the nuclei of uranium and other fissile elements) as well as long-lived radionuclides (radioactive atoms) such as plutonium, which remains dangerously radioactive for tens of thousands of years or more.

High-level waste. Highly radioactive residue created by spent fuel reprocessing (almost entirely for defense purposes in the United States). High-level waste contains most of the radioactive fission products of spent fuel, but most of the uranium and plutonium usually has been removed for re-use. Enough long-lived radioactive elements typically remain, however, to require isolation for 10,000 years or more.

Transuranic (TRU) waste. Relatively low-activity waste that contains more than a certain level of long-lived elements heavier than uranium (primarily plutonium). Shielding may be required for handling of some types of TRU waste. In the United States, transuranic waste is generated almost entirely by nuclear weapons production processes. Because of the plutonium, long-term isolation is required. TRU waste is being sent to a deep underground repository, the Waste Isolation Pilot Plant (WIPP), near Carlsbad, New Mexico.

Low-level waste. Radioactive waste not classified as spent fuel, high-level waste, TRU waste, or byproduct material such as uranium mill tailings (below). Four classes of low-level waste have been established by NRC, ranging from least radioactive and shortest-lived to the longest-lived and most radioactive. Although some types of low-level waste can be more radioactive than some types of high-level waste, in general low-level waste contains relatively low amounts of radioactivity that decays relatively quickly. Low-level waste disposal facilities cannot accept material that exceeds NRC concentration limits.

Uranium mill tailings. Sand-like residues remaining from the processing of uranium ore. Such tailings have very low radioactivity but extremely large volumes that can pose a hazard, particularly from radon emissions or groundwater contamination.

Mixed waste. Chemically hazardous waste that includes radioactive material. High-level, low- level, and TRU waste, and radioactive byproduct material, often falls under the designation of mixed waste. Such waste poses complicated institutional problems, because the radioactive portion is regulated by DOE or NRC under the Atomic Energy Act, while the Environmental Protection Agency (EPA) and states regulate the non-radioactive elements under the Resource Conservation and Recovery Act (RCRA).

Spent Nuclear Fuel

When spent nuclear fuel is removed from a reactor, usually after several years of power production, it is thermally hot and highly radioactive. The spent fuel is in the form of fuel assemblies, which consist of arrays of metal-clad fuel rods 12-15 feet long.

A fresh fuel rod, which emits relatively little radioactivity, contains uranium that has been enriched in the isotope U-235 (usually 3%-5%). But after nuclear fission has taken place in the reactor, most of the U-235 nuclei in the fuel rods have been split into a variety of highly radioactive fission products. Some of the nuclei of the dominant isotope U-238 have absorbed neutrons to become radioactive plutonium, some of which has also split into fission products. Radioactive gases are also contained in the spent fuel rods. Newly withdrawn spent fuel assemblies are stored in deep pools of water adjacent to the reactors to keep them from overheating and to protect workers from radiation. To prevent the pools from filling up, older, cooler spent fuel often is sealed in dry canisters and transferred to radiation-shielded storage facilities elsewhere at reactor sites.

Spent fuel discharged from U.S. commercial nuclear reactors is currently stored at 72 power plant sites around the nation, plus two small central storage facilities. A typical large commercial nuclear reactor discharges an average of 20-30 metric tons of spent fuel per year—an average of about 2,150 metric tons annually for the entire U.S. nuclear power industry. The nuclear industry estimated that the total amount of commercial spent fuel was 62,683 metric tons at the end of 2009, including 13,865 metric tons in dry storage and other separate storage facilities.[23] Counting 7,000 metric tons of DOE spent fuel and high-level waste that had also been planned for disposal at Yucca Mountain, the total amount of existing waste would nearly reach NWPA's 70,000- metric-ton limit for the repository.

As long as nuclear power continues to be generated, the amounts stored at plant sites will continue to grow until an interim storage facility or a permanent repository can be opened—or until alternative treatment and disposal technology is developed. DOE recently updated its estimate of the total amount of U.S. commercial spent fuel that may eventually require disposal from 105,000 metric tons[24] to 130,000 metric tons.[25]

New storage capacity at operating nuclear plant sites or other locations will be required if DOE is unable to begin accepting waste into its disposal system for an indefinite period. Most utilities are expected to construct new dry storage capacity at reactor sites. Forty-nine licensed dry storage facilities are currently operating in the United States.[26] NRC has determined that spent fuel could be stored safely at reactor sites for up to 100 years.[27]

The terrorist attacks of September 11, 2001, heightened concerns about the vulnerability of stored spent fuel. Concerns have been raised that an aircraft crash into a reactor's pool area or acts of sabotage could drain the pool and cause the spent fuel inside to overheat. A report released by NRC January 17, 2001, found that overheating could cause the zirconium alloy cladding of spent fuel to catch fire and release hazardous amounts of radioactivity, although it characterized the probability of such a fire as low.

In a report released April 6, 2005, the National Academy of Sciences (NAS) found that "successful terrorist attacks on spent fuel pools, though difficult, are possible." To reduce the likelihood of spent fuel cladding fires, the NAS study recommended that hotter and cooler spent fuel assemblies be interspersed throughout spent fuel pools, that spray systems be installed above the pools, and that more fuel be transferred from pools to dry cask storage.[28] NRC has agreed to consider some of the recommendations, although it contends that current security measures would prevent successful attacks. The nuclear industry contends that the several hours required for uncovered spent fuel to heat up enough to catch fire would allow ample time for alternative measures to cool the fuel.

Commercial Low-Level Waste

Nearly 2.1 million cubic feet of low-level waste with about 800,000 curies of radioactivity was shipped to commercial disposal sites in 2008, according to DOE.[29] Volumes and radioactivity can vary widely from year to year, based on the status of nuclear decommissioning projects and cleanup activities that can generate especially large quantities.

Low-level radioactive waste is divided into three major categories for handling and disposal: Class A, B, and C. Classes B and C have constituted less than 1% of the volume of U.S. low-level waste disposal during the past five years but contain most of its radioactivity. For more background on radioactive waste characteristics, see CRS Report RL32163, *Radioactive Waste Streams: Waste Classification for Disposal*, by Anthony Andrews.

CURRENT POLICY AND REGULATION

Spent fuel and high-level waste are a federal responsibility, while states are authorized to develop disposal facilities for commercial low-level waste. In general, disposal requirements have grown more stringent over the years, in line with overall national environmental policy and heightened concerns about the hazards of radioactivity.

Spent Nuclear Fuel

Current Program

The Nuclear Waste Policy Act of 1982 (NWPA, P.L. 97-425) established a system for selecting a geologic repository for the permanent disposal of up to 70,000 metric tons (77,000 tons) of spent nuclear fuel and high-level waste. DOE's Office of Civilian Radioactive Waste Management (OCRWM) was created to carry out the program. The Nuclear Waste Fund, holding receipts from a fee on commercial nuclear power and federal contributions for emplacement of high-level defense waste, was established to pay for the program. DOE was required to select three candidate sites for the first national high-level waste repository.

After much controversy over DOE's implementation of NWPA, the act was substantially modified by the Nuclear Waste Policy Amendments Act of 1987 (Title IV, Subtitle A of P.L. 100- 203, the Omnibus Budget Reconciliation Act of 1987). Under the amendments, the only candidate site DOE may consider for a permanent high-level waste repository is at Yucca Mountain, Nevada. If that site cannot be licensed, DOE must return to Congress for further instructions.

The 1987 amendments also authorized construction of a monitored retrievable storage (MRS) facility to store spent fuel and prepare it for delivery to the repository. But because of fears that the MRS would reduce the need to open the permanent repository and become a de facto repository itself, the law forbids DOE from selecting an MRS site until recommending to the President that a permanent repository be constructed. The repository recommendation occurred in February 2002, but DOE has not announced any plans for an MRS.

Along with halting all funding for the Yucca Mountain project, President Obama's FY2011 budget request calls for OCRWM to be eliminated and its remaining functions to be transferred to DOE's Office of Nuclear Energy. The Blue Ribbon Commission on America's Nuclear Future, which held its first meeting March 25-26, 2010, is to issue recommendations on a new nuclear waste strategy within two years.

Private Interim Storage

In response to delays in the federal nuclear waste program, a utility consortium signed an agreement with the Skull Valley Band of the Goshute Indians in Utah on December 27, 1996, to develop a private spent fuel storage facility on tribal land. The Private Fuel Storage (PFS) consortium submitted a license application to NRC on June 25, 1997, and an NRC licensing board recommended approval on February 24, 2005. On September 9, 2005, NRC denied the State of Utah's final appeals and authorized the NRC staff to issue the license. The 20-year license for storing up to 44,000 tons of spent fuel in dry casks was issued on February 21, 2006, although NRC noted that Interior Department approval would also be required.

On September 7, 2006, the Department of the Interior issued two decisions against the PFS project. The Bureau of Indian Affairs disapproved a proposed lease of tribal trust lands to PFS, concluding there was too much risk that the waste could remain at the site indefinitely.[30] The Bureau of Land Management rejected the necessary rights-of-way to transport waste to the facility, concluding that a proposed rail line would be incompatible with the Cedar Mountain Wilderness Area and that existing roads would be inadequate.[31]

In reaction to the Interior Department decisions, Senator Hatch, a staunch opponent of the PFS proposal, declared the project "stone cold dead."[32] However, the Skull Valley Band of Goshutes and PFS filed a federal lawsuit July 17, 2007, to overturn the Interior decisions on the grounds that they were politically motivated.[33]

Regulatory Requirements

NWPA requires that high-level waste facilities be licensed by the NRC in accordance with general standards issued by EPA. Under the Energy Policy Act of 1992 (P.L. 102-486), EPA was required to write new standards specifically for Yucca Mountain. NWPA also requires the repository to meet general siting guidelines prepared by DOE and approved by NRC. Transportation of waste to storage and disposal sites is regulated by NRC and the Department of Transportation (DOT). Under NWPA, DOE shipments to Yucca Mountain must use NRCcertified casks and comply with NRC requirements for notifying state and local governments. Yucca Mountain shipments must also follow DOT regulations on routing, placarding, and safety.

NRC's licensing requirements for Yucca Mountain, at 10 C.F.R. 63, require compliance with EPA's standards (described below) and establish procedures that DOE must follow in seeking a repository license. For example, DOE must conduct a repository performance confirmation program that would indicate whether natural and man-made systems were functioning as intended and assure that other assumptions about repository conditions were accurate.

The Energy Policy Act of 1992 (P.L. 102-486) made a number of changes in the nuclear waste regulatory system, particularly that EPA must issue new environmental standards specifically for the Yucca Mountain repository site. General EPA repository standards previously issued and subsequently revised no longer apply to Yucca Mountain. DOE and NRC had raised concern that some of EPA's general standards might be impossible or impractical to meet at Yucca Mountain.[34]

The new standards, which limit the radiation dose that the repository could impose on individual members of the public, were required to be consistent with the findings of a study by the National Academy of Sciences (NAS), which was issued August 1, 1 995.[35] The NAS study recommended that the Yucca Mountain environmental standards establish a limit on risk to individuals near the repository, rather than setting specific limits for the releases of radioactive material or on radioactive doses, as under previous EPA standards. The NAS study also examined the potential for human intrusion into the repository and found no scientific basis for predicting human behavior thousands of years into the future.

Pursuant to the Energy Policy Act, EPA published its proposed Yucca Mountain radiation protection standards on August 27, 1999. The proposal would have limited annual radiation doses to 15 millirems for the "reasonably maximally exposed individual," and to 4 millirems from groundwater exposure, for the first 10,000 years of repository operation. EPA calculated that its standard would result in an annual risk of fatal cancer for the maximally exposed individual of seven chances in a million. The nuclear industry criticized the EPA proposal as being unnecessarily stringent, particularly the groundwater standard. On the other hand, environmental groups contended that the 10,000-year standard proposed by EPA was too short, because DOE had projected that radioactive releases from the repository would peak after about 400,000 years.

EPA issued its final Yucca Mountain standards on June 6, 2001. The final standards included most of the major provisions of the proposed version, including the 15 millirem overall exposure limit and the 4 millirem groundwater limit. Despite the Department's opposition to the EPA standards, DOE's site suitability evaluation determined that the Yucca Mountain site would be able to meet them. NRC revised its repository regulations September 7, 2001, to conform to the EPA standards.

A three-judge U.S. Court of Appeals panel on July 9, 2004, struck down the 10,000-year regulatory compliance period in the EPA and NRC Yucca Mountain standards.[36] The court ruled that the 10,000-year period was inconsistent with the NAS study on which the Energy Policy Act required the Yucca Mountain regulations to be based. In fact, the court found, the NAS study had specifically rejected a 10,000-year compliance period because of analysis that showed peak radioactive exposures from the repository would take place several hundred thousand years in the future.

In response to the court decision, EPA proposed a new version of the Yucca Mountain standards on August 9, 2005. The proposal would have retained the dose limits of the previous standard for the first 10,000 years but allowed a higher annual dose of 350 millirems for the period of 10,000 years through 1 million years. EPA also proposed to base the post-10,000-year Yucca Mountain standard on the median dose, rather than the mean, potentially making it easier to meet.[37] Nevada state officials called EPA's proposed standard far too lenient and charged that it was "unlawful and arbitrary."[38]

EPA issued its final rule to amend the Yucca Mountain standards on September 30, 2008. The final rule reduces the annual dose limit during the period of 10,000 through 1 million years from the proposed 350 millirems to 100 millirems, which the agency contended was consistent with international standards. Under the final rule, compliance with the post-10,000-year standard will be based on the arithmetic mean of projected doses, rather than the median as proposed. The 4 millirem groundwater standard will continue to apply only to the first 10,000 years.[39] NRC revised its repository licensing regulations to conform to the new EPA standards on April 13, 2009.[40] (For more information, see CRS Report RL34698, *EPA's Final Health and Safety Standard for Yucca Mountain*, by Bonnie C. Gitlin.)

DOE estimated in its June 2008 Final Supplemental Environmental Impact Statement (FSEIS) for the Yucca Mountain repository that the maximum mean annual individual dose after 10,000 years would be 2 millirems. That is substantially below the level estimated by the 2002 Final Environmental Impact Statement, which calculated that the peak doses—occurring after 400,000 years—would be about 150 millirems (Volume 1, Chapter 5). The FSEIS attributed the reduction to changes in DOE's computer model and in the assumptions used, noting that "various elements of DOE's modeling approach may be challenged as part of the NRC licensing process."[41]

Alternative Technologies

Several alternatives to the geologic disposal of spent fuel have been studied by DOE and its predecessor agencies, as well as technologies that might reduce waste disposal risks.

However, most of these technologies involve large technical obstacles, uncertain costs, and potential public opposition.

Among the primary long-term disposal alternatives to geologic repositories are disposal below the seabed and transport into space, neither of which is currently being studied by DOE. Other technologies have been studied that, while probably not replacing geologic disposal, might make geologic disposal safer and more predictable. Chief among these is the reprocessing or "recycling" of spent fuel so that plutonium, uranium, and other long-lived radionuclides could be converted to faster-decaying fission products in special nuclear reactors or particle accelerators.

Funding

President Obama's FY2011 budget would provide no funding for Yucca Mountain or OCRWM. Alternatives to Yucca Mountain are to be evaluated by the Blue Ribbon Commission on America's Nuclear Future, for which $5 million was included in the FY2010 Energy and Water Development Appropriations Act.

DOE's Office of Nuclear Energy (NE) is to take over the remaining functions of OCRWM and "lead all future waste management activities," according to DOE's budget justification. Substantial funding is being requested for NE to conduct research on nuclear waste disposal technologies and options and to provide support for the Blue Ribbon Commission.

President Obama's budget request for FY2010 had called for termination of the Yucca Mountain project but included $198.6 million to continue the Yucca Mountain licensing process and fund the Blue Ribbon Commission. Congress ultimately approved the Administration's OCRWM budget as requested. As a result, all work related solely to preparing for construction and operation of the Yucca Mountain repository is being halted during FY2010, according to DOE. The FY2011 budget request would halt the licensing process as well, and, as noted, DOE has informed the House and Senate Appropriations Committees that it will reprogram OCRWM's FY2010 funding toward shutdown of the program and has moved to withdraw the Yucca Mountain license application.

Table 1. DOE Civilian Spent Fuel Management Funding (in millions of current dollars)

Program	FY2007 Approp.	FY2008 Approp.	FY2009 Approp.	FY2010 Approp.	FY2011 Request
Yucca Mountain	298.1	267.1	183.3	116.1	0
Transportation	35.3	18.3	2.1	0	0
Management and Integration	46.7	26.4	26.2	10.7	0
Program Direction and Other	64.4	69.8	76.8	70.0	0
Total	**445.7**	**386.4**	**288.4**	**196.8**	**0**
Source of Funding					
Nuclear Waste Fund appropriations	99.2	187.3	145.4	98.4	0
Defense waste appropriations	346.5	199.2	143.0	98.4	0

Sources: DOE FY2011 Congressional Budget Request, H.Rept. 111-203, S.Rept. 111-45.

During consideration of the FY2010 budget request, the House Appropriations Committee had stipulated that the Blue Ribbon Commission consider the continuation of the Yucca Mountain project under current law as one of the future waste management alternatives, and the Senate Appropriations Committee had called for the Secretary of Energy to suspend the Nuclear Waste Fee on nuclear power generation, which pays for the waste program. However, both provisions were dropped in conference.

Funding for the nuclear waste program has historically been provided under two appropriations accounts, as shown in Table 1. These accounts are, first, appropriations from the Nuclear Waste Fund, which holds fees paid by nuclear utilities, and, second, the Defense Nuclear Waste Disposal account, which pays for disposal of high-level waste from the nuclear weapons program.

NRC is requesting $10 million from the Nuclear Waste Fund in FY20 11 for the Yucca Mountain licensing process. In light of DOE's motion to withdraw the Yucca Mountain license application, the NRC funding request would cover the costs of adjudicating the license withdrawal motion as well as "work related to an orderly closure of the agency's Yucca Mountain licensing support activities such as archiving material, knowledge capture and management, and maintenance of certain electronic systems," according to NRC's budget presentation.

Although nuclear utilities pay fees to the Nuclear Waste Fund to cover the disposal costs of civilian nuclear spent fuel, DOE cannot spend the money in the fund until it is appropriated by Congress. Through January 31, 2010, utility nuclear waste fees and interest totaled $31.69 billion, of which $7.41 billion had been disbursed to the waste disposal program, according to DOE's program summary report, leaving a balance of $24.276 billion in the Nuclear Waste Fund. In addition to the disbursements from the Nuclear Waste Fund, the waste disposal program received defense waste disposal appropriations totaling $3.974 billion through FY2010, according to DOE.[42]

DOE's most recent update of its Analysis of the Total System Life Cycle Cost of the Civilian Radioactive Waste Management Program was released on August 5, 2008.[43] According to that estimate, the Yucca Mountain program would cost $96.2 billion in 2007 dollars from the beginning of the program in 1983 to repository closure in 2133. DOE's previous estimate, issued in 2001, was $57.5 billion in 2000 dollars. Major factors in the increase are inflation and a higher estimate of spent fuel to be generated by existing reactors. Spent fuel from proposed new reactors is not included in the cost estimate.

Low-Level Radioactive Waste

Current Policy

Selecting disposal sites for low-level radioactive waste, which generally consists of low concentrations of relatively short-lived radionuclides, is authorized to be conducted by states under the 1980 Low-Level Radioactive Waste Policy Act and 1985 amendments. Most states have joined congressionally approved interstate compacts to handle low-level waste disposal. Under the 1985 amendments, the nation's three (at that time) operating commercial low-level waste disposal facilities could start refusing to accept waste from outside their regional interstate compacts after the end of 1992. One of the three sites closed, and the remaining two are using their congressionally granted authority to prohibit waste from outside their regional compacts. Another site, in Utah, has since become available nationwide for most Class A low-level waste, but no site is currently open to nationwide disposal of all major types of low-level waste.

Despite the 1992 deadline, no new disposal sites have been opened under the Low-Level Waste Act. Legislation providing congressional consent to a disposal compact among Texas, Maine, and Vermont was signed by President Clinton September 20, 1998 (P.L. 105-236). However, on October 22, 1998, a proposed disposal site near Sierra Blanca, Texas, was rejected by the Texas Natural Resource Conservation Commission, and Maine has since withdrawn. Texas Governor Perry signed legislation June 20, 2003, authorizing the Texas Commission on Environmental Quality (TCEQ) to license adjoining disposal facilities for commercial and federally generated low-level waste. Pursuant to that statute, an application to build a disposal facility for commercial and federal low-level waste in Andrews County, Texas, was filed August 2, 2004, by Waste Control Specialists LLC. TCEQ voted January 14, 2009, to issue the license after the necessary land and mineral rights have been acquired.[44] Waste Control Specialists has predicted that the facility could start receiving waste by mid-2010.[45]

The Midwestern Compact voted June 26, 1997, to halt development of a disposal facility in Ohio. Nebraska regulators rejected a proposed waste site for the Central Compact December 21, 1998, drawing a lawsuit from five utilities in the region. A U.S. district court judge ruled September 30, 2002, that Nebraska had exercised bad faith in disapproving the site and ordered the state to pay $151 million to the compact. A settlement was reached August 9, 2004, resulting in a payment of $145.8 million,[46] and the compact is seeking access to the planned Texas disposal facility. Most other regional disposal compacts and individual states that have not joined compacts are making little progress toward finding disposal sites.

The disposal facility at Barnwell, South Carolina, is currently accepting all Class A, B, and C low-level waste from the Atlantic Compact (formerly the Northeast Compact), in which South Carolina joined original members Connecticut and New Jersey on July 1, 2000. Under the compact, South Carolina can limit the use of the Barnwell facility to the three compact members, and a state law enacted in June 2000 phased out acceptance of non-compact waste through June 30, 2008. The Barnwell facility previously had stopped accepting waste from outside the Southeast Compact at the end of June 1994. The Southeast Compact Commission in May 1995 twice rejected a South Carolina proposal to open the Barnwell site to waste generators outside the Southeast and to bar access to North Carolina until that state opened a new regional disposal facility, as required by the compact. The rejection of those proposals led the South Carolina General Assembly to vote in 1995 to withdraw from the Southeast Compact and begin accepting waste at Barnwell from all states but North Carolina. North Carolina withdrew from the Southeast Compact July 26, 1999.

The only other existing disposal facility for all three major classes of low-level waste is at Hanford, Washington. Controlled by the Northwest Compact, the Hanford site will continue taking waste from the neighboring Rocky Mountain Compact under a contract. Since the South Carolina facility closed to out-of-region waste, the 36 states and the District of Columbia that are outside the Northwest, Rocky Mountain, and Atlantic Compacts have had no disposal site for Class B and C low-level waste. Waste generators in those states must store their Class B and C waste on site until new disposal sites are available.

Regulatory Requirements

Licensing of commercial low-level waste facilities is carried out under the Atomic Energy Act by NRC or by "agreement states" with regulatory programs approved by NRC. NRC regulations governing low-level waste licenses must conform to general environmental protection standards and radiation protection guidelines issued by EPA. Transportation of low-level waste is jointly regulated by NRC and the Department of Transportation.

Most states considering new or expanded low-level waste disposal facilities, including Texas and Utah, are agreement states. Most states, both agreement and non-agreement, have established substantially stricter technical requirements for low-level waste disposal than NRC's, such as banning shallow land burial and requiring concrete bunkers and other engineered barriers. NRC would issue the licenses in non-agreement states.

CONCLUDING DISCUSSION

Disposal of radioactive waste will be a key issue in the continuing nuclear power debate. Without a national disposal system, spent fuel from nuclear power plants must be stored on-site indefinitely. This situation may raise public concern near proposed reactor sites, particularly at sites without existing reactors where spent nuclear fuel is already stored.

Under current law, the federal government's nuclear waste disposal policy is focused on the Yucca Mountain site. However, President Obama's plan to terminate the Yucca Mountain project and develop a new waste strategy through the Blue Ribbon Commission on America's Nuclear Future has brought most activities in the DOE waste program to a halt. Congress will consider the project's termination during the FY2011 appropriations process.

Because of their waste-disposal contracts with DOE, owners of existing reactors are likely to continue seeking damages from the federal government if disposal delays continue. DOE's 2004 settlement with the nation's largest nuclear operator, Exelon, could require payments of up to $600 million from the federal judgment fund, for example. DOE estimates that payments could rise to $11 billion if the federal government cannot begin taking waste from reactor sites before 2020, as previously planned. The nuclear industry has predicted that future damages could reach tens of billions of dollars if the federal disposal program fails altogether.

Lack of a nuclear waste disposal system could also affect the licensing of proposed new nuclear plants, both because of NRC licensing guidelines and various state laws.[47] In addition, further repository delays could force DOE to miss compliance deadlines for defense waste disposal.

Problems being created by nuclear waste disposal delays are expected to be addressed by the Blue Ribbon Commission. Major options include centralized interim storage, continued storage at existing nuclear sites, reprocessing and waste treatment technology, development of alternative repository sites, or a combination. Given the delays resulting from the ongoing shutdown of the nuclear waste program, longer on-site storage is almost a certainty under any option. Any of the options would also face intense controversy, especially among states and regions that might be potential hosts for future waste facilities. As a result, substantial debate would be expected over any proposals to change the Nuclear Waste Policy Act.

LEGISLATION

H.R. 513 (Forbes)

New Manhattan Project for Energy Independence. Includes grants and prizes for nuclear waste treatment technology. Introduced January 14, 2009; referred to Committee on Science and Technology.

H.R. 2250 (Burton)

Energy Independence Now Act of 2009. Includes a provision prohibiting the Nuclear Regulatory Commission from denying a nuclear reactor license because of a lack of nuclear waste disposal capacity. Introduced May 5, 2009; referred to multiple committees.

H.R. 2300 (Rob Bishop)

Among other provisions, would authorize DOE to enter into temporary spent nuclear fuel storage agreements with volunteer sites, establish payments to settle nuclear utility breach-of-contract claims for DOE waste disposal delays, and prohibit NRC from considering nuclear waste storage when licensing new nuclear facilities. Introduced May 7, 2009; referred to multiple committees.

H.R. 2539 (Thornberry)

No More Excuses Energy Act of 2009. Includes a provision prohibiting the Nuclear Regulatory Commission from denying a nuclear reactor license because of a lack of nuclear waste disposal capacity. Introduced May 5, 2009; referred to multiple committees.

H.R. 3183 (Pastor)

Energy and Water Development and Related Agencies Appropriations Act, 2010. Includes funding for nuclear waste programs. Reported as an original measure by the House Appropriations Committee July 13, 2009. Passed House July 17, 2009, by vote of 320-97 (H.Rept. 111-203); passed Senate July 29, 2009, by vote of 85-9 (S.Rept. 111-45). Signed by the President October 28, 2009 (P.L. 111-85).

H.R. 3385 (Barton)

Would authorize DOE to use the Nuclear Waste Fund to pay for grants or long-term contracts for spent nuclear fuel recycling or reprocessing and place the Waste Fund off-budget. Introduced July 29, 2009; referred to committees on Energy and Commerce and the Budget.

H.R. 3505 (Gary Miller)

American Energy Production and Price Reduction Act. Among other provisions, would prohibit the Nuclear Regulatory Commission from denying a nuclear reactor license because of a lack of nuclear waste disposal capacity. Introduced July 31, 2009; referred to multiple committees.

H.R. 4741 (Fattah)/S. 2776 (Alexander)

Clean Energy Act of 2010. Among other provisions, requires NRC to assume that sufficient disposal capacity will be available for nuclear waste that would be produced from proposed reactors, and authorizes annual appropriations of $150 million to DOE through 2020 for spent nuclear fuel recycling research and development. Senate bill introduced November 16, 2009; referred to Committee on Energy and Natural Resources. House bill introduced March 3, 2010; referred to multiple committees.

S. 807 (Nelson of Nebraska)

SMART Energy Act. Includes provision authorizing DOE to begin construction of a spent fuel recycling research and development facility. Introduced April 2, 2009; referred to Committee on Finance.

S. 861 (Graham)

Rebating America's Deposits Act. Requires the President to certify that the Yucca Mountain site continues to be the designated location for a nuclear waste repository under the Nuclear Waste Policy Act. If such a certification is not made within 30 days after enactment or is subsequently revoked, the Treasury is to refund all payments, plus interest, made by nuclear reactor owners to the Nuclear Waste Fund. DOE is to begin shipping defense-related high-level radioactive waste to Yucca Mountain by 2017 or pay $1 million per day to each state in which such waste is located. Introduced April 22, 2009; referred to Committee on Energy and Natural Resources.

S. 1333 (Barrasso)

Clean, Affordable, and Reliable Energy Act of 2009. Includes provisions to take the Nuclear Waste Fund off-budget, authorize DOE to use the Nuclear Waste Fund to pay for grants or longterm contracts for spent nuclear fuel recycling or reprocessing, and prohibit NRC from denying licenses for new nuclear facilities because of a lack of waste disposal capacity. Introduced June 24, 2009; referred to Committee on Finance.

FOR ADDITIONAL READING

Harvard University. John F. Kennedy School of Government. Belfer Center for Science and International Affairs. *The Economics of Reprocessing vs. Direct Disposal of Spent Nuclear Fuel.* DE-FG26-99FT4028. December 2003.

Nuclear Waste Technical Review Board. *Survey of National Programs for Managing High-Level Radioactive Waste and Spent Nuclear Fuel.* October 2009. http://www.nwtrb.gov /reports/reports.html

University of Illinois. Program in Arms Control, Disarmament, and International Security. *'Plan D ' for Spent Nuclear Fuel.* 2009. http://acdis.illinois.edu/publications/ 207/publicationPlanDforSpentNuclearFuel.html.

U.S. Department of Energy. *Office of Civilian Radioactive Waste Management home page*; covers DOE activities for disposal, transportation, and other management of civilian nuclear waste. http ://www. ocrwm. doe. gov.

U.S. General Accounting Office. *Low-Level Radioactive Waste: Disposal Availability Adequate in the Short Term, but Oversight Needed to Identify Any Future Shortfalls.* GAO-04-604. June 2004. 53 p.

Walker, J. Samuel. *The Road to Yucca Mountain: The Development of Radioactive Waste Policy in the United States.* University of California Press. 2009. 228 p.

End Notes

[1] *U.S. Department of Energy's Motion to Withdraw*, NRC Atomic Safety and Licensing Board, Docket No. 63-0001, March 3, 2010, http://www.energy.gov/news/documents/DOE_Motion_to_Withdraw.pdf.

[2] National Association of Regulatory Utility Commissioners, "NARUC Seeks Party Status at NRC, Says Yucca Review Must Continue," press release, March 16, 2010, http://www.naruc.org/ News/default.c fm?pr=191&pdf=.

[3] Department of Energy, *Blue Ribbon Commission on America's Nuclear Future*, Advisory Committee Charter, Washington, DC, March 1, 2010, http://www.energy.gov/news/documents/BRC_Charter.pdf.

[4] Nuclear Energy Institute, Key Issues, Yucca Mountain, http://www.nei.org/keyissues/nuclearwastedisposal/ yuccamountain/, viewed April 11, 2008.

[5] National Research Council, Board on Radioactive Waste Management, *Rethinking High-Level Radioactive Waste Disposal: A Position Statement of the Board on Radioactive Waste Management* (1990), p. 2.

[6] Senator Bingaman introduced the approval resolution in the Senate April 9, 2002 (S.J.Res. 34), and Representative Barton introduced it in the House April 11, 2002 (H.J.Res. 87). The Subcommittee on Energy and Air Quality of the House Committee on Energy and Commerce approved H.J.Res. 87 on April 23 by a 24-2 vote, and the full Committee approved the measure two days later, 41-6 (H.Rept. 107-425). The resolution was passed by the House May 8, 2002, by a vote of 306-117. The Senate Committee on Energy and Natural Resources approved S.J.Res. 34 by a 13-10 vote June 5, 2002 (S.Rept. 107-159). Following a 60-39 vote to consider S.J.Res. 34, the Senate passed H.J.Res. 87 by voice vote July 9, 2002.

[7] The Standard Contract for Disposal of Spent Nuclear Fuel and/or High-Level Radioactive Waste can be found at 10 CFR 961.11.

[8] Statement of Kim Cawley, Chief, Natural and Physical Resources Costs Estimates Unit, Congressional Budget Office, before the House Committee on the Budget, July 16, 2009, p. 6-7.

[9] Telephone conversation with David K. Zabransky, Nuclear Utility Specialist, Office of Civilian Radioactive Waste Management, U.S. Department of Energy, March 25, 2009.

[10] Statement of Kim Cawley, *op. cit.*

[11] U.S. Department of Energy, Office of Civilian Radioactive Waste Management, *Analysis of the Total System Life Cycle Cost of the Civilian Radioactive Waste Management Program, Fiscal year 2007*, DOE/RW-0591, Washington, DC, July 2008, p. 20, http://ocrwm.doe.gov/about/budget/pdf/TSLCC_2007_8_05_08.pdf.

[12] *Ibid.*, p. B-2.

[13] NARUC, "State Regulators Go to Court with DOE over Nuclear Waste Fees, news release, April 2, 2010, http://www.naruc.org/News/default.cfm?pr=193; *Nuclear Energy Institute et al. v. U.S. DOE*, Joint Petition for Review, U.S. Court of Appeals for the District of Columbia Circuit, April 5, 2010.

[14] Jeff Beattie, "NARUC, Utilities Sue DOE Over Nuke Waste Fee," *Energy Daily*, April 6, 2010, p. 1.

[15] DOE Motion to Withdraw, *op. cit.*

[16] Nicole E. Matthews, "DOE Withdraws Application for Yucca Nuke Dump," *Fox5 Vegas.com*, March 3, 2010, http://www.fox5vegas.com/news/22734591/detail.html.

[17] *Motion for the State of Nevada for Leave to Intervene as Intervenor-Respondent*, U.S. Court of Appeals for the Fourth Circuit, Case No. 10-1229, March 19, 2010, http://www.state.nv.us/nucwaste/licensing/nv100319motion3.pdf.

[18] National Association of Regulatory Utility Commissioners, "NARUC Seeks Party Status at NRC, Says Yucca Review Must Continue," press release, March 16, 2010, http://www.naruc.org/News/ default .cfm?pr=191&pdf=.

[19] NRC Atomic Safety and Licensing Board, Memorandum and Order, ASLBP No. 09-892-HLW-CAB04, April 6, 2010.

[20] George Lobsenz, "Murray Slams Yucca Mountain Withdrawal as 'Irresponsible'," *Energy Daily*, March 5, 2010, p. 1.

[21] Letter from Energy Secretary Steven Chu to Peter J. Visclosky, Chairman, Subcommittee on Energy and Water Development, Committee on Appropriations, U.S. House of Representatives, March 26, 2010, http://www.sustainablefuelcycle.com/resources/20100326DOESecChuLetterToRepViscloskyOnHearngtestimony.pdf.

[22] Statutory definitions for "spent nuclear fuel," "high-level radioactive waste," and "low-level radioactive waste" can be found in Section 2 of the Nuclear Waste Policy Act of 1982 (42 U.S.C. 10101). "Transuranic waste" is defined in Section 11ee. of the Atomic Energy Act (42 U.S.C. 2014); Section 1 1e.(2) of the Act includes uranium mill tailings in the definition of "byproduct material." "Mixed waste" consists of chemically hazardous waste as defined by EPA regulations (40 CFR Part 261, Subparts C and D) that contains radioactive materials as defined by the Atomic Energy Act.

[23] ACI Nuclear Energy Solutions, *2009 Used Fuel Data*, ACI-NES Letter No. L1010001, January 22, 2010.

[24] DOE Office of Civilian Radioactive Waste Management, *OCR WM Annual Report to Congress, Fiscal Year 2002*, DOE/RW-0560, October 2003, Appendix C.

[25] DOE Office of Civilian Radioactive Waste Management, *Draft Supplemental Environmental Impact Statement for a Geologic Repository for the Disposal of Spent Nuclear Fuel and High-Level Radioactive Waste at Yucca Mountain, Nye County, Nevada*, Summary, DOE/EIS-0250F-S1D, October 2007, p. S-47.

[26] ACI Nuclear Energy Solutions, *op. cit.*

[27] Nuclear Regulatory Commission, *Waste Confidence Decision Review*, 55 *Federal Register* 38474, September 18, 1990.

[28] National Academy of Sciences, *Safety and Security of Commercial Spent Nuclear Fuel Storage: Public Report*, released April 6, 2005, p. 2.

[29] U.S. Department of Energy, Management Information Manifest System, http://mims.apps.em.doe.gov/mims.asp#.

[30] Bureau of Indian Affairs, *Record of Decision for the Construction and Operation of an Independent Spent Fuel Storage Installation (ISFSI) on the Reservation of the Skull Valley Band of Goshute Indians (Band) in Tooele County, Utah*, September 7, 2006.

[31] Bureau of Land Management, *Record of Decision Addressing Right-of-Way Applications U 76985 and U 76986 to Transport Spent Nuclear Fuel to the Reservation of the Skull Valley Band of Goshute Indians*, September 7, 2006.

[32] Senator Orrin Hatch, *Utahns Deliver Killing Blow to Skull Valley Nuke Waste Plan*, News Release, September 7, 2006.

[33] Winslow, Ben, "Gosutes, PFS Sue Interior," *Deseret Morning News*, July 18, 2007.

[34] See, for example: NRC, "Analysis of Energy Policy Act of 1992 Issues Related to High-Level Waste Disposal Standards, SECY-93-013, January 25, 1993, attachment p. 4.

[35] National Research Council. *Technical Bases for Yucca Mountain Standards*. National Academy Press. 1995.

[36] *Nuclear Energy Institute v. Environmental Protection Agency*, U.S. Court of Appeals for the District of Columbia Circuit, No. 01-1258, July 9, 2004.

[37] Especially high doses at the upper end of the exposure range would raise the mean, or average, more than the median, or the halfway point in the data set.

[38] Office of the Governor, Agency for Nuclear Projects. *Comments by the State of Nevada on EPA's Proposed New Radiation Protection Rule for the Yucca Mountain Nuclear Waste Repository*. November 2005.

[39] Posted on the EPA website at http://www.epa.gov/radiation/yucca.

[40] Nuclear Regulatory Commission, "Implementation of a Dose Standard After 10,000 Years," 74 *Federal Register* 10811, March 13, 2009.

[41] FSEIS, p. S-42. Posted on the DOE website at http://www.rw.doe.gov/ym_repository/ seis/docs/ 002_Summary.pdf. DOE.

[42] DOE, Office of Civilian Radioactive Waste Management, Office of Program Management, *Monthly Summary of Program Financial and Budget Information*, as of July 1, 2009, available at http://www.rw.doe.gov/about// Monthly _Financial _and _Budget _Summary.shtml. The report notes that some figures may not add due to independent rounding.

[43] Available on the OCRWM website at http://www.rw.doe.gov/about/budget/pdf/TSLCC_2007_8_05_08.pdf.

[44] TCEQ website: http://www.tceq.state.tx.us/permitting/radmat/licensing/wcs_license_app.html#wcs_status.

[45] Weil, Jenny, "Texas Regulators Approve License for LLW Disposal," *Inside NRC*, January 19, 2009, p. 3.

[46] USAToday.com, August 1, 2005, http://www.usatoday.com/news/nation/2005-08-01-nukewaste_x.htm.

[47] Lovell, David L., Wisconsin Legislative Council Staff, *State Statutes Limiting the Construction of Nuclear Power Plants*, October 5, 2006.

In: Nuclear Waste: Disposal and Liability Issues
Editor: Ylenia E. Farrugia

ISBN: 978-1-61761-590-0
© 2011 Nova Science Publishers, Inc.

Chapter 2

NUCLEAR WASTE MANAGEMENT: KEY ATTRIBUTES, CHALLENGES, AND COSTS FOR THE YUCCA MOUNTAIN REPOSITORY AND TWO POTENTIAL ALTERNATIVES[*]

United States Government Accountability Office

WHY GAO DID THIS STUDY

High-level nuclear waste—one of the nation's most hazardous substances—is accumulating at 80 sites in 35 states. The United States has generated 70,000 metric tons of nuclear waste and is expected to generate 153,000 metric tons by 2055. The Nuclear Waste Policy Act of 1982, as amended, requires the Department of Energy (DOE) to dispose of the waste in a geologic repository at Yucca Mountain, about 100 miles northwest of Las Vegas, Nevada. However, the repository is more than a decade behind schedule, and the nuclear waste generally remains at the commercial nuclear reactor sites and DOE sites where it was generated.

This chapter examines the key attributes, challenges, and costs of the Yucca Mountain repository and the two principal alternatives to a repository that nuclear waste management experts identified: storing the nuclear waste at two centralized locations and continuing to store the waste on site where it was generated. GAO developed models of total cost ranges for each alternative using component cost estimates provided by the nuclear waste management experts. However, GAO did not compare these alternatives because of significant differences in their inherent characteristics that could not be quantified.

---

[*] This is an edited, reformatted and augmented edition of a United States Government Accountability Office publication, Report GAO-10-48, dated November 2009.

What GAO Recommends

GAO is making no recommendations in this chapter. In written comments, DOE and NRC generally agreed with the report.

What GAO Found

The Yucca Mountain repository is designed to provide a permanent solution for managing nuclear waste, minimize the uncertainty of future waste safety, and enable DOE to begin fulfilling its legal obligation under the Nuclear Waste Policy Act to take custody of commercial waste, which began in 1998. However, project delays have led to utility lawsuits that DOE estimates are costing taxpayers about $12.3 billion in damages through 2020 and could cost $500 million per year after 2020, though the outcome of pending litigation may affect the government's total liability. Also, the administration has announced plans to terminate Yucca Mountain and seek alternatives. Even if DOE continues the program, it must obtain a Nuclear Regulatory Commission construction and operations license, a process likely to be delayed by budget shortfalls. GAO's analysis of DOE's cost projections found that a repository to dispose of 153,000 metric tons would cost from $41 billion to $67 billion (in 2009 present value) over a 143-year period until the repository is closed. Nuclear power rate payers would pay about 80 percent of these costs, and taxpayers would pay about 20 percent.

Centralized storage at two locations provides an alternative that could be implemented within 10 to 30 years, allowing more time to consider final disposal options, nuclear waste to be removed from decommissioned reactor sites, and the government to take custody of commercial nuclear waste, saving billions of dollars in liabilities. However, DOE's statutory authority to provide centralized storage is uncertain, and finding a state willing to host a facility could be extremely challenging. In addition, centralized storage does not provide for final waste disposal, so much of the waste would be transported twice to reach its final destination. Using cost data from experts, GAO estimated the 2009 present value cost of centralized storage of 153,000 metric tons at the end of 100 years to range from $15 billion to $29 billion but increasing to between $23 billion and $81 billion with final geologic disposal.

On-site storage would provide an alternative requiring little change from the status quo, but would face increasing challenges over time. It would also allow time for consideration of final disposal options. The additional time in on-site storage would make the waste safer to handle, reducing risks when waste is transported for final disposal. However, the government is unlikely to take custody of the waste, especially at operating nuclear reactor sites, which could result in significant financial liabilities that would increase over time. Not taking custody could also intensify public opposition to spent fuel storage site renewals and reactor license extensions, particularly with no plan in place for final waste disposition. In addition, extended on-site storage could introduce possible risks to the safety and security of the waste as the storage systems degrade and the waste decays, potentially requiring new maintenance and security measures. Using cost data from experts, GAO estimated the 2009 present value cost of on-site storage of 153,000 metric tons at the end of 100 years to range from $13 billion to $34 billion but increasing to between $20 billion to $97 billion with final geologic disposal.

ABBREVIATIONS

DOE   Department of Energy
EPA   Environmental Protection Agency
NRC   Nuclear Regulatory Commission
NWPA   Nuclear Waste Policy Act of 1982

November 4, 2009

The Honorable Barbara Boxer
Chairman
Committee on Environment and Public Works
United States Senate

The Honorable Harry Reid
United States Senate

The Honorable John Ensign
United States Senate

High-level nuclear waste consists mostly of spent nuclear fuel removed from commercial power reactors and is considered one of the most hazardous substances on earth. The U.S. national inventory of 70,000 metric tons of nuclear waste—enough to fill a football field more than 15 feet deep—has been accumulating at 80 sites in 35 states since the mid-1940s and is expected to more than double to 153,000 metric tons by 2055. The current national policy of constructing a federal repository to dispose of this waste at Yucca Mountain—which is about 100 miles northwest of Las Vegas, Nevada—has already been delayed more than a decade. As a result, nuclear waste generally remains at the sites where it was generated. Experts and regulators believe the nuclear waste, if properly stored and monitored, can be kept safe and secure on-site for decades; but communities across the country have raised concerns about the waste's lethal nature and the possibility of natural disasters or terrorism, particularly at sites near urban centers or sources of drinking water. Industry has also raised concerns that local communities will not support the expansion of the nuclear energy industry without a final waste disposition pathway. Many experts and communities view nuclear energy as a potential means of meeting future energy demands while reducing reliance on fossil fuels and cutting carbon emissions, a key contributor to climate change.

In addition to the spent nuclear fuel generated by commercial power reactors, the Department of Energy (DOE) owns and manages about 19 percent of the nuclear waste—referred to as DOE-managed spent nuclear fuel and high-level waste—which consists of spent nuclear fuel from power, research, and navy shipboard reactors, and high-level nuclear waste from the nation's nuclear weapons program. (See figure 1 for the locations where nuclear waste is stored.)

Under the Nuclear Waste Policy Act of 1982 (NWPA), as amended, DOE was to evaluate one or more national geologic repositories that would be designated to permanently store commercial spent nuclear fuel and DOE-managed spent nuclear fuel and high-level waste.

NWPA was amended in 1987 to direct DOE to evaluate only the Yucca Mountain site. In 2002, the president recommended and the Congress approved the Yucca Mountain site as the nation's geologic repository. The repository is intended to isolate nuclear waste from humans and the environment for thousands of years, long enough for its radioactivity to decay to near natural background levels. NWPA set January 31, 1998, as the date for DOE to start accepting nuclear waste for disposal. To meet this goal, DOE has spent more than $14 billion for design, engineering, and testing activities.[1] In June 2008, DOE submitted a license application to the Nuclear Regulatory Commission (NRC) for approval to construct the repository. In July 2008, DOE reported that its best achievable date for opening the repository, if it receives NRC approval, is in 2020. Delays in the Yucca Mountain repository have resulted in a need for continued storage of the waste onsite, leaving industry uncertain regarding the licensing of new nuclear power reactors and the nation uncertain regarding a final disposition of the waste.

In March 2009, the Secretary of Energy testified that the administration planned to terminate the Yucca Mountain repository. Since then, the administration has announced plans to study alternatives to geologic disposal at Yucca Mountain before making a decision on a future nuclear waste management strategy, which the administration said could include reprocessing or other complementary strategies.

In this context, you asked us to identify key aspects of DOE's nuclear waste management program and other possible management approaches. Specifically, you asked us to examine (1) the key attributes, challenges, and costs of the Yucca Mountain repository; (2) and identify alternative nuclear waste management approaches; (3) the key attributes, challenges, and costs of storing the nuclear waste at two centralized sites; and (4) the key attributes, challenges, and costs of continuing to store the nuclear waste at its current locations. The centralized storage and onsite storage options—both with disposal scenarios—were the two most likely alternative approaches identified by the experts we interviewed. We are also providing information on what is known about sources of funding—primarily taxpayers and nuclear power rate payers—for the Yucca Mountain repository and the two alternative approaches.

To examine the key attributes, challenges, and costs of the Yucca Mountain repository, we obtained reports and supporting documentation from DOE, NRC, the National Academy of Sciences, and the Nuclear Waste Technical Review Board. Specifically, we used DOE's report on the Yucca Mountain repository's total lifecycle cost to analyze the cost for disposing of either (1) 70,000 metric tons of nuclear waste, which is the statutory cap on the amount of waste that can be disposed of at Yucca Mountain, or (2) 153,000 metric tons, which is the estimated total amount of nuclear waste that has already been generated and will be generated if all currently operating commercial reactors operate for a 60-year lifespan.[2] We then discounted these costs to 2009 present value.

To identify alternative nuclear waste management approaches, we interviewed DOE officials, experts at the National Academy of Sciences and the Nuclear Waste Technical Review Board, and executives at the Nuclear Energy Institute, among others. Based on their comments, we identified two generic alternative approaches for managing this waste for at least a 100-year period before it is disposed in a repository: storing the nuclear waste at two centralized facilities—referred to as centralized storage—and continuing to store the nuclear waste on site at their current facilities—referred to as on-site storage. To examine the key attributes, challenges, and costs of each alternative, we asked nuclear waste management experts from federal agencies, industry, academic institutions, and concerned groups to comment on the attributes and challenges of each alternative, provide relevant cost data, and comment on the assumptions and cost components that we used to develop cost models for the alternatives. We then used the models to produce the total cost ranges for each alternative with and without final disposal in a geologic repository at the end of a 100-year specific time period. In addition, we analyzed onsite storage for longer periods than 100 years. We analyzed costs associated with storing 70,000 metric tons and 153,000 metric tons and discounted the costs to 2009 present value.

We did not compare the Yucca Mountain cost range to the ranges of other alternatives because of significant differences in inherent characteristics of these alternatives that our modeling work could not quantify. For example, the safety, health, and environmental risks for each are very different, which needs to be considered in the policy debate on nuclear waste management decisions. (See app. I for additional information about our scope and methodology, app. II for our methodology for soliciting comments from nuclear waste management experts, and app. III for a list of these experts.)

We conducted this performance audit from April 2008 to October 2009 in accordance with generally accepted government auditing standards. Those standards require that we plan and perform the audit to obtain sufficient, appropriate evidence to provide a reasonable basis for our findings and conclusions based on our audit objectives. We believe that the evidence obtained provides a reasonable basis for our findings and conclusions based on our audit objectives.

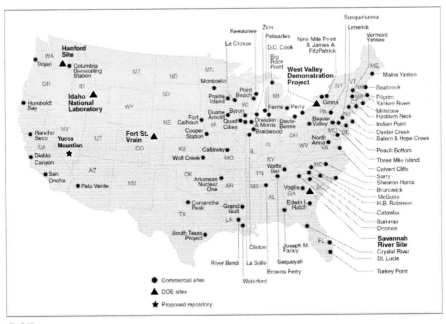

Source: DOE.

Note: Locations are approximate. DOE has reported that it is responsible for managing nuclear waste at 121 sites in 39 states, but DOE officials told us that several sites have only research reactors that generate small amounts of waste that will be consolidated at the Idaho National Laboratory for packaging prior to disposal.

Figure 1. Current Storage Sites and Proposed Repository for High-Level Nuclear Waste

BACKGROUND

Nuclear waste is long-lived and very hazardous—without protective shielding, the intense radioactivity of the waste can kill a person within minutes or cause cancer months or even decades after exposure.[3] Thus, careful management is required to isolate it from humans and the environment. To accomplish this, the National Academy of Sciences first endorsed the concept of nuclear waste disposal in deep geologic formations in a 1957 report to the U.S. Atomic Energy Commission, which has since been articulated by experts as the safest and most secure method of permanent disposal.[4] However, progress toward developing a geologic repository was slow until NWPA was enacted in 1983. Citing the potential risks of the accumulating amounts of nuclear waste, NWPA required the federal government to take responsibility for the disposition of nuclear waste and required DOE to develop a permanent geologic repository to protect public health and safety and the environment for current and future generations. Specifically, the act required DOE to study several locations around the country for possible repository sites and develop a contractual relationship with industry for disposal of the nuclear waste. The Congress amended NWPA in 1987 to restrict scientific study and characterization of a possible repository to only Yucca Mountain. (Figure 2 shows the north crest of Yucca Mountain and a cut-out of the proposed mined repository.)

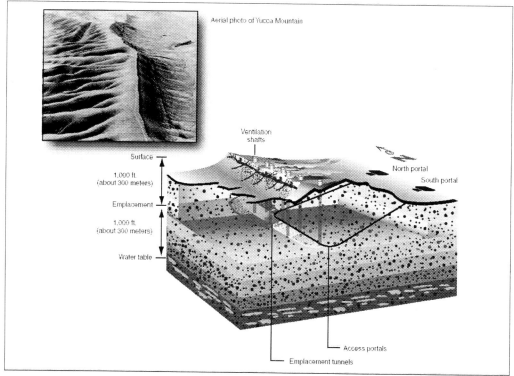

Source: DOE.

Figure 2. Aerial View and Cut-Out of the Yucca Mountain Repository

After the Congress approved Yucca Mountain as a suitable site for the development of a permanent nuclear waste repository in 2002, DOE began preparing a license application for submittal to NRC, which has regulatory authority over commercial nuclear waste management facilities. DOE submitted its license application to NRC in June 2008, and NRC accepted the license application for review in September 2008. NWPA requires NRC to complete its review of DOE's license application for the Yucca Mountain repository in 3 years, although a fourth year is allowed if NRC deems it necessary and complies with certain reporting requirements.

To pay the nuclear power industry's share of the cost for the Yucca Mountain repository, NWPA established the Nuclear Waste Fund, which is funded by a fee of one mill (one-tenth of a cent) per kilowatt-hour of nuclear-generated electricity that the federal government collects from electric power companies. DOE reported that, at the end of fiscal year 2008, the Nuclear Waste Fund contained $22 billion, with an additional $1.9 billion projected to be added in 2009. DOE receives money from the Nuclear Waste Fund through congressional appropriations. Additional funding for the repository comes from an appropriation which provides for the disposal cost of DOE-managed spent nuclear fuel and high-level waste.

NWPA caps nuclear waste that can be disposed of at the Yucca Mountain repository at 70,000 metric tons until a second repository is available. However, the nation has already accumulated about 70,000 metric tons of nuclear waste at current reactor sites and DOE facilities. Without a change in the law to raise the cap or to allow the construction of a second repository, DOE can dispose of only the current nuclear waste inventory. The nation will have to develop a strategy for an additional 83,000 metric tons of waste expected to be generated if NRC issues 20-year license extensions to all of the currently operating nuclear reactors.[5] This amount does not include any nuclear waste generated by new reactors or future defense activities, or greater than class C nuclear waste.[6] According to DOE and industry studies, three to four times the 70,000 metric tons—and possibly more—could potentially be disposed safely in Yucca Mountain, which could address current and some future waste inventories, potentially delaying the need for a second repository for several generations.

Nuclear waste has continued to accumulate at the nation's commercial and DOE nuclear facilities over the past 60 years. Facility managers must actively manage the nuclear waste by continually isolating, confining, and monitoring it to keep humans and the environment safe. Most spent nuclear fuel is stored at reactor sites, immersed in pools of water designed to cool and isolate it from the environment. With nowhere to dispose of the spent nuclear fuel, the racks holding spent fuel in the pools have been rearranged to allow for more dense storage of assemblies. Even with this re-racking, spent nuclear fuel pools are reaching their capacities. Some critics have expressed concern about the remote possibility of an overcrowded spent nuclear fuel pool releasing large amounts of radiation if an accident or other event caused the pool to lose water, potentially leading to a fire that could disperse radioactive material. As reactor operators have run out of space in their spent nuclear fuel pools, they have turned in increasing number to dry cask storage systems that generally consist of stainless steel canisters placed inside larger stainless steel or concrete casks. (See figure 3.) NRC requires protective shielding, routine inspections and monitoring, and security systems to isolate the nuclear waste to protect humans and the environment.

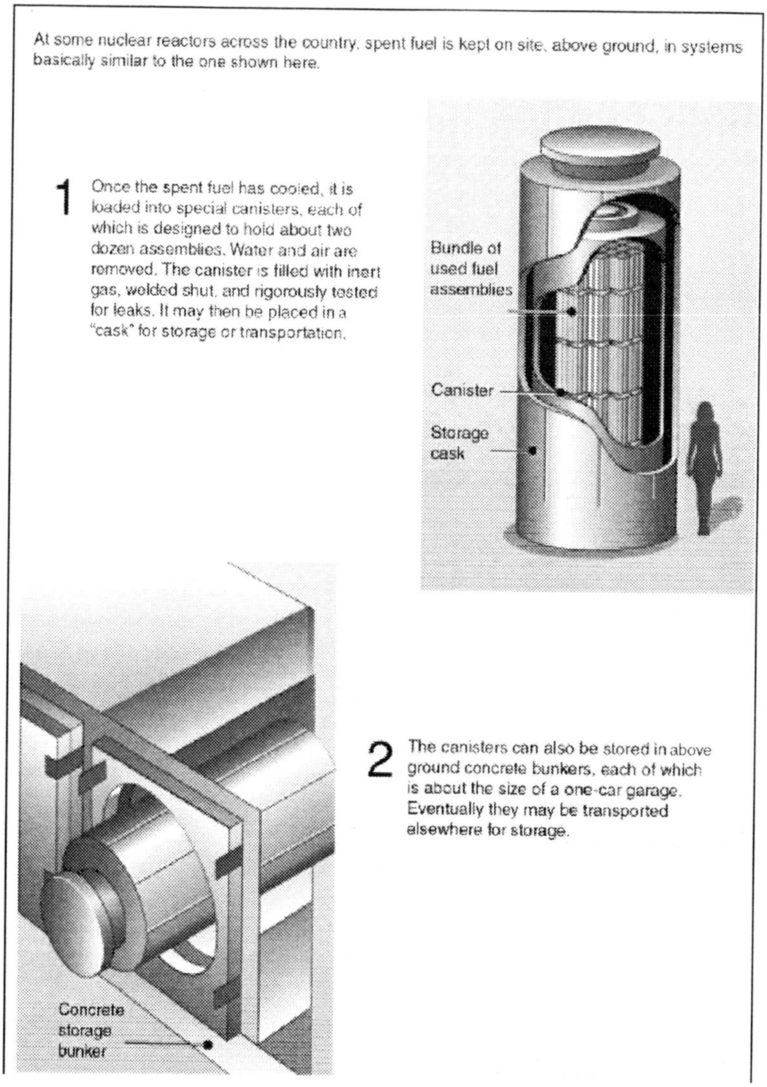

Source: NRC.

Figure 3. Dry Cask Storage System for Spent Nuclear Fuel

NRC has determined that these dry cask storage systems can safely store nuclear waste, but NRC considers them to be interim measures. In 1990, NRC issued a revised waste confidence rule, stating that it had confidence that the waste generated by a reactor can be safely stored in either wet or dry storage for 30 years beyond a reactor's life, including license extensions. NRC further determined that it had reasonable assurance that safe geologic disposal was feasible and that a geologic repository would be operational by about 2025. More recently, NRC has published a notice of proposed rulemaking to revise that rule, proposing that waste generated by a reactor can be safely stored for 60 years beyond the life of a reactor and that geologic disposal would be available in 50 to 60 years beyond a reactor's life.[7] NRC is currently considering whether to republish its proposed rule to seek additional public input on certain issues. Forty-five reactor sites or former reactor sites in 30 states have dry storage facilities for their spent nuclear fuel as of June 2009, and the number of reactor sites storing spent nuclear fuel is likely to continue to grow until an alternative is implemented.

Implementing a permanent, safe, and secure disposal solution for the nuclear waste is of concern to the nation, particularly state governments and local communities, because many of the 80 sites where nuclear waste is currently stored are near large populations or major water sources or consist of shutdown reactor sites that tie up land that could be used for other purposes. In addition, states that have DOE facilities with nuclear waste storage are concerned because of possible contamination to aquifers, rivers, and other natural resources. DOE's Hanford Reservation, located near Richland, Washington, was a major component of the nation's nuclear weapons defense program from 1943 until 1989, when operations ceased. In the settlement of a lawsuit filed by the state of Washington in 2003, DOE agreed not to ship certain nuclear waste to Hanford until environmental reviews were complete. In August 2009, the U.S. government stated that the preferred alternative in DOE's environmental review would include limitations on certain nuclear waste shipments to Hanford until the process of immobilizing tank waste in glass begins, expected in 2019.[8] Moreover, some commercial and DOE sites where the nuclear waste is stored may not be able to accommodate much additional waste safely because of limited storage space or community objections. These sites will require a more immediate solution.

The nation has considered proposals to build centralized storage facilities where waste from reactor sites could be consolidated. The 1987 amendment to NWPA established the Office of the Nuclear Waste Negotiator to try to broker an agreement for a community to host a repository or interim storage facility. Two negotiators worked with local communities and Native American tribes for several years, but neither was able to conclude a proposed agreement with a willing community by January 1995, when the office's authority expired. Subsequently, in 2006 after a 9-year licensing process, a consortium of electric power companies called Private Fuel Storage obtained a NRC license for a private centralized storage facility on the reservation of the Skull Valley Band of the Goshute Indians in Utah. NRC's 20-year license—with an option for an additional 20 years—allows storage of up to 40,000 metric tons of commercial spent nuclear fuel. However, construction of the Private Fuel Storage facility has been delayed by Department of the Interior decisions not to approve the lease of tribal lands to Private Fuel Storage and declining to issue the necessary rights-of-way to transport nuclear waste to the facility through Bureau of Land Management land. Private Fuel Storage and the Skull Valley Band of Goshutes filed a federal lawsuit in 2007 to overturn Interior's decisions.

Reprocessing nuclear waste could potentially reduce, but not eliminate, the amount of waste for disposal. In reprocessing, usable uranium and plutonium are recovered from spent nuclear fuel and are used to make new fuel rods. However, current reprocessing technologies separate weapons usable plutonium and other fissionable materials from the spent nuclear fuel, raising concerns about nuclear proliferation by terrorists or enemy states. Although the United States pioneered the reprocessing technologies used by other countries, such as France and Russia, presidents Gerald Ford and Jimmy Carter ended government support for commercial reprocessing in the United States in 1976 and 1977, respectively, primarily due to proliferation concerns. Although President Ronald Reagan lifted the ban on government support in 1981, the nation has not embarked on any reprocessing program due to proliferation and cost concerns—the Congressional Budget Office recently reported that current reprocessing technologies are more expensive than direct disposal of the waste in a geologic repository.[9] DOE's Fuel Cycle Research and Development program is currently performing research in reprocessing technologies that would not separate out weapons usable plutonium, but it is not certain whether these technologies will become cost-effective.[10]

The general consensus of the international scientific community is that geologic disposal is the preferred long-term nuclear waste management alternative. Finland, Sweden, Canada, France, and Switzerland have decided to construct geologic disposal facilities, but none have yet completed any such facility, although DOE reports that Finland and Sweden have announced plans to begin emplacement operations in 2020 and 2023, respectively. Moreover, some countries employ a mix of complementary storage alternatives in their national waste management strategies, including on-site storage, consolidated interim storage, reprocessing, and geologic disposal. For example, Sweden plans to rely on on-site storage until the waste cools enough to move it to a centralized storage facility, where the waste will continue to cool and decay for an additional 30 years. This waste will then be placed in a geologic repository for disposal. France reprocesses the spent nuclear fuel, recycling usable portions as new fuel and storing the remainder for eventual disposal.

THE YUCCA MOUNTAIN REPOSITORY WOULD PROVIDE A PERMANENT SOLUTION FOR NUCLEAR WASTE, BUT ITS IMPLEMENTATION FACES CHALLENGES AND SIGNIFICANT UPFRONT COSTS

The Yucca Mountain repository—mandated by NWPA, as amended—would provide a permanent nuclear waste management solution for the nation's current inventory of about 70,000 metric tons of waste. According to DOE and industry studies, the repository potentially could be a disposal site for three to four times that amount of waste. However, the repository lacks the support of the administration and the state of Nevada, and faces regulatory and other challenges. Our analysis of DOE's cost projections found that the Yucca Mountain repository would cost from $41 billion to $67 billion (in 2009 present value) for disposing of 153,000 metric tons of nuclear waste.[11] Most of these costs are up-front capital costs. However, once the Yucca Mountain repository is closed—in 2151 for our 153,000-metric-ton model—it is not expected to incur any significant additional costs, according to DOE.

As Designed, the Yucca Mountain Repository Would Be a Permanent Solution and Would Reduce the Uncertainty Associated with Future Nuclear Waste Safety

The Yucca Mountain repository is designed to isolate nuclear waste in a safe and secure environment long enough for the waste to degrade into a form that is less harmful to humans and the environment. As nuclear waste ages, it cools and decays, becoming less radiologically dangerous. In October 2008, after years of legal challenges, the Environmental Protection Agency (EPA) promulgated standards that require DOE to ensure that radioactive releases from the nuclear waste disposed of at Yucca Mountain do not harm the public for 1 million years.[12] This is because some waste components, such as plutonium 239, take hundreds of thousands of years to decay into less harmful materials. To meet EPA's standards and keep the waste safely isolated, DOE's license application proposes the use of both natural and engineered barriers. Key natural barriers of Yucca Mountain include its dry climate, the depth and isolation of the Death Valley aquifer in which the mountain resides, its natural physical shape, and the layers of thick rock above and below the repository that lie 1,000 feet below the surface of the mountain and 1,000 feet above the water table. Key engineered barriers include the solid nature of the nuclear waste; the double-shelled transportation, aging, and disposal canisters that encapsulate the waste and prevent radiation leakage; and drip shields that are composed of corrosion-resistant titanium to ward off any dripping water inside the repository for many thousands of years.

The construction of a geologic repository at Yucca Mountain would provide a permanent solution for nuclear waste that could allow the government to begin taking possession of the nuclear waste in the near term—about 10 to 30 years. The nuclear power industry sees this as an important consideration in obtaining the public support necessary to build new nuclear power reactors. The industry is interested in constructing new nuclear power reactors because, among other reasons, of the growing demand for electricity and pressure from federal and state governments to reduce reliance on fossil fuels and curtail carbon emissions. Some electric power companies see nuclear energy as an important option for noncarbon emitting power generation. According to NRC, 18 electric power companies have filed license applications to construct 29 new nuclear reactors.[13] Nuclear industry representatives, however, have expressed concerns that investors and the public will not support the construction of new nuclear power reactors without a final safe and secure disposition pathway for the nuclear waste, particularly if that waste is generated and stored near major waterways or urban centers. Moreover, having a permanent disposal option may allow reactor operators to thin-out spent nuclear fuel assemblies from densely packed spent fuel pools, potentially reducing the risk of harm to humans or the environment in the event of an accident, natural disaster, or terrorist event.

In addition, disposal is the only alternative for some DOE and commercial nuclear waste—even if the United States decided to reprocess the waste—because it contains nuclear waste residues that cannot be used as nuclear reactor fuel. This nuclear waste has no safe, long-term alternative other than disposal, and the Yucca Mountain repository would provide a near-term, permanent disposal pathway for it. Moreover, DOE has agreed to remove spent nuclear fuel from at least two states by certain dates or face penalties. Specifically, DOE has an agreement with Colorado stating that if the spent nuclear fuel at Fort St. Vrain is not removed by January 1, 2035, the government will, subject to certain conditions, pay the state $15,000 per day until the waste is removed. In addition, the state of Idaho sued DOE to remove inventories of spent nuclear fuel stored at DOE's Idaho National Laboratory. Under the resulting settlement DOE agreed to (1) remove the spent nuclear fuel by January 1, 2035, or incur penalties of $60,000 per day and (2) curtail or suspend future shipments of spent nuclear fuel to Idaho.[14] Some of the spent nuclear fuel stored at the Idaho National Laboratory comes from refueling the U.S. Navy's submarines and aircraft carriers, all of which are nuclear powered. Special facilities are maintained at the Idaho National Laboratory to examine naval spent nuclear fuel to obtain information for improving future fuel performance and to package the spent nuclear fuel following examination to make it ready for rail shipment to its ultimate destination. According to Navy officials, refueling these warships, which necessitates shipment of naval spent nuclear fuel from the shipyards conducting the refuelings to the Idaho National Laboratory, is part of the Navy's national security mission. Consequently, curtailing or suspending shipments of spent nuclear fuel to Idaho raises national security concerns for the Navy.

The Yucca Mountain repository would help the government fulfill its obligation under NWPA to electric power companies and ratepayers to take custody of the commercial spent nuclear fuel and provide a permanent repository using the Nuclear Waste Fund. When DOE missed its 1998 deadline to begin taking custody of the waste, owners of spent fuel with contracts for disposal services filed lawsuits asking the courts to require DOE to fulfill its statutory and contractual obligations by taking custody of the waste. Though a court decided that it would not order DOE to begin taking custody of the waste, the courts have, in subsequent cases, ordered the government to compensate the utilities for the cost of storing the waste. DOE projected that, based on a 2020 date for beginning operations at Yucca Mountain, the government's liabilities from the 71 lawsuits filed by electric power companies could sum to about $12.3 billion, though the outcome of pending and future litigation could substantially affect the ultimate total liability.[15] DOE estimates that the federal government's future liabilities will average up to $500 million per year. Furthermore, continued delays in DOE's ability to take custody of the waste could result in additional liabilities. Some experts noted that without immediate plans for a permanent repository, reactor operators and ratepayers may demand that the Nuclear Waste Fund be refunded.[16]

Finally, disposing of the nuclear waste now in a repository facility would reduce the uncertainty about the willingness or the ability of future generations to monitor and maintain multiple surface waste storage facilities and would eliminate the need for any future handling of the waste. As a 2001 report of the National Academies noted, continued storage of nuclear waste is technically feasible only if those responsible for it are willing and able to devote adequate resources and attention to maintaining and expanding the storage facilities, as required to keep the waste safe and secure.[17] DOE officials noted that the waste packages at Yucca Mountain are designed to be retrievable for more than 100 years after emplacement, at which time DOE would begin to close the repository, allowing future generations to consider retrieving spent nuclear fuel for reprocessing or other uses. However, the risks and costs of retrieving the nuclear waste from Yucca Mountain are uncertain because planning efforts for retrieval are preliminary. Once closed, Yucca Mountain will require minimal monitoring and little or no maintenance, and all future controls will be passive.[18] Some experts stated that the current generation has a moral obligation to not pass on to future generations the extensive technical and financial responsibilities for managing nuclear waste in surface storage.

Yucca Mountain Faces Many Challenges, Including a Lack of Key Support and License Approval

There are many challenges to licensing and constructing the Yucca Mountain repository, some of which could delay or potentially terminate the program. First, in March 2009, the Secretary of Energy stated that the administration planned to terminate the Yucca Mountain repository and to form a panel of experts to review alternatives. During the testimony, the

Secretary stated that Yucca Mountain would not be considered as one of the alternatives. The administration's fiscal year 2010 budget request for Yucca Mountain was $197 million, which is $296 million less than what DOE stated it needs to stay on its schedule and open Yucca Mountain by 2020.

In July 2009 letters to DOE, the Nuclear Energy Institute and the National Association of Regulatory Utility Commissioners raised concerns that, despite the announced termination of Yucca Mountain, DOE still intended on collecting fees for the Nuclear Waste Fund.[19] The letters requested that DOE suspend collection of payments to the Nuclear Waste Fund. Some states have raised similar concerns and legislators have introduced legislation that could hold payments to the Nuclear Waste Fund until DOE begins operating a federal repository.[20]

Nevertheless, NWPA still requires DOE to pursue geologic disposal at Yucca Mountain. If the administration continues the licensing process for Yucca Mountain, DOE would face a variety of other challenges in licensing and constructing the repository. Many of these challenges—though unique to Yucca Mountain—might also apply in similar form to other future repositories, should they be considered.

One of the most significant challenges facing DOE is to satisfy NRC that Yucca Mountain meets licensing requirements, including ensuring the repository meets EPA's radiation standards over the required 1 million year time frame, as implemented by NRC regulation. For example, NRC's regulations require that DOE model its natural and engineered barriers in a performance assessment, including how the barriers will interact with each other over time and how the repository will meet the standards even if one or more barriers do not perform as expected. NRC has stated that there are uncertainties inherent in the understanding of the performance of the natural and engineered barriers and that demonstrating a reasonable expectation of compliance requires the use of complex predictive models supported by field data, laboratory tests, site-specific monitoring, and natural analog studies. The Nuclear Waste Technical Review Board has also stated that the performance assessment may be "the most complex and ambitious probabilistic risk assessment ever undertaken" and the Board, as well as other groups or individuals, have raised technical concerns about key aspects of the engineered or natural barriers in the repository design.

DOE and NRC officials also stated that budget constraints raise additional challenges. DOE officials told us that past budget shortfalls and projected future low budgets for the Yucca Mountain repository create significant challenges in DOE's ability to meet milestones for licensing and for responding to NRC's requests for additional information related to the license application. In addition, NRC officials told us budget shortfalls have constrained their resources. Staff members they originally hired to review DOE's license application have moved to other divisions within NRC or have left NRC entirely. NRC officials stated that the pace of the license review is commensurate with funding levels. Some experts have questioned whether NRC can meet the maximum 4-year time requirement stipulated in NWPA for license review and have pointed out that the longer the delays in licensing Yucca Mountain, the more costly and politically vulnerable the effort becomes.

In addition, the state of Nevada and other groups that oppose the Yucca Mountain repository have raised technical points, site-specific concerns, and equity issues and have taken steps to delay or terminate the repository. For example, Nevada's Agency for Nuclear Projects questioned DOE's reliance on engineered barriers in its performance assessment, indicating that too many uncertainties exist for DOE to claim human-made systems will perform as expected over the time frames required. In addition, the agency reported that

Yucca Mountain's location near seismic and volcanic zones creates additional uncertainty about DOE's ability to predict a recurrence of seismic or volcanic events and to assess the performance of its waste isolation barriers should those events occur some time during the 1-million-year time frame. The agency also has questioned whether Yucca Mountain is the best site compared with other locations and has raised issues of equity, since Nevada is being asked to accept nuclear waste generated in other states. In addition to the Agency for Nuclear Projects' issues, Nevada has taken other steps to delay or terminate the project. For example, Nevada has denied the water rights DOE needs for construction of a rail spur and facility structures at Yucca Mountain. DOE officials told us that constructing the rail line or the facilities at Yucca Mountain without those water rights will be difficult.

Based on DOE's Cost Estimates, Yucca Mountain Will Likely Cost from $41 Billion to $67 Billion for 153,000 Metric Tons of Nuclear Waste, but Costs Could Increase

Our analysis of DOE's cost estimates found that (1) a 70,000 metric ton repository is projected to cost from $27 to $39 billion in 2009 present value over 108 years and (2) a 153,000 metric ton repository is projected to cost from $41 to $67 billion and take 35 more years to complete. These estimated costs include the licensing, construction, operation, and closure of Yucca Mountain for a period commensurate with the amount of waste. Table 1 shows each scenario with its estimated cost range over time.

As shown in figure 4, the Yucca Mountain repository costs are expected to be high during construction, followed by reduced, but consistent costs during operations, substantially reduced costs for monitoring, then a period of increased costs for installation of the drip shields, and finally costs tapering off for closure. Once the drip shields are installed, by design, the waste packages will no longer be retrievable. After closure, Yucca Mountain is not expected to incur any significant additional costs.

Table 1. Estimated Cost of the Yucca Mountain Scenarios

Dollars in billions		
Amount of nuclear waste disposed	Time period covered[a]	Present value estimate range[a]
70,000 metric tons	2009 to 2116 (108 years)	$27 to $39
153,000 metric tons	2009 to 2151 (143 years)	$41 to $67

Source: GAO analysis based on DOE data.

[a] These costs are in 2009 present value and thus different than the values presented by DOE which are in constant 2007 dollars. Also, these costs do not include more than $14 billion, in constant fiscal year 2009 dollars, that DOE spent from 1983 through 2008 for the Yucca Mountain repository. In addition, we did not include potential schedule delays and costs associated with licensing. DOE reported that each year of delay could cost DOE about $373 million in constant 2009 dollars.

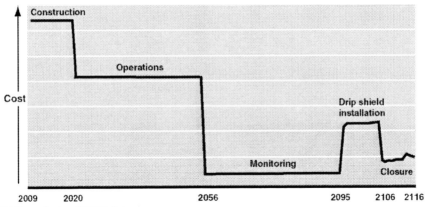

Source: GAO analysis of DOE data.

Figure 4. Cost Profile for the Yucca Mountain Repository, Assuming 70,000 Metric Tons

Costs for the construction of a repository, regardless of location, could increase based on a number of different scenarios, including delays in license application, funding shortfalls, and legal or technical issues that cause delays or changes in plans. For example, we asked DOE to assess the cost of a year's delay in license application approval from the current 3 years to 4 years, the maximum allowed by NWPA. DOE officials told us that each year of delay would cost DOE about $373 million in constant 2009 dollars. Although the experts with whom we consulted did not agree on how long the licensing process for Yucca Mountain might take, several experts told us that the 9 years it took Private Fuel Storage to obtain its license was not unreasonable. This licensing time frame may not directly apply to the Yucca Mountain repository because the repository has a significantly different licensing process and regulatory scheme, including extensive pre-licensing interactions, a federal funding stream, and an extended compliance period and, because of the uncertainties, could take shorter or longer than the Private Fuel Storage experience. A nine-year licensing process for construction authorization would add an estimated $2.2 billion to the cost of the repository, mostly in costs to maintain current systems, such as project support, safeguards and security, and its licensing support network. In addition to consideration of the issuance of a construction authorization, NRC's repository licensing process involves two additional licensing actions necessary to operate and close a repository, each of which allows for public input and could potentially adversely affect the schedule and cost of the repository. The second action is the consideration of an updated DOE application for a license to receive and possess high-level radioactive waste. The third action is the consideration of a DOE application for a license amendment to permanently close the repository. Costs could also increase if unforeseen technical issues developed. For example, some experts told us that the robotic emplacement of waste packages could be difficult because of the heat and radiation output from the nuclear waste, which could impact the electronics on the machinery. DOE officials acknowledged the challenges and told us the machines would have to be shielded for protection. They noted, however, that industry has experience with remote handling of shielded robotic machinery and DOE should be able to use that experience in developing its own machinery.

The responsibility for Yucca Mountain's costs would come from the Nuclear Waste Fund and taxpayers through annual appropriations. NWPA created the Nuclear Waste Fund as a mechanism for the nuclear power industry to pay for its share of the cost for building and operating a permanent repository to dispose of nuclear waste. NWPA also required the federal taxpayers to pay for the portion of permanent repository costs for DOE-managed spent nuclear fuel and high-level waste. DOE has responsibility for determining on an annual basis whether fees charged to industry to finance the Nuclear Waste Fund are sufficient to meet industry's share of costs. As part of that process, DOE developed a methodology in 1989 that uses the total system life cycle cost estimate as input for determining the shares of industry and the federal government by matching projected costs against projected assets. The most recent published assessment, published in July 2008, showed that 80.4 percent of the disposal costs would come from the Nuclear Waste Fund and 19.6 percent would come from appropriations for the DOE-managed spent nuclear fuel and high-level waste.

In addition, the Department of the Treasury's judgment fund will pay the government's liabilities for not taking custody of the nuclear waste in 1998, as required by DOE's contract with industry. Based on existing judgments and settlements, DOE has estimated these costs at $12.3 billion through 2020 and up to $500 million per year after that, though the outcome of pending litigation could substantially affect the government's ultimate liability. The Department of Justice has also spent about $150 million to defend DOE in the litigation.

WE IDENTIFIED TWO NUCLEAR WASTE MANAGEMENT ALTERNATIVES AND DEVELOPED COST MODELS BY CONSULTING WITH EXPERTS

We used input from experts to identify two nuclear waste management alternatives that could be implemented if the nation does not pursue disposal at Yucca Mountain—centralized storage and continued on-site storage, both of which could be implemented with final disposal, according to experts. To understand the implications and likely assumptions of each alternative, as well as the associated costs for the component parts, we systematically solicited facts, advice, and opinions from experts in nuclear waste management. Finally, we used the data and assumptions that the experts provided to develop large-scale cost models that estimate ranges of likely total costs for each alternative.

We Consulted with Experts to Identify and Develop Assumptions for Two Generic Alternatives to Analysis

To identify waste management alternatives that could be implemented if the waste is not disposed of at Yucca Mountain, we solicited facts, advice, and opinions from nuclear waste management experts. Specifically, we interviewed dozens of experts from DOE, NRC, the Nuclear Energy Institute, the National Association of Regulatory Utility Commissioners, the National Conference of State Legislatures, and the State of Nevada Agency for Nuclear Projects. We also reviewed documents they provided or referred us to.

Based on this information, we chose to analyze (1) centralized interim dry storage and (2) on-site dry storage (both interim and long-term). Centralized storage has been attempted to varying degrees in the United States, and on-site storage has become the country's status quo.

Consequently, the experts believe these two alternatives are currently among the most likely for this country in the near-term, in conjunction with final disposal in the long-term. The experts also told us that current nuclear waste reprocessing technologies raise proliferation concerns and are not considered commercially feasible, but they noted that reprocessing has future potential as a part of the nation's nuclear waste management strategy. Because nuclear waste is not reprocessed in this country, we found a lack of sufficient and reliable data to provide meaningful analysis for this alternative. Experts have largely dismissed other alternatives that have been identified, such as disposal of waste in deep boreholes, because of cost or technical constraints.

We developed a set of key assumptions to establish the scope of our alternatives by initially consulting with a small group of nuclear waste management experts. For example, we asked the experts about how many storage sites should be used and whether waste would have to be repackaged. These discussions occurred in an iterative manner—we followed up with experts with specific expertise to refine our assumptions as we learned more. Based on this input, we formulated several key assumptions and defined the alternatives in a generic manner by taking into account some, but not all, of the complexities involved with nuclear waste management (see table 2). We made this choice because experts advised us that trying to consider all of the variability among reactor sites would result in unmanageable models since each location where nuclear waste is currently stored has a unique set of environmental, management, and regulatory considerations that affect the logistics and costs of waste management. For example, reactor sites use different dry cask storage systems with varying costs that require different operating logistics to load the casks.

Table 2. Key Assumptions Used to Define Alternatives

Centralized storage	
Type of storage	Conventional dry cask storage (for commercial spent nuclear fuel).
Number of sites	Two centralized interim storage sites, located in different geographic regions of the country.
Reactor operations	All currently operating reactors receive a 20-year license extension and continue operating until the extensions expire. Reactors will be decommissioned when operations cease, and only spent nuclear fuel dry storage will remain on site.
Transportation	Transportation to the centralized site will be via rail using dedicated trains.
Repackaging	Waste will not be repackaged at the centralized facilities.
Final disposition[a]	After 100 years, the waste will be disposed of in a geologic repository.
On-site storage	
Type of storage	Conventional dry cask storage (for commercial spent nuclear fuel).
Number of sites	Commercial spent nuclear fuel will be stored on independent spent fuel storage installations at 75 reactor sites, which includes operating reactor sites, decommissioned reactor sites, and the Morris facility.[b] DOE high-level waste and spent nuclear fuel will remain at five current sites.[c]

Table 2. (Continued)

On-site storage	
	DOE spent nuclear fuel will be moved to dry storage. DOE high-level waste will be vitrified and stored in facilities like the Glass Waste Storage Building at the Savannah River Site.
Reactor operations	All currently operating reactors receive a 20-year license extension and continue operating until the extensions expire. Reactors will be decommissioned when operations cease, and only spent nuclear fuel dry storage will remain on site.
Transportation	Waste will not be transported between reactor sites.
Repackaging	Dry cask storage systems will need to be replaced after 100 years, requiring repackaging into new inner canisters and outer casks. Only our 500-year on-site storage model assumes repackaging.
Final disposition or long-term management[c]	We analyzed two final disposition scenarios: The waste will be disposed of in a geologic repository after 100 years or the waste will remain on site for 500 years and be repackaged every 100 years.

Source: GAO analysis based on expert-provided data.

[a] We analyzed some scenarios associated with these alternatives that did not include final disposition of the waste.

[b] The Morris facility is an independent spent nuclear fuel storage installation located in Illinois that is operated by General Electric Corporation, which originally intended to operate a fuel reprocessing plant at the site. The Morris facility is the only spent nuclear fuel pool licensed by NRC that is not at a reactor site.

[c] Hanford Reservation, Washington; Idaho National Laboratory, Idaho; Fort St. Vrain, Colorado; West Valley, New York; and Savannah River Site, South Carolina.

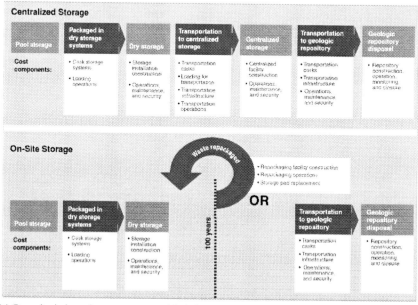

Source: GAO analysis based on expert-provided data.

Figure 5. Process Assumptions and Cost Components for Hypothetical Nuclear Waste Management Alternatives

In addition, there were some instances in which we made assumptions that, while not entirely realistic, were necessary to keep our alternatives generic and distinct from one another. For example, some electric power companies would likely consolidate nuclear waste from different locations by transporting it between reactor sites, but to keep the on-site storage alternative generic and distinct from the centralized storage alternative, we assumed that there would be no consolidation of waste. These simplifying assumptions make our alternatives hypothetical and not entirely representative of their real-world implementation.

We also consulted with experts to formulate more specific assumptions about processes that reflect the sequence of activities that would occur within each alternative (see figure 5). In addition, we identified the components of these processes that have associated costs. For example, one of the processes associated with both alternatives is packaging the nuclear waste in dry storage canisters from the pools of water where they are stored. The component costs associated with this process include the dry storage canisters and operations to load the spent nuclear fuel into the canisters.

We then began to gather data on specific processes and component costs, such as the kind of cask systems we would use in our model and their cost. We gathered initial data from a core group of experts with specialized knowledge in different aspects of nuclear waste management, such as cask systems, waste loading operations, and transportation. We then solicited comments on the initial data from a broader group of experts using a data collection instrument that asked specific questions about how reasonable the data were. We received almost 70 sets of comments and used them to refine or modify our assumptions and component costs and develop the input data that we would use to estimate the overall costs of the alternatives. (See app. I for additional information about our scope and methodology, app. II for our methodology for soliciting comments from nuclear waste management experts, and app. III for these experts.)

We Developed Cost Ranges for Each Alternative Using Large-scale Cost Models that Addressed Uncertainties and Discounted Future Costs

To generate cost ranges for the centralized storage and on-site storage alternatives, we developed four large-scale cost models that analyzed the costs for each alternative of storing 70,000 metric tons and 153,000 metric tons of nuclear waste and created scenarios within these models to analyze different storage durations and final dispositions. (See table 3.) We generated cost ranges for each alternative for storing 153,000 metric tons of waste for 100 years followed by disposal in a geologic repository. We also generated cost ranges for each alternative of storing 70,000 metric tons and 153,000 metric tons of nuclear waste for 100 years, and for storing 153,000 metric tons of waste on site for 500 years without including the cost of subsequent disposal in a geologic repository. For each of the models, which rely upon data and assumptions provided by nuclear waste management experts, the cost range was based on the annual volume of commercial spent nuclear fuel that became ready to be packaged and stored in each year.[21] In general, each model started in 2009 by annually tracking costs of initial packaging and related costs for the first 100 years and for every 100 years thereafter if the waste was to remain on site and be repackaged. Since our models analyzed only the costs associated with storing commercial nuclear waste management, we augmented them with DOE's cost data for (1) managing its spent nuclear fuel and high-level waste and (2) constructing and operating a permanent repository. Specifically, we used DOE's estimated costs for the Yucca Mountain repository to represent cost for a hypothetical permanent repository.[22]

One of the inherent difficulties of analyzing the cost of any nuclear waste management alternative is the large number of uncertainties that need to be addressed. In addition to general uncertainty about the future, there is uncertainty because of the lack of knowledge about the waste management technologies required, the type of waste and waste management systems that individual reactors will eventually employ, and cost components that are key inputs to the models and could occur over hundreds or thousands of years. Given these numerous uncertainties, it is not possible to precisely determine the total costs of each alternative. However, much of the uncertainty that we could not easily capture within our models can be addressed through the use of several alternative models and scenarios. As shown in table 3, we developed two models for each alternative to address the uncertainty regarding the total volume of waste for disposal. We then developed different scenarios within each model to address different time frames and disposal paths. Furthermore, we used a risk analysis modeling technique that recognized and addressed uncertainties in our data and assumptions. Given the different possible scenarios and uncertainties, we generated ranges, rather than point estimates, for analyzing the cost of each alternative.

One of the most important uncertainties in our analysis was uncertainty over component costs. To address this, we used a commercially available risk analysis software program that enabled us to model specific uncertainties associated with a large number of cost inputs and assumptions. Using a Monte Carlo simulation process,[23] the program explores a wide range of values, instead of one single value, for each cost input and estimates the total cost. By repeating the calculations thousands of times with a different set of randomly chosen input values, the process produces a range of total costs for each alternative and scenario. The process also specifies the likelihood associated with values in the estimated range.

Table 3. Models and Scenarios Used for Cost Ranges

Model		Scenario	
Nuclear waste management alternative	Waste volume (metric tons)	Storage duration (years)	Final disposition or long-term management
On-site storage	153,000	100	None
		100	Permanent repository
		500	Waste repackaged every 100 years
On-site storage	70,000	100	None
Centralized storage	153,000	100	None
		100	Permanent repository
Centralized storage	70,000	100	None

Source: GAO analysis.

Another inherent difficulty in estimating the cost of nuclear waste management alternatives is the fact that the costs are spread over hundreds or thousands of years. The economic concept of discounting is central to such long-term analysis because it allows us to convert costs that occur in the distant future to present value—equivalent values in today's dollars. Although the concept of discounting is an accepted and standard methodology in economics, the concept of discounting values over a very distant future—known as "intergenerational discounting"—is still subject to considerable debate. Furthermore, no consensus exists among economists regarding the exact value of the discount rate that should be used to discount values that are spread over many hundreds or thousands of years.

To develop an appropriate discounting methodology and to choose the discount rates for our analysis, we reviewed a number of economic studies published in peer-reviewed journals that addressed intergenerational discounting. Based on our review, we designed a discounting methodology for use in our models. Because our review did not find a consensus on discount rates, we used a range of values for discount rates that we developed based on the economic studies we reviewed, rather than using one single rate. Consequently, because we used ranges for the discount rate along with the Monte Carlo simulation process, the present value of estimated costs does not depend on one single discount rate, but rather reflect a range of discount rate values taken from peer-reviewed studies. (See app. IV for details of our modeling and discounting methodologies, assumptions, and results.)

CENTRALIZED STORAGE WOULD PROVIDE A NEAR-TERM ALTERNATIVE, ALLOWING OTHER OPTIONS TO BE STUDIED, BUT FACES IMPLEMENTATION CHALLENGES

Centralized storage would provide a near-term alternative for managing nuclear waste, allowing the government to begin taking possession of the waste within approximately the next 30 years, and giving additional time for the nation to consider long-term waste management options. However, centralized storage does not preclude the need for final disposal of the waste. In addition, centralized storage faces several implementation challenges including that DOE (1) lacks statutory authority to provide centralized storage under NWPA, (2) is expected to have difficulty finding a location willing to host a centralized storage facility, and (3) faces potential transportation risks. The estimated cost of implementing centralized storage for 100 years ranges from $15 billion to $29 billion for 153,000 metric tons of nuclear waste, and the total cost ranges from $23 billion to $81 billion if the nuclear waste is centrally stored and then disposed in a geologic repository.

Centralized Storage Would Provide a Near-Term Alternative to Managing Nuclear Waste but Does Not Eliminate the Need for Final Disposal

As the administration re-examines the Yucca Mountain repository and national nuclear waste policy, centralized dry cask storage could provide a near-term alternative for managing the waste that has accumulated and will continue to accumulate. This would provide additional time—NRC has stated that spent nuclear fuel storage is safe and environmentally acceptable for a period on the order of 100 years—to consider other long-term options that may involve alternative policies and new technologies and allow some flexibility for their implementation. For example, centralized storage would maintain nuclear waste in interim dry storage configurations so that it could be easily accessible for reprocessing in case the nation decided to pursue reprocessing as a waste management option and developed technologies that address current proliferation and cost concerns. In fact, reprocessing facilities could be built near or adjacent to centralized facilities to maximize efficiencies. However, even with reprocessing, some of the spent nuclear fuel and high-level waste in current inventories would require final disposal.

Centralized storage would consolidate the nation's nuclear waste after reactors are decommissioned, thereby decreasing the complexity of securing and overseeing the waste and increasing the efficiency of waste storage operations. This alternative would remove nuclear waste from all DOE sites and nine shutdown reactor sites that have no operations other than nuclear waste storage, allowing these sites to be closed. Some of these storage sites occupy land that potentially could be used for other purposes, imposing an opportunity cost on states and communities that no longer receive the benefits of electricity generation from the reactors. To compensate for this loss, industry officials noted that at least two states where decommissioned sites are located have tried to raise property taxes on the sites, and at one site, the state collects a per cask fee for storage. In addition, the continued storage of nuclear waste at decommissioned sites can cost the power companies between about $4 million and $8 million per year, according to several experts.

Centralized storage could allow reactor operators to thin-out spent nuclear fuel assemblies from densely packed spent fuel pools and may also prevent operating reactors from having to build the additional dry storage capacity they would need if the nuclear waste remained on site. According to an industry official, 28 reactor sites could have to add dry storage facilities over the next 10 years in order to maintain a desired capacity in their storage pools. These dry storage facilities could cost about $30 million each, but this cost would vary widely by site. In addition, some current reactor sites use older waste storage systems and are near large cities or large bodies of fresh water used for drinking or irrigation. Although NRC's licensing and inspection process is designed to ensure that these existing facilities appropriately protect public health and safety, new centralized facilities could use state-of-the-art design technology and be located in remote areas with fewer environmental hazards, in order to protect public health and enhance safety.

Finally, if DOE uses centralized facilities to store commercial spent nuclear fuel, this alternative could allow DOE to fulfill its obligation to take custody of the commercial spent nuclear fuel until a long-term strategy is implemented. As a result, DOE could curtail its liabilities to the electric power companies, potentially saving the government up to $500 million per year after 2020, as estimated by DOE. The actual impact of centralized storage on the amount of the liabilities would depend on several factors, including when centralized storage is available, whether reactor sites had already built on-site dry storage facilities for which the government may be liable for a portion of the costs, how soon waste could be transported to a centralized site, and the outcome of pending litigation that may affect the government's total liability. DOE estimates that if various complex statutory, regulatory, siting, construction, and financial issues were expeditiously resolved, a centralized facility to accept nuclear waste could begin operations as early as 6 years after its development began.

However, a centralized storage expert estimated that the process from site selection until a centralized facility opens could take between 17 and 33 years.

Although centralized storage has a number of positive attributes, it provides only an interim alternative and does not eliminate the need for final disposal of the nuclear waste. To keep the waste safe and secure, a centralized storage facility relies on active institutional controls, such as monitoring, maintenance, and security. Over time, the storage systems may degrade and institutional controls may be disrupted, which could result in increased risk of radioactive exposure to humans or the environment. For example, according to several experts on dry cask systems, the vents on the casks—which allow for passive cooling—must be periodically inspected to ensure no debris clogs them, particularly during the first several decades when the spent nuclear fuel is thermally hot. If the vents become clogged, the temperature in the canister could rise, which could impact the life of the dry cask storage system. Over a longer time frame, concrete on the exterior casks could degrade, requiring more active maintenance. Although some experts stated that the risk of radiation being released into the environment may be low, such risks can be avoided by permanently isolating the waste in a manner that does not require indefinite, active institutional controls, such as disposal in a geologic repository.

Legal and Community Challenges Contribute to the Complexity of Implementing Centralized Storage

A key challenge confronting the centralized storage alternative is the lack of authority under NWPA for DOE to provide such storage. Provisions in NWPA that allow DOE to arrange for centralized storage have either expired or are unusable because they are tied to milestones in repository development that have not been met. For example, NWPA authorized DOE to provide temporary storage for a limited amount of spent nuclear fuel until a repository was available, but this authority expired in 1990. Some industry representatives have stated that DOE still has the authority to accept and store spent nuclear fuel under the Atomic Energy Act of 1954, as amended, but DOE asserts that NWPA limits its authority under the Atomic Energy Act.[24] In addition, NWPA provided authority for DOE to site, construct, and operate a centralized storage facility, but such a facility could not be constructed until NRC authorized construction of the Yucca Mountain repository, and the facility could only store up to 10,000 metric tons of nuclear waste until the repository started accepting spent nuclear fuel. Therefore, unless provisions in NWPA were amended, centralized storage would have to be funded, owned, and operated privately. A privately operated centralized storage facility alternative, such as the proposed Private Fuel Storage Facility in Utah, would not likely resolve DOE's liabilities with the nuclear power companies.[25]

A second, equally important, challenge to centralized storage is the likelihood of opposition during site selection for a facility. Experts noted that affected states and communities would raise concerns about safety, security, and the likelihood that an interim centralized storage facility could become a de facto permanent storage site if progress is not being made on a permanent repository. Even if a local community supports a centralized storage facility, the state may not. For example, the Private Fuel Storage facility was generally supported by the Skull Valley Band of the Goshute Indians, on whose reservation the facility was to be located, but the state of Utah and some tribal members opposed its licensing and construction. Other states have indicated their opposition to involuntarily hosting a centralized facility through means such as the Western Governors' Association, which issued a resolution stating that "no such facility, whether publicly or privately owned, shall be located within the geographic boundaries of a Western state without the written consent of the governor."[26] Some experts noted that a state or community may be willing to serve as a host if substantial economic incentives were offered and if the party building the site undertook a time-consuming and expensive process of site characterization and safety assessment. However, DOE officials stated that in their previous experience—such as with the Nuclear Waste Negotiator about 15 to 20 years ago—they have found no incentive package that has successfully encouraged a state to voluntarily host a site.

A third challenge to centralized storage is that nuclear waste would likely have to be transported twice—once to the centralized site and once to a permanent repository—if a centralized site were not colocated with a repository.[27] Therefore, the total distance over which nuclear waste is transported is likely to be greater than with other alternatives, an important factor because, according to one expert, transportation risk is directly tied to this distance. However, according to DOE, nuclear waste has been safely transported in the United States since the 1960s and National Academy of Sciences, NRC, and DOE-sponsored reports have found that the associated risks are well understood and generally low. Yet, there are also perceived risks associated with nuclear waste transportation that can result in lower property values along transportation routes, reductions in tourism, and increased anxiety that create community opposition to nuclear waste transportation. According to experts, transportation risks could be mitigated through such means as shipping the least radioactive fuel first, using trains that only transport nuclear waste, and identifying routes that minimize possible impacts on highly populated areas. In addition, the hazards associated with transportation from a centralized facility to a repository would decline as the waste decayed and became less radioactive at the centralized facility.

Cost Ranges for Centralized Storage Will Vary Depending on Waste Volume and Final Disposition

As shown in table 4, our models generated cost ranges from $23 billion to $81 billion for the centralized storage of 153,000 metric tons of spent nuclear fuel and high-level waste for 100 years followed by geologic disposal. For centralized storage without disposal, costs would range from $12 billion to $20 billion for 70,000 metric tons of waste and from $15 billion to $29 billion for 153,000 metric tons of waste. These centralized model scenarios include the cost of on-site operations required to package and prepare the waste for transportation, such as storing the waste in dry-cask storage until it is transported off site, developing and operating a system to transport the waste to centralized storage, and constructing and operating two centralized storage facilities. (See app. IV for information about our modeling methodology, assumptions, and results.)

Table 4. Estimated Cost Range for Each Centralized Storage Scenario

Dollars in billions		
Centralized storage scenario	Time period covered[a]	2009 present value estimate range
Storage of 70,000 metric tons	2009 to 2108 (100 years)	$12 to $20
Storage of 153,000 metric tons	2009 to 2108 (100 years)	$15 to $29
Storage of 153,000 metric tons, with disposal in a permanent repository after 100 years	2009 to 2240 (232 years[b])	$23 to $81

Source: GAO analysis of data provided by nuclear waste management experts and DOE.
[a] See appendix IV for an explanation of the periods covered by the scenarios.
[b] This period was chosen to capture costs of the hypothetical geologic repository through closure.

Actual centralized storage costs may be more or less than these cost ranges if a different centralized storage scenario is implemented. For example, our models assume that there would be two centralized facilities, but licensing, construction, and operations and maintenance costs would be greater if there were more than two facilities and lower if there was only one facility. Some experts told us that centralized storage would likely be implemented with only one facility because it would be too difficult to site two. But other experts noted that having more sites could reduce the number of miles traveled by the waste and provide a greater degree of geographic equity. The length of time the nuclear waste is stored could also impact the cost ranges, particularly if the nuclear waste were stored for less than or more than the time period assumed in our model. For periods longer than 100 years, experts told us that the dry storage cask systems may be subject to degradation and require repackaging, substantially raising the costs, as well as the level of uncertainty in those costs. Transportation is another area where costs could vary if, for example, transportation was not by rail or if the transportation system differed significantly from what is assumed in our models.

Furthermore, costs could be outside our ranges if the final disposition of the waste is different. Our scenario that includes geologic disposal is based on the current cost projections for Yucca Mountain, but these costs could be significantly different for another repository site or if much of the nuclear waste is reprocessed. A different geologic repository would have unique site characterization costs, may use an entirely different design than Yucca Mountain, and may be more or less difficult to build. Also, reprocessing could contribute significantly to the cost of an alternative.

For example, we previously reported that construction of a reprocessing plant with an annual production throughput of 3,000 metric tons of spent nuclear fuel could cost about $44 billion.[28] Studies analyzed by the Congressional Budget Office estimate that once a reprocessing plant is constructed, spent nuclear fuel could be reprocessed at between $610,000 and $1.4 million per-metric-ton, when adjusted to 2009 constant dollars.[29] This would result in an annual cost of about $2 billion to $4 billion, assuming a throughput of 3,000 metric tons per year.

Finally, the actual cost of implementing one of our centralized storage scenarios would likely be higher than our estimated ranges indicate because our models omit several location-specific costs. These costs could not be quantified in our generic models because we did not make an assumption about the specific location of the centralized facilities. For example, a few experts noted that incentives may be given a state or locality as a basis for allowing a centralized facility to be built, but the incentive amount may vary from location to location based on what agreement is reached. Also, several experts said that rail construction may be required for some locations, which could add significant cost depending on the distance of new rail line required at a specific location. Experts could not provide data for these location-dependent costs to any degree of certainty, so we did not use them in our models. Also, the funding source for government-run centralized storage is unclear. The Nuclear Waste Fund, which electric power companies pay into, was established by NWPA to fund a permanent repository and cannot be used to pay for centralized storage without amending the act. Without such a change, the cost for the federal government to implement this alternative would likely have to be borne by the taxpayers.

ON-SITE STORAGE WOULD PROVIDE AN INTERMEDIATE OPTION WITH MINIMAL EFFORT BUT POSES CHALLENGES THAT COULD INCREASE OVER TIME

On-site storage of nuclear waste provides an intermediate option to manage the waste until the government can take possession of it, requiring minimal effort to change from what the nation is currently doing to manage its waste. In the meantime, other longer term policies and strategies could be considered. Such strategies would eventually be required because the on-site storage alternative would not eliminate the need for final disposal of the waste. Some experts believe that legal, community, and technical challenges associated with on-site storage will intensify as the waste remains on site without plans for final disposition because, for example, communities are more likely to oppose recertification of on-site storage. The estimated cost to continue storing 153,000 metric tons of nuclear waste on site for 100 years range from $13 billion to $34 billion, and total costs would range from $20 billion to $97 billion if the nuclear waste is stored on site for 100 years and then disposed in a geologic repository.

On-Site Storage Would Require Minimal Near-Term Logistics and Provide Time to Decide on Long-Term Waste Management Strategies

Because of delays in the Yucca Mountain repository, on-site storage has continued as the nation's strategy for managing nuclear waste, thus its continuation would require minimal near-term effort and allow time for the nation to consider alternative long-term nuclear waste management options. This alternative maintains the waste in a configuration where it is readily retrievable for reprocessing or other disposition, according to an expert. However, like centralized storage, on-site storage is an interim strategy that relies on active institutional controls, such as monitoring, maintenance, and security. To permanently isolate the waste from humans and the environment without the need for active institutional controls some form of final disposal would be required, even if some of the waste were reprocessed.

The additional time in on-site storage may also make the waste safer to handle because older spent nuclear fuel and high-level waste has had a chance to cool and become less radioactive. As a result, on-site storage could reduce transportation risks, particularly in the near-term, since the nuclear waste would be cooler and less radioactive when it is finally transported to a repository. In addition, some experts state that older, cooler waste may provide more predictability in repository performance and be some degree safer than younger, hotter waste. However, NRC cautioned that the ability to handle the waste more safely in the future also depends on other factors, including how the waste or waste packages might degrade over time. In particular, NRC stated that there are many uncertainties with the behavior of spent nuclear fuel as it ages, such as potential fracturing of the structural assemblies, possibly increasing the risks of release. If the waste has to be repackaged, for example, the process may require additional safety measures. Some experts noted that continuing to store nuclear waste on site would be more equitable than consolidating it in one or a few areas. As a result, the waste, along with its associated risks, would be kept in the location where the electrical power was generated, leaving the responsibility and risks of the waste in the communities that benefited from its generation.

On-Site Storage Poses Legal, Community, and Technical Challenges that Are Likely to Intensify over Time

With on-site storage of DOE-managed spent nuclear fuel and high-level waste, DOE would have difficulty meeting enforceable agreements with states, which could result in significant costs being incurred the longer spent nuclear fuel remains on site. In addition to Idaho's agreement to impose a penalty of $60,000 per day if spent nuclear fuel is not removed from the state by 2035, DOE has an agreement with Colorado stating that if the spent fuel at Fort St. Vrain is not removed by January 1, 2035, the government will, subject to certain conditions, pay the state $15,000 per day until it is removed. Other states where DOE spent nuclear fuel and high-level waste are currently stored may seek similar penalties if the spent fuel and waste remain on-site with no progress toward a permanent repository or centralized storage facility.

A second challenge is the cost due to the government's possible legal liabilities to commercial reactor operators. Leaving waste on site under the responsibility of the electric power companies does not relieve the government of its obligation to take custody of the waste, thus the liability debt could continue to mount. For every year after 2020 that DOE fails to take custody of the waste in accordance with its contracts with the reactor operators, DOE estimates that the government will continue to accumulate up to $500 million per year beyond the estimated $12 billion in liabilities that will have accrued up to that point; however, the outcome of pending litigation could substantially affect the government's total liability.[30] The government will no longer incur these costs if DOE takes custody of the waste. Some representatives from industry have stated that it is not practical for DOE to take custody of the waste at commercial reactor sites. Moreover, some electric power company executives have stated that their ratepayers are paying for DOE to provide a geologic repository through their contributions to the Nuclear Waste Fund, and the executives believe that simply taking custody of the waste is not sufficient. A DOE official stated that if DOE were to take custody of the waste on site, it would be a complex undertaking due to considerations such as liability for accidents.

Third, continued use of on-site storage would likely also face community opposition. Some experts noted that without progress on a centralized storage facility or repository site to which waste will be moved, some state and local opposition to reactor storage site recertification will increase, and so will challenges to nuclear power companies' applications for reactor license extensions and combined licenses to construct and operate new reactors. Also, experts noted that many commercial reactor sites are not suitable for long-term storage, and none has had an environmental review to assess the impacts of storing nuclear waste at the site beyond the period for which it is currently licensed. One expert noted that if on-site storage were to become a waste management policy, the long-term health, safety, and environmental risks at each site would have to be evaluated. Because waste storage would extend beyond the life of nuclear power reactors, decommissioned reactor sites would not be available for other purposes, and the former reactor operators may have to stay in business for the sole purpose of storing nuclear waste.

Finally, although dry cask storage is considered reliable in the short term, the longer-term costs, maintenance requirements, and security requirements are not well understood. Many experts said waste packages will likely retain their integrity for at least 100 years, but eventually dry storage systems may begin to degrade and the waste in those systems would have to be repackaged. However, commercial dry storage systems have only been in existence since 1986, so nuclear utilities have little experience with long-term system degradation and requirements for repackaging. Some experts suggested that only the outer protective cask would require replacement, but the inner canister would not have to be replaced. Yet, other experts said that, over time, the inner canister would also be exposed to environmental conditions by vents in the outer cask, which could cause corrosion and require a total system replacement. In addition, experts disagreed on the relative safety risks and costs associated with using spent fuel pools to transfer the waste during repackaging compared to using a dry transfer system, which industry representatives said had not been used on a commercial scale. Finally, future security requirements for extended storage are uncertain because as spent nuclear waste ages and becomes cooler and less radioactive, it becomes less lethal to anyone attempting to handle it without protective shielding. For example, a spent nuclear fuel assembly can lose nearly 80 percent of its heat 5 years after it has been removed from a reactor, thereby reducing one of the inherent deterrents to thieves and terrorists attempting to steal or sabotage the spent nuclear fuel and potentially creating a need for costly new security measures.

Cost Ranges for On-Site Storage Will Vary Depending on Waste Volume, Final Disposition, and Duration of Storage

As shown in table 5, our models generated cost ranges from $20 billion to $97 billion for the on-site storage of 153,000 metric tons of spent nuclear fuel and high-level waste for 100 years followed by geologic disposal. For only on-site storage for 100 years without disposal, costs would range from \$10 billion to \$26 billion for 70,000 metric tons of waste and from \$13 billion to \$34 billion for 153,000 metric tons of waste. On-site storage costs would increase significantly if the waste were stored for longer periods—storing 153,000 metric tons on site for 500 years would cost from \$34 billion to \$225 billion—because it would have to be repackaged every 100 years for safety. The on-site storage model scenarios include the costs of on-site operations required to package the waste into dry canister storage, build additional dry storage at the reactor sites, prepare the waste for transportation, and operate and maintain the on-site storage facilities. Most of the costs for the first 100 years would result from the initial loading of materials into dry storage systems. (See app. IV for information on our modeling methodology, assumptions, and results.)

Actual on-site storage costs may be more or less than these cost ranges if a different on-site storage scenario is implemented. For example, to keep it distinct from the centralized storage models, our on-site storage models assume that there would be no transportation or consolidation of waste between the reactor sites. However, several experts noted that in an actual on-site storage scenario, reactor operators would likely consolidate their waste to make operations more efficient and reduce costs. Also, as with the centralized storage alternative, costs for the on-site storage scenario that includes geologic disposal could differ for a repository site other than Yucca Mountain or for additional waste management technologies.

Finally, our models did not include certain costs that were either location-specific or could not be predicted sufficiently to be quantified for our purposes, which would make the actual costs of on-site storage higher than our cost ranges. For example, the taxes and fees associated with on-site storage could vary significantly by state and over time. Also, repackaging operations in our 500-year on-site storage scenario would generate low-level waste that would require disposal. However, the amount of waste generated and the associated disposal costs could vary depending on the techniques used for repackaging. Finally, the total amount of the government's liability for failure to begin taking spent nuclear fuel for disposal in 1998 will depend on the outcome of pending and future litigation.

Table 5. Estimated Cost Range for Each On-site Storage Scenario

Dollars in billions		
On-site storage scenario	Period covered[a]	2009 present value estimate range
Storage of 70,000 metric tons	2009 to 2108 (100 years)	\$10 to \$26
Storage of 153,000 metric tons	2009 to 2108 (100 years)	\$13 to \$34
Storage of 153,000 metric tons, with disposal in a permanent repository after 100 years	2009 to 2240 (232 years[b])	\$20 to \$97
Storage of 153,000 metric tons with repackaging every 100 years	2009 to 2508 (500 years)	\$34 to \$225

Source: GAO analysis of data provided by nuclear waste management experts and DOE.

[a] See appendix IV for an explanation of the periods covered by the scenarios.

[b] This period was chosen to capture costs of the hypothetical geologic repository through closure.

Like the centralized storage alternative, the funding source for the on-site storage alternative is uncertain. Currently, the reactor operators have been paying for the cost to store the waste, but have filed lawsuits to be compensated for storage costs of waste that the federal government was required to take title to under standard contracts. Payments resulting from these lawsuits have come from the Department of the Treasury's judgment fund, which is funded by the taxpayer, because a court determined that the Nuclear Waste Fund could not be used to compensate electric power companies for their storage costs. Without legislative or contractual changes—such as allowing the Nuclear Waste Fund to be used for on-site storage—taxpayers would likely bear the ultimate costs for on-site storage.

CONCLUDING OBSERVATIONS

Developing a long-term national strategy for safely and securely managing the nation's high-level nuclear waste is a complex undertaking that must balance health, social, environmental, security, and financial factors. In addition, virtually any strategy considered will face many political, legal, and regulatory challenges in its implementation. Any strategy selected will need to have geologic disposal as a final disposition pathway. In the case of the Yucca Mountain repository, these challenges have left the nation with nearly three decades of experience. In moving forward, whether the nation commits to the same or a different waste management strategy, federal agencies, industry, and policy makers at all levels of government can benefit from the lessons of Yucca Mountain. In particular, stakeholders can better understand the need for a sustainable national focus and community commitment. Federal agencies, industry, and policymakers may also want to consider a strategy of complementary and parallel interim and long-term disposal options—similar to those being pursued by some other nations—which might provide the federal government with maximum flexibility, since it would allow time to work with local communities and to pursue research and development efforts in key areas, such as reprocessing.

APPENDIX I: SCOPE AND METHODOLOGY

For this chapter we examined (1) the key attributes, challenges, and costs of the Yucca Mountain repository; (2) alternative nuclear waste management approaches; (3) the key attributes, challenges, and costs of storing the nuclear waste at two centralized sites; and (4) the key attributes, challenges, and costs of continuing to store the nuclear waste at its current locations.

Developing Information on Key Attributes, Challenges, and Costs of Yucca Mountain

To provide information on the key attributes and challenges of the Yucca Mountain repository, we reviewed documents and interviewed officials from the Department of Energy's (DOE) Office of Civilian Radioactive Waste Management and Office of

Environmental Management; the Nuclear Regulatory Commission's (NRC) Division of Spent Fuel Storage and Transportation and Division of High Level Waste Repository Safety, both within the Office of Nuclear Material Safety and Safeguards; and the Department of Justice's Civil Division. We also reviewed documents and interviewed representatives from the National Academy of Sciences, the Nuclear Waste Technical Review Board, and other concerned groups. Once we developed our preliminary analysis of Yucca Mountain's key attributes and challenges, we solicited input from nuclear waste management experts. (See app. II for our methodology for soliciting comments from nuclear waste management experts and app. III for a list of these experts.)

To analyze the costs for the Yucca Mountain repository through to closure, we started with the cost information in DOE's Yucca Mountain Total System Lifecycle Cost report, which used 122,100 metric tons of nuclear waste in its analysis.[31] We asked DOE officials to provide a breakdown of the component costs on a per-metric-ton basis that DOE used in the Total System Lifecycle Cost report. We used this information to calculate the costs of a repository at Yucca Mountain for 70,000 metric tons and 153,000 metric tons, changing certain component costs based on the ratio between 70,000 and 122,100 or 153,000 and 122,100. For example, we modified the cost of constructing the tunnels for emplacing the waste for the 70,000-metric-ton scenario by 0.57, the ratio of 70,000 metric tons to 122,100 metric tons. We applied this approach to component costs that would be impacted by the ratio difference, particularly for transporting and emplacing the waste and installing drip shields. We also incorporated DOE's cost estimates for potential delays to licensing the Yucca Mountain repository into our analysis and made modifications to the analysis based on comments by cognizant DOE officials. Finally, we discounted DOE's costs, which were in 2008 constant dollars, to 2009 present value using the methodology described in appendix IV.

Examining and Identifying Nuclear Waste Management Alternatives

To examine and identify alternatives, we started with a series of interviews among federal and state officials and industry representatives. We also gathered and reviewed numerous studies and reports on managing nuclear waste— along with interviewing the authors of many of these studies—from federal agencies, the National Academy of Sciences, the Nuclear Waste Technical Review Board, the Massachusetts Institute of Technology, the American Physical Society, Harvard University, the Boston Consulting Group, and the Electric Power Research Institute. To better understand how commercial spent nuclear fuel is stored, we visited the Dresden Nuclear Power Plant in Illinois and the Hope Creek Nuclear Power Plant in New Jersey, which both store spent nuclear fuel in pools and in dry cask storage. We also visited DOE's Savannah River Site in South Carolina and Fort St. Vrain site in Colorado to observe how DOE-managed spent nuclear fuel and high-level waste are processed and stored.

As we began to identify potential alternatives to analyze, we shared our initial approach and methodology with nuclear waste management experts—including members of the National Academy of Sciences and the Nuclear Waste Technical Review Board to obtain their feedback—and revised our approach accordingly. Many of these experts advised us to develop generic, hypothetical alternatives with clearly defined assumptions about technology and environmental conditions. Industry representatives and other experts advised us that trying to account for the thousands of variables relating to geography, the environment, regional regulatory differences, or differences in business models would result in infeasible and unmanageable models. They also advised us against trying to predict changes in the future for technologies or environmental conditions because they would purely conjectural and fall beyond the scope of this analysis.

Based on this information, we identified two generic, hypothetical alternatives to use as the basis of our analysis: centralized storage and on-site storage. Within each of these alternatives, we identified different scenarios that examined the costs associated with the management of 70,000 metric tons and 153,000 metric tons of nuclear waste and whether or not the waste is shipped to a repository for disposal after 100 years.

Once we identified the alternatives, we again consulted with experts to establish assumptions regarding commercial spent nuclear fuel management and its associated components to define the scope and specific processes that would be included in each alternative. To identify a more complete, qualified list of nuclear waste management experts with relevant experience who could provide and critique this information, we used a technique known as snowballing. We started with experts in the field who were known to us, primarily from DOE, NRC, National Council of State Legislators, the State of Nevada Agency for Nuclear Projects, the Nuclear Energy Institute, and the National Association of Regulatory Utility Commissioners and asked them to refer us to other experts, focusing on U.S.-based experts. We then contacted these individuals and asked for additional referrals. We continued this iterative process until additional interviews did not lead us to any new names or we determined that the qualified experts in a given technical area had been exhausted.

We conducted an initial interview with each of these experts by asking them questions about the nature and extent of their expertise and their views on the Yucca Mountain repository. Specifically, we asked each expert:

- What is the nature of your expertise? How many years have you been doing work in this area? Does your expertise allow you to comment on planning assumptions and costs of waste management related to storage, disposal, or transport?
- If you were to classify yourself in relation to the Yucca Mountain repository, would you classify yourself as a proponent, an opponent, an independent, an undecided or uncommitted, or some combination of these?

We then narrowed our list down to those individuals who identified themselves or whom others identified as having current, nationally recognized expertise in areas of nuclear waste management that were relevant to our analysis. For balance, we ensured that we included experts who reflected (1) key technical areas of waste management; (2) a range of industry, government, academia, and concerned groups; and (3) a variety of viewpoints on the Yucca Mountain repository. (See app. III for 147 experts we contacted.) Once we developed our list of experts, we classified them into three groups:

- Those whose expertise would allow them to provide us with specific information and advice on the processes that should be included in each alternative and the best estimates of expected cost ranges for the components of each alternative, such as a typical or reasonable price for a dry cask storage.

- Those who could weigh in on these estimates, as well as give us insight and comments on assumptions that we planned to use to define our alternatives.
- Those whose expertise was not in areas of component costs, but who could nonetheless give us valuable information on other assumptions, such as transportation logistics.

To define our alternatives and develop the assumptions and cost components we needed for our analysis, we started with the experts from the first group who had the most direct and reliable knowledge of the processes and costs associated with the alternatives we identified. This group consisted of seven experts and included federal government officials and representatives from industry. We worked closely with these experts to identify the key assumptions that would establish the scope of our alternatives, the more specific assumptions to identify the processes associated with each alternative, the components of these processes that we could quantify in terms of cost, and the level of uncertainty associated with each component cost. For example, two of the experts in this first group told us that for the on-site alternative, commercial reactor sites that did not already have independent spent nuclear fuel storage installations would have to build them during the next 10 years and that the cost for licensing, design, and construction of each installation would range from $24 million to $36 million. Once we had gathered our initial assumptions and cost components, we used a data collection instrument to solicit comments on them from all of our experts. We then used the experts' comments to refine our assumptions and component costs. (See app. II for our methodology for consulting with this larger group of nuclear waste management experts.)

DOE officials provided assumptions and cost data for managing DOE spent nuclear fuel and high-level waste, which we incorporated into our analysis of the centralized storage and on-site storage alternatives. These assumptions and cost information covered management of spent nuclear fuel and high-level waste at DOE's Idaho National Laboratory, Hanford Reservation, Savannah River Site, and West Valley site.

Developing Information on Key Attributes, Challenges, and Costs of the Centralized Storage and On-Site Storage Alternatives

To gather information on the key attributes and challenges of our alternatives, we interviewed agency officials and nuclear waste management experts from industry, academic institutions, and concerned groups. We also reviewed the reports and studies and visited the locations that were mentioned in the previous section. To ensure that the attributes and challenges we developed were accurate, comprehensive, and balanced, we asked our snowballed list of experts to provide their comments on our work, using the data collection instrument that is described in appendix II. We used the comments that we received to expand the attributes or challenges on our list or, where necessary, to modify our characterization of individual attributes or challenges.

To generate cost ranges for the centralized storage and on-site storage alternatives, we developed four large-scale cost models that analyzed the costs for each alternative of storing 70,000 metric tons and 153,000 metric tons of nuclear waste for 100 years followed by disposal in a geologic repository. (See app. IV.) We also generated cost ranges for each alternative of storing the waste for 100 years without including the cost of subsequent disposal in a geologic repository for storing 153,000 metric tons of waste on site for 500 years. For each model, which rely upon data and assumptions provided by nuclear waste management experts, the cost range was based on the annual volume of commercial spent nuclear fuel that became ready to be packaged and stored in each year. In general, each model started in 2009 by annually tracking costs of initial packaging and related costs for the first 100 years and for every 100 years thereafter if the waste was to remain on site and be repackaged. Since our models analyzed only the costs associated with storing commercial nuclear waste management, we augmented them with DOE's cost data for (1) managing its spent nuclear fuel and high-level waste and (2) constructing and operating a permanent repository. Specifically, we used DOE's estimated costs for the Yucca Mountain repository to represent cost for a hypothetical permanent repository.[32]

We conducted this performance audit from April 2008 to October 2009 in accordance with generally accepted government auditing standards. These standards require that we plan and perform the audit to obtain sufficient, appropriate evidence to provide a reasonable basis for our findings and conclusions based on our audit objectives. We believe that the evidence obtained provides a reasonable basis for our findings and conclusions based on our audit objectives.

APPENDIX II: OUR METHODOLOGY FOR OBTAINING COMMENTS FROM NUCLEAR WASTE MANAGEMENT EXPERTS

As discussed in appendix I, we gathered the assumptions and associated component costs used to define our nuclear waste management alternatives by consulting with experts in an iterative process of identifying initial assumptions and component costs and revising them based on expert comments. This appendix (1) describes the data collection instrument we used to obtain comments on the initial assumptions and component costs, (2) describes how we analyzed the comments and revised our assumptions, and (3) provides a list of the assumptions and cost data that we derived through this process and used in our cost models.

To obtain comments from a broad group of nuclear waste management experts, we compiled the initial assumptions and component costs that we gathered from a small group of experts into a data collection instrument that included

- a description of the Yucca Mountain repository and our proposed nuclear waste management alternatives—on-site storage and centralized storage—and attributes and challenges associated with them;
- our initial assumptions that would identify and define the processes, time frames, and major components used to bound our hypothetical centralized and on-site storage alternatives;
- the major component costs of each alternative, including definitions and initial cost data; and
- components associated with each alternative with a high degree of uncertainty that we did not attempt to quantify in terms of costs.

Table 6. Our Data Collection Instrument for Nuclear Waste Management Experts

Section of the data collection instrument	Questions asked of the experts
Description of each alternative and its attributes and challenges	What additional issues do you suggest we consider, or is there one listed that you would modify?
List of initial assumptions for each alternative	To what extent to you think this assumption is reasonable or unreasonable?[a] If this assumption does not seem reasonable, please describe.[a] Are there additional assumptions defining our scenario not mentioned above that you would recommend GAO consider? Please describe.
List of component costs and initial cost data	Is this estimate reasonable or unreasonable?[a] If this estimate is not reasonable, please describe why (estimate too high, estimate too low, range too broad, range too narrow) and, if possible, provide specific alternative cost estimates.[a] Please tell us anything about this cost item that might make it difficult (or not difficult) to estimate accurately?[a] Are there additional cost categories not mentioned above that you would recommend GAO consider? Please provide a generic cost estimate or potential source of such an estimate, if possible.
List of uncertain components	In your opinion, do you think any of these items can be quantified? If so, please provide suggestions for how to quantify them, along with supporting data, if available.

Source: GAO.

[a] This question was asked after each assumption or component.

The data collection instrument asked the experts to answer specific questions about each piece of information that we provided (see table 6).

We pretested our instrument with several individual experts to ensure that our questions were clear and would provide us with the information that we needed, and then refined the instrument accordingly. Next; we sent the instrument to 114 experts who were identified through our snowballing methodology (see apps. I and III). Each expert received the sections of our data collection instrument that included the attributes and challenges of the alternatives and the initial assumptions, but only those experts with the type and level of expertise to comment on costs received the cost component sections.

We received 67 sets of comments from independent experts and experts representing industry, federal government, state governments, and other concerned groups.[33] These experts also represented a range of viewpoints on the Yucca Mountain repository. Each of their responses was compiled into a database organized by each individual assumption or cost element for the on-site storage and centralized interim storage alternatives.

To arrive at the final assumptions and cost component data for our models, we qualitatively analyzed the experts' comments. The comments we received on the assumptions differed in nature from those we received on the component costs, so our analysis and disposition of comments differed slightly. For the assumptions, we took the comments on each assumption that were made when an expert did not believe it was entirely reasonable and grouped comments that were similar. We determined the relevance of a comment to our assumption based on whether the comment provided a basis upon which we could modify the assumption or was within the scope or capability of our models. For example, we received several comments about how an assumption may be affected by nuclear waste from new reactors, including potential liabilities if the Department of Energy (DOE) does not take custody of that waste, but in the key assumptions defining our alternatives, we explicitly excluded new reactors because we could not predict how many new reactors would be built, when they would operate, and the amount of waste that they would generate. For those comments that were relevant, we weighed the expertise of those making the comments and determined whether the balance of the comments warranted a modification to our preliminary assumption. In some instances, we conducted followup interviews with selected experts to clarify issues that the broad group of experts raised.

For the component costs, we organized the comments on a particular component based on whether an expert thought the cost and uncertainty range was reasonable, too high, too low, the range was too broad, or the range was too narrow. We developed a ranking system to identify which experts had the greatest degree of direct experience or knowledge with the cost and weighed their comments accordingly to determine whether our preliminary cost should be modified. Also, we took into account the incidence of expert agreement or disagreement when deciding how much uncertainty to apply to a particular cost.

Table 7. Initial Assumptions and Component Cost Estimates for Our Centralized Storage and On-site Storage Alternatives and Modifications Made Based on Experts' Responses to Our Data Collection Instrument

Centralized storage		
Key aspect of the alternative	**Initial key assumption**	**Modification based on expert comments**
Number of sites	Two sites located in different geographic regions of the country.	None
Reactor operations	Current reactors will receive, if they have not already, a 20-year license extension and will operate until the end of their licensed life.	None
	When reactors cease operations, they will be decommissioned and only spent nuclear fuel dry storage will remain on site.	None
Transportation	Transportation will be the similar to what is assumed for the Yucca Mountain repository—via rail, using dedicated trains.	None
Repackaging	Waste will not be repackaged at the centralized facilities.[a]	None
Final disposition	Waste will be stored at the centralized sites until 100 years from now and then be disposed of in a geologic repository.[b]	None

Table 7. (Continued)

Process	Initial process assumption	Modification based on expert comments
Waste packaged into dry storage casks	Reactor operators will only move the amount of waste from pools into dry storage that is necessary to preserve full-core offload capability—the capacity in their spent nuclear fuel pools to store all of the fuel in the reactor core.	None
	The overall amount of fuel moved from the pools to dry storage will be equal to estimated annual rates at which fuel is discharged from the reactors.	None
	Dual-purpose canister systems will be used until Transportation, Aging and Disposal systems become widely available.	Only dual-purpose systems will be used.
	Transportation, Aging and Disposal systems will have a capacity of 8.5 metric tons plus or minus 5 percent.	None (although this assumption became obsolete when we no longer assumed transportation, aging, and disposal systems would be used).
Centralized storage		
Reactor site dry storage	All reactor sites without dry storage facilities will construct them at the time they lose full-core offload capability—the capacity in their spent nuclear fuel pools to store all of the fuel in the reactor core.	None
	Dry storage operations and maintenance costs vary by nature of the site, such as operating versus decommissioned.	None
	On average, 1.5 decommissioned reactor sites will be cleared of their waste each year.	None
Transportation to centralized storage	Once running at full capacity, transportation rates will be approximately 3,000 metric tons per year (what is assumed for Yucca Mountain).	None
	Waste from decommissioned sites and GE Morris will be transported before waste from operating sites. This waste would not be converted to dry storage prior to transportation.	None
	133 transportation casks will be required (what is assumed for Yucca Mountain) and will be acquired over a 7-year period.	None
	No new rail construction will be required.	None

Table 7. (Continued)

Process	Initial process assumption	Modification based on expert comments
	Transportation system infrastructure, system support, and operations will be analogous to what DOE assumes for Yucca Mountain.	None
Centralized storage	The two centralized facilities will begin accepting waste in 2028.	None
	The sites will be built at existing federal facilities and be owned and operated by DOE.	None
Geologic disposal	Waste will not be repackaged before being disposed of in a permanent repository.	None
	Any spent nuclear fuel not originally packaged into a Transportation, Aging and Disposal canister will be repackaged at the geologic repository.	This assumption became obsolete when we no longer assumed transportation, aging, and disposal canisters would be used.
Process component	**Initial component cost estimate**	**Modification based on expert comments**
Dry cask storage systems: • transportation, aging, and disposal • dual-purpose	• $1.1 million plus or minus 10 percent • $900,000 plus or minus 5 percent	• Obsolete • $900,000 plus or minus 25 percent
Loading operations: • cost per cask to load fuel into dry storage canisters • loadingcampaign consisting, on average, of five casks (including set-up, clean up, training, and labor)	• $150,000 plus or minus 5 percent • $750,000 plus or minus 5 percent	• $275,000 plus or minus 45 percent • None
Centralized storage		
Design, licensing, and construction of dry storage installations at reactor sites	$30 million plus or minus 20 percent	$30 million plus or minus 40 percent
Annual operations and maintenance:	• $100,000 plus or minus 20 percent • $3 million plus or minus 20 percent • $10 million plus or minus 20 percent	• $100,000 plus or minus 50 percent

Table 7. (Continued)

Process component	Initial component cost estimate	Modification based on expert comments
• operating reactor site dry storage • decommissioned reactor site dry storage • decommissioned reactor site wet storage		• $4.5 million plus or minus 40 percent • None
Transportation casks	$4.5 million plus or minus 10 percent	None
Loading for transportation cost per canister	$250,000 plus or minus 5 percent	$150,000 plus or minus 40 percent
Transportation infrastructure: • rolling stock and facilities • transportation system support	• $400 million plus or minus 10 percent • $2.5 billion plus or minus 10 percent	• None • None
Transportation operations per-metric-ton	$26,000 plus or minus 10 percent	None
Centralized facility licensing and construction: • 70,000 metric ton facility • 153,000 metric ton facility	• $168 million plus or minus 10 percent • $232 million plus or minus 10 percent	• $218 million plus or minus 20 percent • $302 million plus or minus 20 percent
Centralized facility annual operations and maintenance	$8.8 million plus or minus 10 percent	None
On-site storage		
Key aspect of the alternative	Initial key assumption	Modification based on expert comments
Number of commercial sites	Commercial spent nuclear fuel spent nuclear fuel will be stored at 75 reactor sites.	None
Number of DOE sites	DOE high-level waste and spent nuclear fuel will remain at five current sites.	None
Reactor operations	Current reactors will receive, if they have not already, a 20-year license extension and will operate until the end of their licensed life.	None

Table 7. (Continued)

Key aspect of the alternative	Initial key assumption	Modification based on expert comments
	When reactors cease operations, they will be decommissioned and only spent nuclear fuel dry storage will remain on site.	None
Transportation	There will be no transportation of waste between sites.	None
Repackaging	Dry cask storage systems would require repackaging every 100 years.	None

On-site storage

Process	Initial process assumption	Modification based on expert comments
Waste packaged into dry storage casks	Reactor operators will use generic dual-purpose canisters for dry storage with a capacity of 13 metric tons plus or minus 5 percent.	Range increased to plus or minus 15 percent.
	Reactor operators will only move the amount of waste from pools into dry storage that is necessary to preserve full-core offload capability.	None
	The overall amount of fuel moved from the pools to dry storage will be equal to estimated annual rates at which fuel is discharged from the reactors.	None
Reactor site dry storage	All reactor sites without dry storage facilities will construct them at the time they lose full-core offload capability.	None
	Dry storage operations and maintenance costs vary by nature of the site, such as operating versus decommissioned.	None
Repackaging	Wet transfer facilities will need to be built at each site for every packaging interval (i.e. every 100 years).	We will assume a generic transfer system that could be either wet or dry.
	All sites will need to replace their dry storage pad and infrastructure every 100 years when they repackage.	None

Process component	Initial component cost estimate	Modification based on expert comments
Dry cask storage system	$900,000 plus or minus 5 percent	$900,000 plus or minus 25 percent
Loading operations: • cost per cask to load fuel into dry storage canisters	• $150,000 plus or minus 5 percent • $750,000 plus or minus 5 percent	• $275,000 plus or minus 45 percent • None

Table 7. (Continued)

Process	Initial process assumption	Modification based on expert comments
• loading campaign consisting, on average, of five casks (including set-up,clean up, training, and labor)		
Design, licensing, and construction of dry storage installations at reactor sites	$30 million plus or minus 20 percent	$30 million plus or minus 40 percent
Annual operations and maintenance: • operating reactor site dry storage	• $100,000 plus or minus 20 percent	• $200,000 plus or minus 50 percent
• decommissioned reactor site dry storage • decommissioned reactor site wet storage	• $3 million plus or minus 20 percent • $10 million plus or minus 20 percent	• $4.5 million plus or minus 40 percent • None
Construction of a transfer facility for repackaging	$300 million plus or minus 50 percent (for a wet transfer facility)	$300 million plus or minus 50 percent (for either a wet or a dry transfer facility)
On-site Storage		
Repackaging operations:		
• repackaging costs per cask • repackaging campaign consisting, on average, of 5 casks (including set-up, clean up, training, and labor)	• $1.2 million plus or minus 10 percent • $750,000 plus or minus 10 percent	• $1.6 million plus or minus 10 percent • None
Storage pad replacement	$30 million plus or minus 20 percent	$30 million plus or minus 40 percent

Source: GAO analysis based on expert-provided data.

Note: Unless specifically noted, all assumptions and costs apply specifically to commercial nuclear power sites. We used information provided by DOE for the assumptions and costs related to DOE-managed spent nuclear fuel and high-level waste.

[a] We did not explicitly solicit comment on this assumption in the data collection instrument for the centralized storage alternative because we solicited comments on the repackaging requirements in the on-site alternative.

[b] This assumption applies only to the version of our centralized storage alternative that includes final disposal.

Through this analysis, we determined that the preponderance of our preliminary assumptions and cost data were reasonable for use in our models either because the experts generally agreed it was reasonable, or the experts who thought it was reasonable had a greater degree of relevant expertise or knowledge than those who commented otherwise. However, some of the experts' responses indicated that a modification to our model was needed. Table 7 presents a summary of the modifications we made to our model assumptions and cost data based on the expert comments received.

APPENDIX III: NUCLEAR WASTE MANAGEMENT EXPERTS WE INTERVIEWED

	Name	Affiliation
1	Mark D. Abkowitz	U.S. Nuclear Waste Technical Review Board (member)
2	John Ahearne	Sigma Xi
3	Joonhong Ahn	National Academy of Sciences/Nuclear and Radiation Studies Board
4	David Applegate	U.S. Geological Survey
5	Wm. Howard Arnold	U.S. Nuclear Waste Technical Review Board (member)
6	Tom Baillieul	The Chamberlain Group
7	James David Ballard	California State University, Northridge
8	William D. Barnard	U.S. Nuclear Waste Technical Review Board (retired) (staff)
9	Lake Barrett	DOE/Office of Civilian Radioactive Waste Management (retired)
10	Barbara Beller	DOE/Office of Environmental Management
11	David W. Bland	TriVis Incorporated
12	Ted Borst	CH2M-WG Idaho, LLC
13	David C. Boyd	Minnesota Public Utilities Commission
14	Michele Boyd	Physicians for Social Responsibility
15	William Boyle	DOE/Office of Civilian Radioactive Waste Management
16	E. William Brach	Nuclear Regulatory Commission (NRC)/Division of Spent Fuel Storage and Transportation
17	Bruce Breslow	State of Nevada Agency for Nuclear Projects
18	Philip Brochman	NRC/Office of Nuclear Security and Incident Response
19	Tom Brookmire	Dominion Resources, Inc.
20	Robert J. Budnitz	Lawrence Berkeley National Laboratory
21	Susan Burke	Idaho Department of Environmental Quality
22	Barbara Byron	Western Interstate Energy Board
23	Robert Capstick	The Yankee Nuclear Power Companies
24	Thure E. Cerling	U.S. Nuclear Waste Technical Review Board (member)
25	Margaret Chu	M.S. Chu & Associates
26	Tom Clements	Friends of the Earth

(Continued)

	Name	Affiliation
27	Jean Cline	University of Nevada Las Vegas
28	Thomas Cochran	Natural Resources Defense Council
29	Marshall Cohen	Nuclear Energy Institute
30	Kevin Crowley	Nuclear and Radiation Studies Board, National Research Council of the National Academies
31	Jeanne Davidson	U.S. Department of Justice/Civil Division
32	Bradley Davis	DOE/Office of Nuclear Energy
33	Jack Davis	NRC/Division of High Level Waste Repository Safety
34	Jay C. Davis	Lawrence Livermore National Laboratory (retired) Nuclear and Radiation Studies Board, National Research Council of the National Academies
35	Scott DeClue	DOE/Office of Environmental Management
36	Edgardo DeLeon	DOE/Office of Environmental Management
37	Fred Dilger	Black Mountain Research
38	David J. Duquette	U.S. Nuclear Waste Technical Review Board (member)
39	Doug Easterling	Wake Forest University
40	Steven Edwards	Progress Energy
41	Randy Elwood	CH2M-WG Idaho, LLC
42	Rod Ewing	University of Michigan
43	Steve Fetter	University of Maryland
44	James Flynn	Pacific World History Institute
45	Charles Forsberg	Massachusetts Institute of Technology
46	Derrick Freeman	Nuclear Energy Institute
47	Steve Frishman	State of Nevada Nuclear Waste Project Office
48	Robert Fronczak	Association of American Railroads
49	B. John Garrick	U.S. Nuclear Waste Technical Review Board (chairman)
50	Ron Gecan	U.S. Congressional Budget Office
51	Lynn Gelhar	Massachusetts Institute of Technology
52	Christine Gelles	DOE/Office of Environmental Management
53	Robert Gisch	Department of Defense/Department of the Navy
54	Aubrey Godwin	Arizona Radiation Regulatory Agency
55	Charles R. Goergen	Washington Savannah River Company[a]
56	Stephen Goldberg	Argonne National Laboratory
57	Steven Grant	Bechtel SAIC Company, LLC[b]
58	Paul Gunter	Beyond Nuclear
59	Brian Gustems	PSEG Nuclear, LLC
60	Brian Gutherman	ACI Nuclear Energy Solutions
61	Roger L. Hagengruber	University of New Mexico Nuclear and Radiation Studies Board, National Research Council of the National Academies
62	R. Scott Hajner	Bechtel SAIC Company, LLC[b]
63	Robert Halstead	Transportation Advisor, State of Nevada Agency for Nuclear Projects

(Continued)

	Name	Affiliation
64	Paul Harrington	DOE/Office of Civilian Radioactive Waste Management
65	Ronald Helms	Bechtel SAIC Company, LLC[b]
66	Damon Hindle	Bechtel SAIC Company, LLC[b]
67	James Hollrith	DOE/Office of Civilian Radioactive Waste Management
68	Greg Holden	Department of Defense/Department of the Navy
69	Mark Holt	U.S. Congressional Research Service
70	George M. Hornberger	U.S. Nuclear Waste Technical Review Board (member)
71	William Hurt	Idaho National Laboratory
72	Thomas H. Isaacs	Stanford University Lawrence Livermore National Laboratory Nuclear and Radiation Studies Board, National Research Council of the National Academies
73	Lisa R. Janairo	Council of State Governments, Midwestern Office
74	Andrew C. Kadak	U.S. Nuclear Waste Technical Review Board (member)
75	Kevin Kamps	Beyond Nuclear
76	Anthony Kluk	DOE/Office of Environmental Management
77	Lawrence Kokajko	NRC/Division of High Level Waste Repository Safety
78	Leonard Konikow	U.S. Geological Survey
79	Christopher Kouts	DOE/Office of Civilian Radioactive Waste Management
80	Steven Kraft	Nuclear Energy Institute
81	Darrell Lacy	Nye County, State of Nevada
82	Gary Lanthrum	DOE/Office of Civilian Radioactive Waste Management
83	Doug Larson	Western Interstate Energy Board
84	Ned Larson	DOE/Office of Civilian Radioactive Waste Management
85	Ronald M. Latanision	U.S. Nuclear Waste Technical Review Board (member)
86	Thomas Leschine	University of Washington
87	Adam H. Levin	Exelon Corporation
88	David Little	Washington Savannah River Company[c]
89	David Lochbaum	Union of Concerned Scientists
90	Bob Loux	Consultant
91	Edwin Lyman	Union of Concerned Scientists
92	Allison Macfarlane	George Mason University
93	Arjun Makhijani	Institute for Energy and Environmental Research
94	Zita Martin	Tennessee Valley Authority
95	Rodney McCullum	Nuclear Energy Institute
96	John McKenzie	Department of Defense/Department of the Navy
97	Richard A. Meserve	Carnegie Institution for Science Nuclear and Radiation Studies Board, National Research Council of the National Academies
98	Barry Miles	Department of Defense/Department of the Navy
99	Thomas Minvielle	Department of Defense/Department of the Navy

(Continued)

	Name	Affiliation
100	Bob Mitchell	Yankee Rowe
101	Ali Mosleh	U.S. Nuclear Waste Technical Review Board (member)
102	William M. Murphy	U.S. Nuclear Waste Technical Review Board (member)
103	Connie Nakahara	Utah Department of Environmental Quality
104	Irene Navis	Clark County, Nevada
105	Tara Neider	Transnuclear, Inc.
106	Brian O'Connell	National Association of Regulatory Utility Commissioners
107	Mary Olson	Nuclear Information and Resource Service
108	Pierre Oneid	Holtec International
109	Ronald S. Osteen	DOE/Office of Environmental Management
110	Jean Ridley	DOE/Office of Environmental Management
111	John Parkyn	Private Fuel Storage
112	Stan Pedersen	Bechtel SAIC Company, LLC[b]
113	Charles W. Pennington	NAC International
114	Mark Peters	Argonne National Laboratory
115	Per Peterson	University of California at Berkeley
116	Henry Petroski	U.S. Nuclear Waste Technical Review Board (member)
117	Max Power	Oregon Hanford Cleanup Board
118	Kenneth Powers	DOE/Office of Civilian Radioactive Waste Management
119	Jay Ray	DOE/Office of Environmental Management
120	Jeffrey Ray	Washington Savannah River Company[c]
121	Everett Redmond II	Nuclear Energy Institute
122	James Robert	Tennessee Valley Authority
123	Gene Rowe	U.S. Nuclear Waste Technical Review Board (staff)
124	Karyn Severson	U.S. Nuclear Waste Technical Review Board (staff)
125	David Shoesmith	University of Western Ontario
126	Linda Sikkema	National Conference of State Legislators
127	Kris Singh	Holtec International
128	Brian M. Smith	Department of Defense/Department of the Navy
129	Susan Smith	DOE/Office of Civilian Radioactive Waste Management
130	Joseph D. Sukaskas	Maine Public Utilities Commission
131	Jane Summerson	DOE/Office of Civilian Radioactive Waste Management
132	Eileen Supko	Energy Resources International, Inc.
133	Bill Swift	Washington Savannah River Company[c]
134	Peter Swift	Sandia National Laboratories
135	Raymond Termini	Exelon Corporation
136	Mike Thorne	Mike Thorne and Associates Limited
137	John Till	Risk Assessment Corporation
138	Richard Tosetti	Bechtel SAIC Company, LLC[b]
139	Brian Wakeman	Dominion Resources, Inc.

(Continued)

	Name	Affiliation
140	John Weiss, Jr.	Entergy Corporation
141	Christopher U. Wells	Southern States Energy Board
142	Chris Whipple	ENVIRON International Corporation
143	James Williams	Western Interstate Energy Board
144	Wayne Worthington	Progress Energy
145	David Zabransky	DOE/Civilian Radioactive Waste Management Board
146	Paul L. Ziemer	Purdue University (retired) Nuclear and Radiation Studies Board, National Research Council of the National Academies
147	Louis Zeller	Blue Ridge Environmental Defense League

Source: GAO.

[a] On August 1, 2008, Savannah River Nuclear Solutions, LLC replaced Washington Savannah River Company as the primary contractor for DOE's Savannah River site. Expert affiliation was with Washington Savannah River Company at the time of our interviews.

[b] On April 1, 2009, USA Repository Services, LLC, replaced Bechtel SAIC Company, LLC, as the primary contractor for the Yucca Mountain repository. Expert affiliation was with Bechtel SAIC Company, LLC at the time of our interviews.

[c] On July 1, 2009, Savannah River Remediation, LLC replaced Washington Savannah River Company as the liquid waste program contractor. Expert affiliation was with Washington Savannah River Company at the time of our interviews.

APPENDIX IV: MODELING METHODOLOGY, ASSUMPTIONS, AND RESULTS

The methodology and results of the models we developed to analyze the total costs of two alternatives for managing nuclear waste are based on cost data and assumptions we gathered from experts. Specifically, this appendix contains information on the following:

- The modeling methodology we developed to generate a range of total costs for the two nuclear waste management alternatives with two different volumes of waste.
- The Monte Carlo simulation process we used to address uncertainties in input data.
- The discounting methodology we developed to derive the present value of total costs in 2009 dollars.
- The individual models and scenarios within each model.
- The results of our cost estimations for each scenario.
- Caveats to our modeling work.

Appendixes I and II describe our methodology for collecting cost data and assumptions and how we ensured their reliability.

Modeling Methodology

The general framework for our models was an Excel spreadsheet that annually tracked all costs associated with packaging, transportation, construction, operation, and maintenance of nuclear waste facilities as well as repackaging of nuclear waste every 100 years when applicable. The starting time period for all models was the year 2009, but the end dates vary depending on the specifics of the scenario. The cost inputs were collected in constant 2008 dollars, but the range of total costs for each scenario was converted to and reported in 2009 present value dollars. Our analysis began with an estimate of existing and future annual volume of nuclear waste ready to be packaged and stored. We chose to model two amounts of waste: 70,000 metric tons and 153,000 metric tons.[34] For ease of calculation, we converted all input costs to cost per-metric-ton of waste, when applicable.

The total cost range for each scenario was developed in four steps. First, we developed the total costs for commercial spent nuclear fuel volumes of about 63,000 metric tons and 140,000 metric tons, respectively. Second, we added DOE cost data for its managed waste.[35] Third, we discounted all annual costs to 2009 present value by a discounting methodology discussed later in this appendix. Finally, for scenarios where we assumed that the waste would be moved to a permanent repository after 100 years, we added DOE's cost estimate for the Yucca Mountain repository to represent cost for a permanent repository.[36] To ensure compatibility of cost data that DOE provided with cost ranges generated by our models, we converted DOE cost data to 2009 present value.

Monte Carlo Simulation Process

To address the uncertainties inherent in our analysis, we used a commercially available risk analysis software program called Crystal Ball to incorporate uncertainties associated with the data. This program allowed us to explore a wide range of possible values for all the input costs and assumptions we used to build our models. The Crystal Ball program uses a Monte Carlo simulation process, which repeatedly and randomly selects values for each input to the model from a distribution specified by the user. Using the selected values for cells in the spreadsheet, Crystal Ball then calculates the total cost of the scenario. By repeating the process in thousands of trials, Crystal Ball produces a range of estimated total costs for each scenario as well as the likelihood associated with any specific value in the range.

Discount Rates and Present Value Analysis

One of the inherent difficulties in developing the cost for a nuclear waste disposal option is that costs are spread over thousands of years. The economic concept of discounting is central to such analyses as it allows costs incurred in the distant future to be converted to present equivalent worth. We selected discount rates primarily based on results of studies published in peer reviewed journals. That is, rather than subjectively selecting a single discount rate, we developed our discounting approach based on a methodology and values for discount rates that were recommended by a number of published studies.

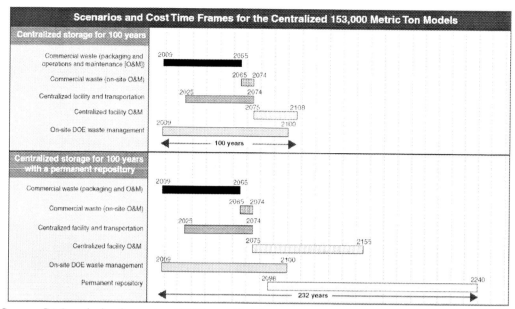

Source: GAO analysis of expert and DOE-provided data.

Figure 6. Scenario and Cost Time Frames for the Centralized 153,000 Metric Ton Models

We selected studies that addressed issues related to discounting activities whose costs and effects spread across the distant future or many generations, also known as "intergenerational discounting." In general, we found that these studies were in near consensus on two points: (1) discounting is an appropriate methodology when analyzing projects and policies that span many generations and (2) rates for discounting the distant future should be lower than near term discount rates and/or should decline over time. However, we found no consensus among the studies as to any specific discount rate that should be used. Consequently, we developed a discounting methodology using the following steps:

- We divided the entire time frame of our analysis into five different discounting intervals: immediate, near future, medium future, far future, and far-far future.
- We assumed that within each interval the discount rates were distributed with a triangular distribution.
- Based on all published rates, we developed the maximum, minimum, and mode values for each of the five specified intervals.
- We discounted all costs, using Crystal Ball to randomly and repeatedly select a rate from the appropriate interval and discount cost values using a different rate for each trial.
- Using these steps, we discounted all annual costs to 2009 present value.

Our methodology builds on a wide range of published rates from a number of different sources in concert with the Crystal Ball program. This enabled us, to the extent possible, to address the general lack of consensus on any specific discount rate and, at the same time, address the uncertainties that were inherent in intergenerational discounting and long-term analyses of nuclear waste management alternatives.

Individual Models

We developed the following four models to estimate the cost of several hypothetical nuclear waste disposal alternatives, and we incorporated a number of scenarios within each model to address all uncertainties that we could not easily capture with Crystal Ball:

- **Model I:** Centralized storage for 153,000 metric tons, which included the following scenarios:
  - *Scenario 1:* Centralized storage for 100 years.
  - *Scenario 2:* Centralized storage for 100 years plus a permanent repository after 100 years.
- **Model II:** Centralized storage for 70,000 metric tons, which included one scenario:
  - *Scenario 1:* Centralized storage for 100 years.
- **Model III:** On-site storage using total waste volume of 153,000 metric tons which included the following scenarios:
  - *Scenario 1:* On-site storage for 100 years.
  - *Scenario 2:* On-site storage for 100 years plus a permanent repository after 100 years.
  - *Scenario 3:* On-site storage for 500 years.
- **Model IV:** On-site storage using total waste volume of 70,000 metric tons, which included one scenario:
  - *Scenario 1:* On-site storage for 100 years.

Model I: Centralized Storage (153,000 metric tons)

For this model we assumed that nuclear waste would remain on site until interim facilities are constructed and ready to receive the waste. Two centralized storage facilities would be constructed over 3 years—from 2025 through 2027—and then start accepting waste. The first scenario for this model includes the costs to store waste at the centralized facilities through 2108. In the second scenario, these facilities would stay in operation through 2155, or 47 years after a permanent repository for the waste would become available. The total analysis period for the cost of this alternative plus permanent repository continues until 2240, when a permanent repository would be expected to close. In general, the costs include the following:

- Initial costs, which include costs of casks, costs for loading of casks, cost of loading campaigns, and operating and maintenance costs by three types of nuclear sites, i.e., operating sites with dry storage, decommissioned sites with dry storage, and decommissioned sites with wet storage. The uncertainty ranges for these costs were from plus or minus 5 percent to plus or minus 50 percent, depending on specific cost variable.
- Costs associated with centralized facilities, including construction costs for centralized facilities, transportation cost for transfer of nuclear waste to centralized facilities, capital and operation and maintenance costs for transportation of waste to centralized facilities and operation and maintenance of centralized facilities. The uncertainty ranges for these costs are from plus or minus 10 percent to plus or minus 40 percent, depending on the cost category.

Model II: Centralized Storage (70,000 metric tons)

This model was developed under the assumption that total existing and newly generated waste from the private sector and DOE will be 70,000 metric tons. The stream of new annual waste ready to be moved to dry storage will continue through 2030. The cost categories and uncertainty ranges assumed for this storage alternative are the same as those assumed in the centralized storage model for 153,000 metric tons.

Model III: On-Site Storage (153,000 metric tons)

We developed this model under the assumption that total existing and newly generated nuclear waste by the private sector and DOE would be 153,000 metric tons. The stream of new waste ready to be moved to dry storage would continue through 2065. In general, the costs include the following:

- Initial costs, which include costs of casks, costs for loading of casks, cost of loading campaigns, and operating and maintenance costs by three types of nuclear sites, i.e., operating sites with dry storage, decommissioned sites with dry storage, and decommissioned sites with wet storage. The uncertainty ranges for these costs were from plus or minus 5 percent to plus or minus 50 percent, depending on specific cost variable.
- Repackaging costs, which include the costs for casks; construction of transfer facilities, site pools, and other needed infrastructure; and repackaging campaigns. Because these costs are first incurred after 100 years and then every 100 years thereafter, they are included only in the model scenarios covering more than 100 years. The uncertainty for these costs range from plus or minus 10 percent to plus or minus 50 percent, depending on the specific cost variable.
- Dry storage pad costs, including initial costs when dry storage is first established, as well as replacement costs. Because the replacement costs are first incurred after 100 years and then every 100 years thereafter, they are included only in the model scenarios covering more than 100 years. The cost of these pads, collectively referred to as independent spent fuel storage installations, include costs related to licensing, design, and construction of dry storage. The independent spent nuclear fuel storage installation costs have an uncertainty range of plus or minus 40 percent.

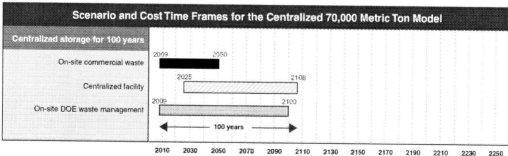

Source: GAO analysis of expert and DOE-provided data.

Figure 7. Scenario and Cost Time Frames for the Centralized 70,000 Metric Ton Model

Model IV: On-Site Storage (70,000 metric tons)

We developed this model under the assumption that total existing and newly generated nuclear waste by the private sector and DOE will be 70,000 metric tons. The stream of new annual waste ready to be moved to dry storage will continue through 2030. The cost categories and uncertainty ranges assumed for this storage alternative are the same as those for the on-site model for storing 153,000 metric tons for 100 years.

Costs for a Permanent Repository

For two scenarios, we assumed that at the end of 100 years the nuclear waste would be transferred to a permanent repository for disposal. To estimate the cost for a repository, we used DOE's cost data for the Yucca Mountain repository and made three adjustments to ensure compatibility with costs generated by our models. First, we included only DOE's future cost estimates for the Yucca Mountain repository. Second, because DOE provided costs in 2008 constant dollars, we converted all costs for the permanent repository to costs to 2009 present value using corresponding ranges of interest rates as previously described in this appendix. Finally, we assumed that repository construction and operating costs would be incurred from 2098 to 2240 when we added these cost ranges to our alternatives after 100 years.

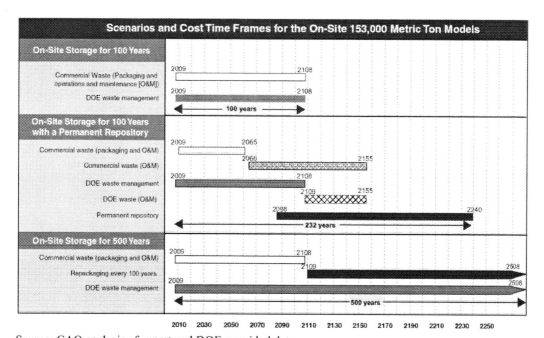

Source: GAO analysis of expert and DOE-provided data.

Figure 8. Scenarios and Cost Time Frames for the On-Site 153,000 Metric Ton Models

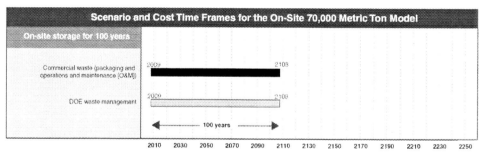

Source: GAO analysis of expert and DOE-provided data.

Figure 9. Scenario and Cost Time Frames for the On-Site 70,000 Metric Ton Model

Modeling Results

Table 8 shows the results of our analysis for all scenarios.

Table 8. Model Results for All Scenarios

Dollars in billions		
Models and scenarios	Range of total costs[a]	Mean[a]
Permanent repository (153,000 metric tons)		
Permanent repository[b]	$41 to $67	$53
Permanent repository (70,000 metric tons)		
Permanent repository[b]	$27 to $39	$32
Model I: centralized storage (153,000 metric tons)		
Centralized 100 years	$15 to $29	$21
Centralized 100 years plus permanent repository	$23 to $81	$47
Model II: centralized storage (70,000 metric tons)		
Centralized 100 years	$12 to $20	$15
Model III: on-site storage (153,000 metric tons)		
On-site 100 years	$13 to $34	$22
On-site 100 years plus permanent repository	$20 to $97	$51
On-site for 500 years	$34 to $225	$89
Model IV: on-site storage (70,000 metric tons)		
On-site 100 years	$10 to $26	$18

Source: GAO.

Note: All costs are in 2009 present value and represent costs regardless of who will pay or is legally responsible to pay for them and as such do not address the issue of liabilities. Furthermore, these costs do not include other potential costs, such as decommissioning and environmental costs and the government's penalties for delays in moving waste from the Idaho National Laboratory under the settlement agreement with Idaho.

[a] The cost estimates do not present exact values rather order-of-magnitude estimates as both the maximum and minimum as well as mean values will be somewhat different each time the simulation is repeated. This is because the Monte Carlo methodology will randomly select a different set of input data from one simulation run to the next.

[b] While our cost ranges for a permanent repository are based on DOE's estimate for the Yucca Mountain repository, our cost ranges differ from DOE's of $96 billion estimate for the following reasons: First, our cost ranges are in 2009 present value, while DOE uses 2007 constant dollars, which are not discounted. Our present value analysis reflects the time value of money—costs incurred in the future are worth less today—so that streams of future costs become smaller. Second, our cost ranges do not include about $14 billion in previously incurred costs. Third, our cost ranges are for 153,000 metric tons and 70,000 metric tons of nuclear waste, while DOE's estimated cost is for 122,100 metric tons. Finally, we use ranges while DOE provides a point estimate.

Figures 10 and 11 show ranges of total costs, as well as the probabilities for two selected scenarios. In the figures, each bar indicates a range of values for total cost and the height of the each bar indicates the probability associated with those values.

Figure 12 shows the present value of the total cost ranges of storing the nuclear waste on site over 2,000 years. The shaded areas indicate the probability that the values fall within the indicated ranges and are the result of combinations of uncertainties from a large number of input data. Specifically, we estimate that these costs could range from $34 billion to $225 billion over 500 years, from $41 billion to $548 billion over 1,000 years, and from $41 billion to $954 billion over 2,000 years, indicating and substantial level of uncertainty in making long-term cost projections.

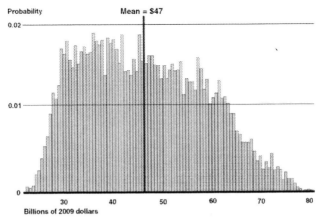

Source: GAO analysis of expert and DOE provided data.
Note: The values on the horizontal axis of the figure are to provide a scale and do not correspond exactly to the ranges for total costs which are provided in table 8.

Figure 10. Total Cost Ranges for Centralized Storage for 100 Years with Final Disposition

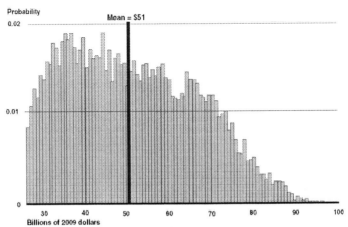

Source: GAO analysis of expert and DOE provided data.
Note: The values on the horizontal axis of the figure are to provide a scale and do not correspond exactly to the ranges for total costs which are provided in table 8.

Figure 11. Total Cost Ranges for On-site Storage for 100 years with Final Disposition

Modeling Caveats

Our models are based on ranges of average costs for each major cost category that is applicable to the alternative under analysis. As a result, the costs do not reflect storage costs for any specific site. Since we did not attempt to capture specific characteristics of each site, our values for any cost factor, if applied to any specific site, are likely incorrect. Nevertheless, since we used ranges rather than single values for a wide range of cost inputs to the models, we expect that our cost range for each variable includes the true cost for any specific site. Moreover, we expect the total cost point estimate for any scenario is within the range of total costs we developed.

Our models are designed to develop total cost ranges for each scenario within each alternative, regardless of who will pay or is legally responsible for the costs. Issues related to assignment of the costs and potentially responsible entities are discussed elsewhere in this chapter but are not incorporated into our ranges. Also, our cost ranges focus on actual expenditures that would be incurred over the period of analysis and do not assume a particular funding source and do not necessarily represent costs to the federal government. Finally, because a number of cost categories are not included in our final estimated ranges, we cannot predict their impact on our final costs ranges. For example, we did not include (1) decontamination and decommissioning costs for existing facilities or facilities yet to be built within each scenario and (2) estimates for local and state taxes or fees, which would be required to establish new sites or for continued operation of on-site storage facilities after nuclear reactors are decommissioned.

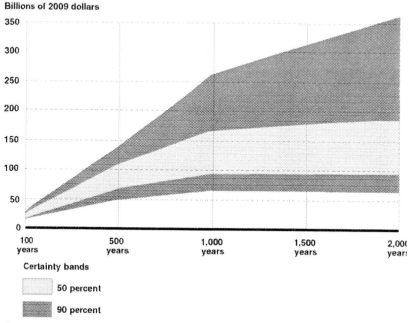

Source: GAO analysis of expert and DOE-provided data.
Note: The values on the vertical axis of the figure are to provide a scale and do not correspond exactly to the total cost ranges presented in table 8.

Figure 12. Total Cost Ranges of On-Site Storage over 2,000 Years

Table 8 and figures 10 and 11 present the results of our analysis by individual scenario. Because the purpose of our analysis was primarily to provide cost ranges for various nuclear waste management alternatives, we did not attempt to provide a comparison of results across scenarios. For a number of reasons, we believe such a comparison would have been misleading. The alternatives we have considered are inherently different in a large number of characteristics that could not be captured in our modeling work or they were not within the scope of our analysis. For example, differences in safety, health, and environmental effects, and ease of implementation characteristics of these alternatives should have an integral role in the policy debate on waste management decisions. However, because these effects cannot be readily quantified, they were outside the scope of our modeling work and are not reflected in the total cost ranges we generated.

APPENDIX V: COMMENTS FROM THE DEPARTMENT OF ENERGY

Department of Energy
Washington, DC 20585

October 28, 2009

Mr. Mark E. Gaffigan
Director, Natural Resources and Environment
U.S. Government Accountability Office
441 G Street, NW
Washington, D.C. 20548

Dear Mr. Gaffigan:

Thank you for the opportunity to review and submit comments on the draft report, "NUCLEAR WASTE MANAGEMENT: Key Attributes, Challenges and Costs for the Yucca Mountain Repository and Two Potential Alternatives" (GAO-10-48). The U.S. Department of Energy appreciates the amount of time and effort that you and your staff have taken to review this important topic.

Specific comments from Naval Reactors, the Office of General Counsel, and the Office of Environmental Management on the draft report are enclosed. If you have any questions, please feel free to call me on 202-586-6850.

Sincerely,

Christopher A. Kouts
Acting Director
Office of Civilian Radioactive
   Waste Management

Enclosure

APPENDIX VI: COMMENTS FROM THE NUCLEAR REGULATORY COMMISSION

**UNITED STATES
NUCLEAR REGULATORY COMMISSION**
WASHINGTON, D.C. 20555-0001

October 26, 2009

Mr. Richard Cheston
Assistant Director
U.S. Government Accountability Office
441 G Street, N.W.
Washington, DC 20548

Dear Mr. Cheston:

Thank you for providing the U.S. Nuclear Regulatory Commission (NRC) the opportunity to review and comment on the U.S. Government Accountability Office's (GAO) draft report GAO-10-48, "NUCLEAR WASTE MANAGEMENT – Key Attributes, Challenges, and Costs for the Yucca Mountain Repository and Two Potential Alternatives." The NRC staff has reviewed the draft report. Although we did not identify any significant issues regarding accuracy, completeness, or sensitivity of information, we have separately transmitted several technical and editorial comments to your staff.

If you have any questions regarding this response, please contact Mr. Jesse Arildsen of my staff, at (301) 415-1785.

Sincerely,

R. W. Borchardt
Executive Director
for Operations

Enclosure:
NRC Staff Comments on Draft
Report GAO-10-48

End Notes

[1] In constant fiscal year 2009 dollars. Funding comes primarily from fees collected from electric power companies operating commercial reactors and appropriations for DOE-managed spent nuclear fuel and high-level waste.

[2] DOE, *Analysis of the Total System Lifecycle Cost of the Civilian Radioactive Waste Management Program, Fiscal Year 2007*, DOE/RW-0591 (Washington, D.C., July 2008).

[3] For the purposes of our report, nuclear waste includes both spent nuclear fuel—fuel that has been withdrawn from a nuclear reactor following irradiation—and high-level radioactive waste—generally the material resulting from the reprocessing of spent nuclear fuel. Nuclear waste—specifically spent nuclear fuel—is also very thermally hot. As the radioactive elements in spent nuclear fuel decay, they give off heat. However, according to DOE data, a spent nuclear fuel assembly can lose nearly 80 percent of its heat 5 years after it has been removed from a reactor and about 95 percent of its heat after 100 years.

[4] National Academy of Sciences, *The Disposal of Radioactive Waste on Land*, (Washington, D.C., September 1957). This chapter suggested several potential alternatives for disposal of nuclear waste, stressing that although there are many potential sites for geologic disposal of waste at various depths and in various geologic formations, further research was needed regarding specific waste forms and specific geologic formations, including disposal in deep underground formations. The report stated, "the hazard related to radioactive waste is so great that no element of doubt should be allowed to exist regarding safety." Subsequent reports by the National Academy of Sciences and others have continued to endorse geologic isolation of nuclear waste and have suggested that engineered barriers, such as corrosion-resistant containers, can provide additional layers of isolation.

[5] NRC has already issued license extensions for 54 reactors, enabling them to operate for a total of 60 years. Extension requests for 21 units are currently under review and requests for as many as 25 more are anticipated through 2017.

[6] As of October 2009, NRC has received 18 applications for 29 new reactors. In addition to spent nuclear fuel and DOE-managed high-level waste, the nation also generates so-called greater than class C nuclear waste from the maintenance and decommissioning of nuclear power plants, from radioactive materials that were once used for food irradiation or for medical purposes, and from miscellaneous radioactive waste, such as contaminated equipment from industrial research and development. DOE, which is required to dispose of this nuclear waste, has not issued an environmental impact statement describing potential options, which could include disposal of the waste at the Yucca Mountain repository.

[7] See 73 Fed. Reg. 59551-59570 (Oct. 9, 2008).

[8] The U.S. government made this statement in a letter related to a tentative settlement agreement in the lawsuit of *State of Washington v. Chu*, No. CV-08-5085-FVS (E.D. Washington, filed Nov. 26, 2008). In 2008, the state of Washington filed suit claiming DOE had violated the Tri-Party Agreement among DOE, the state, and the Environmental Protection Agency by failing to meet enforceable cleanup milestones in the agreement. On August 10, 2009, DOE and the state announced they had reached a tentative settlement, including new cleanup milestones and a 2047 completion date for certain key cleanup activities. We have questioned DOE's ability to meet this date. See GAO, *Nuclear Waste: Uncertainties and Questions about Costs and Risks Persist with DOE's Tank Waste Cleanup Strategy at Hanford*, GAO-09-913 (Washington, D.C.: Sept. 30, 2009).

[9] Congressional Budget Office, *Costs of Reprocessing Versus Directly Disposing of Spent Nuclear Fuel: Testimony before the Committee on Energy and Natural Resources* (Washington, D.C.: Nov. 14, 2007).

[10] DOE changed the name of this program from the Advanced Fuel Cycle Initiative to the Fuel Cycle Research and Development program in its fiscal year 2010 budget submission.

[11] Our cost range for a permanent repository differs from DOE's most recent estimate of $96 billion for the following reasons: First, our cost range is in 2009 present value, while DOE uses 2007 constant dollars, which are not discounted. Our present value analysis reflects the time value of money—costs incurred in the future are worth less today—so that streams of future costs become smaller. Second, our cost range does not include about $14 billion in previously incurred costs. Third, our cost range is for 153,000 metric tons of nuclear waste while DOE's estimated cost is for 122,100 metric tons. Finally, we use a range while DOE provides a point estimate.

[12] The Energy Policy Act of 1992 directed EPA to base its health standards on a National Academy of Sciences study of the health issues related to radioactive releases. NRC has promulgated rules based on EPA's October 2008 standards that require the Yucca Mountain repository to limit the annual radiation dose of the public to at most 15 millirem for the first 10,000 years after disposal and at most 100 millirem from 10,001 years to 1 million years after disposal. In contrast, the average American is exposed to about 360 millirem of radiation annually, mainly from natural background sources.

[13] As of October 2, 2009, NRC had suspended or deferred five applications to build and operate six reactors at the request of the applicants.

[14] The penalties in the settlement agreement specifically apply to spent nuclear fuel and not to other high-level waste. However, the agreement specifies that DOE must have the other high-level waste treated and ready for

shipment out of Idaho for disposal by 2035. DOE officials acknowledged that Idaho could take further court action if its milestones toward meeting these goals are not being met.

[15] As of July 2009, of the 71 lawsuits filed by electric power companies, 51 cases were pending either in the Court of Federal Claims or in the Court of Appeals for the Federal Circuit, 10 had been settled, 6 were voluntarily withdrawn, and 4 had been litigated through final unappealable judgment.

[16] DOE estimated the Nuclear Waste Fund at about $23 billion in June 2009, some of which is interest that has accrued. DOE is required to invest the Nuclear Waste Fund in U.S. Treasury securities, resulting in the government paying about $11.2 billion interest to the fund. Both the principal and the interest might be returned, if the fund is returned to the electric power companies.

[17] National Research Council of the National Academies, *Disposition of High-Level Waste and Spent Nuclear Fuel: The Continuing Societal and Technical Challenges*, (Washington, D.C., 2001).

[18] Section 801 (c) of the Energy Policy Act of 1992 requires DOE to provide indefinite oversight to prevent any activity at the site that poses an unreasonable risk of (1) breaching the repository's engineered or geologic barriers or (2) increasing the exposure of the public to radiation beyond allowable limits. Pub. L. No. 102-486, 106 Stat. 2776, 2921-2922.

[19] The Nuclear Energy Institute represents the nuclear power industry and the National Association of Regulatory Utility Commissioners represents state public utility commissions that regulate the electric power industry.

[20] Minnesota House File No. 894, introduced February 16, 2009, and Michigan Senate Concurrent Resolution No. 8, introduced March 25, 2009.

[21] NWPA caps the amount of nuclear waste that can be disposed of at Yucca Mountain at 70,000 metric tons. The estimated amount of current waste plus additional commercial spent nuclear fuel that would be generated if all currently operating commercial reactors received license extensions is 153,000 metric tons. Our analysis did not consider new reactors because of the uncertainty if or when new reactors would be built, how many would be built, and their impact on waste streams.

[22] We excluded historical costs for the Yucca Mountain repository because these costs represent challenges unique to Yucca Mountain and may not be applicable to a future repository. However, the bulk of future cost for construction, operation, and closure may be representative of a new repository.

[23] We used a commercially available risk analysis program called Crystal Ball for our Monte Carlo simulation. Crystal Ball is a commonly used spreadsheet-based software for predictive modeling and forecasting.

[24] DOE acknowledged that the Atomic Energy Act of 1954, as amended, does provide the authority for DOE to accept and store spent nuclear fuel under certain circumstances, which DOE has used in the past to accept and store spent nuclear fuel.. For example, pursuant to the Atomic Energy Act authority, DOE has accepted and stored U.S.-supplied spent nuclear fuel from foreign reactors, as well as damaged spent nuclear fuel from the Three Mile Island reactor site. However, DOE asserts that the NWPA's detailed statutory scheme limits its authority to accept spent nuclear fuel under Atomic Energy Act authority except in compelling circumstances, such as an emergency involving spent nuclear fuel threatening public health.

[25] In addition, lawsuits filed against the government by nuclear reactor owners have included claims to recover the cost of the Private Fuel Storage facility. At least one utility has recovered these costs from the government, while a court did not allow another utility to recover these costs.

[26] Western Governors' Association Policy Resolution 09-5: Interim Storage and Transportation of Commercial Spent Nuclear Fuel.

[27] NWPA prohibits development of a centralized storage facility in any state where a site is being characterized for development of a repository.

[28] GAO, *Global Nuclear Energy Partnership: DOE Should Reassess Its Approach to Designing and Building Spent Nuclear Fuel Recycling Facilities*, GAO-08-483 (Washington, D.C.: April 2008).

[29] The studies used in the Congressional Budget Office's analysis were: Boston Consulting Group, *Economic Assessment of Used Nuclear Fuel Management in the United States* (study prepared for AREVA Inc., July 2006); and Matthew Bunn and others, *The Economics of Reprocessing vs. Direct Disposal of Spent Nuclear Fuel*, Belfer Center for Science and International Affairs, John F. Kennedy School of Government, Harvard University, (Cambridge, Massachusetts, December 2003).

[30] Legislative action by the Congress could also affect the amount of compensation the government ultimately pays to the reactor operators. For example, the Congress could amend NWPA to change contract provisions that would be applicable to newly constructed reactors.

[31] DOE, *Analysis of the Total System Lifecycle Cost of the Civilian Radioactive Waste Management Program, Fiscal Year 2007*, DOE/RW-0591 (Washington, D.C., July 2008). The 122,100 metric tons of nuclear waste included the spent nuclear fuel expected to be generated from all commercial nuclear reactors that had received NRC license extensions through January 2007.

[32] We excluded historical costs for the Yucca Mountain repository because these costs represent challenges unique to Yucca Mountain and may not be applicable to a future repository. However, the bulk of future cost for construction, operation, and closure may be representative of a new repository.

[33] The 67 sets of comments do not reflect the total number of experts who responded because some groups of affiliated experts compiled their comments into a single response. For example, DOE's Office of Civilian Radioactive Waste Management provided a consolidated set of comments for its nine experts.

[34] The 70,000 metric tons is the statutory limit placed on the amount of waste that can be disposed of at Yucca Mountain. The 153,000 metric tons is the estimated amount of current waste plus additional commercial spent nuclear fuel that would be generated by 2055 if all currently operating commercial reactors received license extensions.

[35] DOE management costs include spent nuclear fuel managed at the Hanford Reservation, Idaho National Laboratory, and Fort St. Vrain, in Colorado, and high-level waste at the Hanford Reservation, Savannah River Site, Idaho National Laboratory, and West Valley.

[36] We used DOE estimates for Yucca Mountain to represent the cost of a permanent repository. We, however, did not include historical costs for Yucca Mountain as we felt that these historical costs represent challenges unique to Yucca Mountain and may not be applicable to a future repository whereas the bulk of future cost for construction, operation, and closure would be replicated for a new repository.

In: Nuclear Waste: Disposal and Liability Issues
Editor: Ylenia E. Farrugia

ISBN: 978-1-61761-590-0
© 2011 Nova Science Publishers, Inc.

Chapter 3

NUCLEAR WASTE DISPOSAL: ALTERNATIVES TO YUCCA MOUNTAIN[*]

Mark Holt

SUMMARY

Congress designated Yucca Mountain, NV, as the nation's sole candidate site for a permanent high-level nuclear waste repository in 1987, following years of controversy over the site-selection process. Over the strenuous objections of the State of Nevada, the Department of Energy (DOE) submitted a license application for the proposed Yucca Mountain repository in June 2008 to the Nuclear Regulatory Commission (NRC). During the 2008 election campaign, now-President Obama lent support to Nevada's fight against the repository, contending in an issue statement that he and now-Vice President Biden "do not believe that Yucca Mountain is a suitable site."

Under the current nuclear waste program, DOE hopes to begin transporting spent nuclear fuel and other highly radioactive waste to Yucca Mountain by 2020. That schedule is 22 years beyond the 1998 deadline established by the Nuclear Waste Policy Act (NWPA). Because U.S. nuclear power plants will continue to generate nuclear waste after a repository opens, DOE estimates that all waste could not be removed from existing reactors until about 2066 even under the current Yucca Mountain schedule. Not all the projected waste could be disposed of at Yucca Mountain, however, unless NWPA's current limit on the repository's capacity is increased.

If the Obama Administration decides to halt the Yucca Mountain project, it has a variety of tools available to implement that policy. Although the President cannot directly affect NRC proceedings, the Secretary of Energy could withdraw the Yucca Mountain license application under NRC rules. The President could also urge Congress to cut or eliminate funding for the Yucca Mountain project, and propose legislation to restructure the nuclear waste program.

---

[*] This is an edited, reformatted and augmented edition of a United States Congressional Research Service publication, Report R40202, dated February 6, 2009.

Abandonment of Yucca Mountain would probably further delay the federal government's removal of nuclear waste from reactor sites and therefore increase the government's liabilities for missing the NWPA deadline. DOE estimates that such liabilities will reach $11 billion even if Yucca Mountain opens as currently planned. DOE's agreements with states to remove defense-related high-level waste could also be affected. If the Yucca Mountain project were halted without a clear alternative path for waste management, the licensing of proposed new nuclear power plants could be affected as well. NRC has determined that waste can be safely stored at reactor sites for at least 30 years after a reactor shuts down and is proposing to extend that period to 60 years. While that proposal would allow at least 100 years for waste to remain at reactor sites (including a 40-year reactor operating period), NRC's policy is that new reactors should not be licensed without "reasonable confidence that the wastes can and will in due course be disposed of safely."

Current law provides no alternative repository site to Yucca Mountain, and it does not authorize DOE to open temporary storage facilities without a permanent repository in operation. Without congressional action, therefore, the default alternative to Yucca Mountain would be indefinite on-site storage of nuclear waste at reactor sites and other nuclear facilities. Private central storage facilities can also be licensed under current law; such a facility has been licensed in Utah but its operation has been blocked by the Department of the Interior.

Congress has considered legislation repeatedly since the mid-1990s to authorize a federal interim storage facility for nuclear waste but none has been enacted. Reprocessing of spent fuel could reduce waste volumes and long-term toxicity, but such facilities are costly and raise concerns about the separation of plutonium that could be used in nuclear weapons. Storage and reprocessing would still eventually require a permanent repository, and a search for a new repository site would need to avoid the obstacles that have hampered previous U.S. efforts.

PROPOSALS FOR A NEW DIRECTION

Nevada's Yucca Mountain has been the sole candidate site for the nation's first permanent high-level nuclear waste repository since Congress singled it out in 1987 and halted consideration of any other location. After numerous delays, the Department of Energy (DOE), which was supposed to open a waste repository by 1998, submitted a repository license application for Yucca Mountain to the Nuclear Regulatory Commission (NRC) in June 2008. If NRC approves the license, DOE hopes to begin shipping nuclear waste to the repository by 2020.

The congressional decision to focus solely on Yucca Mountain was highly controversial and continues to face harsh criticism, particularly from the State of Nevada. Yucca Mountain opponents dispute DOE's determination that the site is suitable for long-term disposal of nuclear waste and call for fundamental change in the program. Nonetheless, the proposed Yucca Mountain repository has consistently maintained sufficient congressional support to continue moving forward. Congress explicitly rejected a Nevada "state veto" of the site in 2002, has blocked repeated efforts to halt the program's funding, and has not taken up any of numerous legislative proposals to delay the program or find a new site. President George W. Bush also steadfastly supported the Yucca Mountain project.

But Administration support for Yucca Mountain will apparently change under President Obama. In their campaign statement on nuclear energy policy, Obama and Vice President Biden laid out the following position:

> In terms of waste storage, Barack Obama and Joe Biden do not believe that Yucca Mountain is a suitable site. They will lead federal efforts to look for safe, long-term disposal solutions based on objective, scientific analysis. In the meantime, they will develop requirements to ensure that the waste stored at current reactor sites is contained using the most advanced dry-cask storage technology available.[1]

The Obama-Biden campaign statement on Yucca Mountain raises numerous questions about the future direction of U.S. nuclear waste policy. In particular, what type of long-term disposal solutions could be considered? Every option for handling nuclear waste ultimately requires a method of long-term isolation from the environment. If Yucca Mountain were rejected, it would appear that a new repository site search would need to be undertaken at some point. Given the criticism that DOE has drawn over its handling of the waste program, pressure may intensify for such a search to be handed over to a new organization entirely.

The current effort to develop a repository at Yucca Mountain began with the enactment of the Nuclear Waste Policy Act of 1982 (NWPA, P.L. 97-425), and opening a repository at a different location could take a long time as well, even if the process were started right away. During such an indefinite time period, how would the licensing of new nuclear power plants be affected? Would spent nuclear fuel and other highly radioactive waste remain at commercial reactors and other existing nuclear facilities, or would it be moved to centralized interim storage? Previous U.S. efforts to develop interim central nuclear waste storage facilities have drawn fierce opposition.

Since the 1970s, U.S. nuclear waste policy has been based on the "once through" fuel cycle, in which nuclear fuel is to be used once in a reactor and then permanently disposed of. The major alternative is the "closed" fuel cycle, in which spent nuclear fuel would be reprocessed into new fuel for advanced reactors or particle accelerators. Fast reactors or accelerators would destroy the longest-lived radioactive components of the fuel, leaving only relatively short-lived radioactive isotopes, which would decay to background levels within 1,000 years, for permanent disposal. Under that scenario, spent fuel could be stored at reprocessing facilities while awaiting its turn to be made into new fuel, and the relatively short life of the resulting waste could make it easier to site a permanent repository. However, the material for nuclear fuel that results from reprocessing (primarily plutonium) can also be used for nuclear explosives, raising concerns about nuclear weapons proliferation.

Because current law specifies that Yucca Mountain is the sole candidate site for a high-level waste repository, legislation would probably be needed if a major change in direction in the nuclear waste program is sought. But the Obama Administration does have authority under current law to withdraw the Yucca Mountain license application, propose reductions in the program's funding, and take other administrative actions to delay or halt the development of a repository at the Yucca Mountain site. This chapter discusses those options and the likely impact of indefinite delays in the waste program. It then discusses the mid- and long-term alternatives to the existing waste program, and finally reviews the history of U.S. efforts to site nuclear waste facilities.

BASELINE: CURRENT WASTE PROGRAM PROJECTIONS

DOE's latest schedules for nuclear waste shipments and projected costs under the existing program provide a baseline for analyzing Yucca Mountain alternatives. Although the planned opening of the Yucca Mountain repository is at least 22 years later than NWPA's 1998 deadline, and removing waste from existing storage sites would require many decades, a major redirection of the waste program would probably involve even longer time frames. Of course, there is no certainty that DOE will be able to meet its current schedules, or that the Yucca Mountain repository will receive a license from NRC under the current program. Moreover, policymakers could conclude that the benefits of redirecting the nuclear waste program now would outweigh the almost certain delays in developing a permanent repository and the increased costs of interim storage.

Under DOE's current schedule, about 400 metric tons of spent nuclear fuel would be shipped to Yucca Mountain from reactor sites in 2020. Shipments would rise to 600 metric tons in 2021, 1,200 metric tons in 2022, and 2,000 metric tons in 2023, and reach the planned maximum annual capacity of 3,000 metric tons in 2024.[2] Because the total U.S. commercial reactor fleet discharges an average of about 2,000 metric tons of spent fuel per year, the above shipment schedule would not begin reducing the backlog of spent fuel stored at reactor sites until 2024.

DOE estimates that the amount of commercial spent fuel stored in pools of water and dry casks at reactor sites and other facilities was 57,700 metric tons at the end of 2007.[3] If commercial spent fuel continues to accumulate at the rate of 2,000 metric tons per year, then inventories would reach 81,000 metric tons before shipments are to begin in 2020 and peak at nearly 85,000 in 2023, after which shipments to Yucca Mountain would exceed reactor discharges by 1,000 tons per year. DOE projections indicate that shipments of all spent fuel from previous and existing U.S. nuclear power plants would continue until about 2066, totaling 109,300 metric tons (under existing reactor license periods and extensions). In addition, the equivalent of 12,800 metric tons of defense-related spent nuclear fuel and high-level radioactive waste would be received at Yucca Mountain during the same period, for a total of 122,100 metric tons.[4]

Although DOE's cost projections assume that all spent fuel from existing reactors, plus defense waste, will be shipped to the planned Yucca Mountain repository, NWPA section 114(d) caps Yucca Mountain's capacity at the equivalent of 70,000 metric tons of spent fuel until a second repository begins operating. No such repository is currently authorized. A recent DOE report on the need for a second repository concludes that all existing and anticipated spent fuel and high- level waste could be physically accommodated at Yucca Mountain.[5] Legislation to lift the 70,000- ton limit proposed by the Bush Administration was introduced during the 109th (H.R. 5360) and 110th (S. 37) Congresses but not acted upon.

As amended in 1987, NWPA provides no backup plan for spent fuel management if the Yucca Mountain repository were to be halted. A "monitored retrievable storage" (MRS) facility is authorized by NWPA section 142, but construction is prohibited until NRC has authorized the construction of the Yucca Mountain repository.

Section 302 of NWPA requires nuclear power plant operators to sign contracts with DOE under which the nuclear plants must pay fees to the federal government in return for DOE's spent fuel disposal services. The nuclear power plant fees are deposited in a Treasury account called the Nuclear Waste Fund to pay for the DOE waste program but cannot be spent without congressional appropriation. The Fund's balance was about $20 billion at the end of FY2008.[6] Because the DOE waste program will also handle defense-related waste, Congress typically supplements annual appropriations from the Nuclear Waste Fund with appropriations from general revenues.

Annual spending for the nuclear waste program, focusing on Yucca Mountain site studies and the license application, has averaged about $400 million in recent years. However, DOE projects that to build the repository and develop a transportation system within the next 12 years, annual funding would need to increase to nearly $2 billion during the peak of construction. Disposal of all 122,100 metric tons of currently anticipated waste at Yucca Mountain is projected to cost $96.18 billion (in 2007 dollars) through 2133.[7]

NWPA section 302(d) restricts the use of the Nuclear Waste Fund to disposal activities and research authorized by the act. The section specifically prohibits DOE from expending the funds for any facility besides those expressly authorized by NWPA or subsequent act of Congress. As amended in 1987, NWPA currently authorizes only a repository at Yucca Mountain and a monitored retrievable storage facility tied to the operation of a Yucca Mountain repository.

The contracts that DOE signed with nuclear utilities required DOE to begin taking waste from reactor sites by January 31, 1998. Because that deadline was missed, DOE has been ruled liable for all waste storage costs that nuclear utilities would not have incurred had shipments to the planned repository begun on time. The U.S. Court of Federal Claims has already issued several judgments against DOE. Claims are paid from the federal judgment fund, rather than the Nuclear Waste Fund, and require no congressional appropriations. DOE calculates that its nuclear waste liabilities to nuclear reactor operators under current law will ultimately total $11 billion if shipments begin by 2020 as currently planned and potentially much more if waste operations are further delayed.[8]

OPTIONS FOR HALTING OR DELAYING YUCCA MOUNTAIN

The Yucca Mountain repository is now in the final stages of the lengthy approval process established by NWPA. Therefore, if the Obama Administration does "not believe that Yucca Mountain is a suitable site," what options are available at this point to stop the project?

NWPA sections 113-116 prescribed the following actions by the Secretary of Energy, the President, and the Nuclear Regulatory Commission toward developing a nuclear waste repository at the Yucca Mountain site:

- The Secretary were to determine whether the site is suitable for a repository, and, if so, notify the State of Nevada and recommend that the President approve the project.

- If the President agreed with the Secretary's recommendation, the President were to submit an approval recommendation to Congress.
- After the presidential recommendation, the Nevada Legislature or Governor were allowed to submit a notice of disapproval to Congress.
- State disapproval would block the repository unless Congress voted within 90 days for an approval resolution that was signed by the President.
- Once the presidential site designation took effect, the Secretary were required to submit a repository license application to NRC.

All these steps have now taken place, and the Yucca Mountain license application has been docketed by NRC for consideration. NRC is an independent regulatory body not directly under the President's control. But the President has a variety of tools at his disposal that could dramatically affect the nuclear waste program.

Withdraw License Application

To stop further action on Yucca Mountain, perhaps the most dramatic step would be for DOE to withdraw the repository license application, as allowed by NRC procedures.[9] Such a withdrawal could be temporary, pending completion of some of the study options described below, or it could be permanent, with the intention of completely ending the Yucca Mountain project. If the license application were permanently withdrawn, the previous presidential site designation may have to be reversed as well, because NWPA section 114 requires that the license application be submitted 90 days after the presidential designation takes effect (a deadline that was missed by more than five years). The fact that, as noted above, the presidential designation of the Yucca Mountain site took effect pursuant to a congressional override of Nevada's "state veto" could be a complicating factor.

Reduce Appropriations

Restricting funding for the Yucca Mountain Project could be another approach. Congressional opponents of the waste program have succeeded in cutting its funds in recent years, although not enough to prevent DOE from submitting the license application. The Bush Administration requested an appropriation of $37.3 million from the Nuclear Waste Fund for NRC's license review activities during FY2009,[10] and substantial reductions could force significant delays in the planned four-year licensing schedule.

As noted above, DOE contends that it will need large funding increases to design and build the Yucca Mountain repository by 2020, so even steady funding would probably push back that schedule by many years. Of course, eliminating funding altogether for NRC licensing and DOE repository construction would halt further work on the project. The Obama Administration's ability to reduce or eliminate Yucca Mountain funding, if it so desired, would depend on its influence with Congress.

Key Policy Appointments

Although NRC is independent of the Administration, and Commissioners cannot be removed by the President without cause, the President can change the makeup of the Commission over time. Significant changes in the Commission could affect the Yucca Mountain licensing process and its ultimate outcome. The five NRC Commissioners serve five-year terms that are staggered so that one expires each year, on June 30. No more than three Commissioners may be from the same political party. One of the five slots is currently vacant. The President can also redesignate the Chairmanship of the NRC to a different Commissioner at any time.

Other presidential appointments could also have a strong effect on the Yucca Mountain project, the Secretary of Energy in particular. Senate Majority Leader Harry Reid had promised to block any nominee for that post who supported the Yucca Mountain site.[11] The Energy Secretary could initiate a redirection of the nuclear waste program, revisit DOE's complex computer models that predict low radioactive releases from Yucca Mountain, or, as noted above, withdraw the license application.

Senator Reid expressed support for President Obama's Energy Secretary, former Lawrence Berkeley National Laboratory Director Steven Chu, contending that "Dr. Chu also knows, like most Nevadans, that Yucca Mountain is not a viable solution for dumping and dealing with nuclear waste."[12] In a 2005 interview posted on the Lawrence Berkeley National Laboratory website, Chu noted projections from his lab that waste canisters in Yucca Mountain would begin to fail after about 5,000 years, which would require the underlying rock formations to prevent unacceptable migration of radioactive material into the groundwater.[13] However, Chu also signed a nuclear policy statement with other national laboratory directors in August 2008 that called for "licensing of the Yucca Mountain Repository as a long-term resource."[14]

Another important appointment for Yucca Mountain is the Administrator of the Environmental Protection Agency (EPA), Lisa Jackson, who was confirmed January 22, 2009. Under NWPA, EPA sets the radiation protection standard that NRC must use in licensing Yucca Mountain. After an earlier version of the standard was struck down by a federal court, EPA published a final standard October 15, 2008, which sets individual radiation exposure limits of 15 millirems for the first 10,000 years after disposal and 100 millirems after 10,000 through one million years.[15] The State of Nevada has sued to overturn the EPA regulations, contending that there is no justification for a higher limit after 10,000 years.[16] If the EPA standard is overturned, licensing of the Yucca Mountain site could become more difficult.[17]

Waste Program Review

Rather than moving immediately to halt the Yucca Mountain repository, the Obama Administration could delay or suspend the project through the approaches described above and then initiate a major program review – a step implied by the Obama-Biden campaign policy statement. The scope of the review could include such topics as management issues, research and development needs, foreign waste management experience, and broad policy options.

Such a review could be conducted by an interagency task force within the new Administration or by an outside entity such as the National Academy of Sciences (NAS) or a presidential commission. Independent scientific reviews of the waste program are currently provided by the Nuclear Waste Technical Review Board (NWTRB), which, under NWPA Title V, the President appoints from nominees provided by NAS. However, the President does not set the agenda for independent agencies such as NWTRB, so it is not clear what role the Board might play in a major policy review.

CONSEQUENCES OF A YUCCA MOUNTAIN POLICY SHIFT

A decision by the incoming Administration to halt or delay development of the Yucca Mountain repository could have significant impact on the federal budget, proposed new U.S. nuclear power plants, waste storage at existing reactor sites, and disposal of defense-related nuclear waste. Such consequences could be most pronounced if such a policy shift involved simply a halt of Yucca Mountain without legislation to forge a new direction – legislation that presumably would address the issues discussed below.

No matter what decision is made on Yucca Mountain, there is a broad scientific consensus that long-term isolation of nuclear waste from the environment – for at least 1,000 years – will still be required. In other words, if Yucca Mountain were abandoned, another repository site in the United States would almost certainly have to be found eventually. Reprocessing and recycling of nuclear spent fuel can reduce the amount of long-lived radioactive waste requiring isolation but cannot entirely eliminate the need for such isolation. Alternatives to deep geologic waste isolation have been studied, such as space and subseabed disposal, but they face daunting technical obstacles, and none has ever been developed beyond the conceptual stage.

If development of the Yucca Mountain repository were delayed or halted, commercial spent fuel and defense-related nuclear waste would almost certainly remain at numerous on-site storage facilities longer than currently planned. A new repository to replace Yucca Mountain would be unlikely to open by 2020 to prevent delays in DOE's current shipping schedule. Federal centralized interim storage has been proposed repeatedly as a solution, including the MRS facility authorized by NWPA, but no such facility has been developed. If new legislation were to authorize a central interim storage facility, it possibly could begin receiving waste by 2020 and prevent further delays. Another possibility is a private spent fuel storage facility in Utah that has already received an NRC license and might be opened relatively quickly if other administrative approvals were granted (as discussed in a subsequent section). However, the Utah facility's licensed capacity is limited to 40,000 metric tons of spent fuel, which could be stored at the site for no longer than 40 years.

Federal Liabilities for Disposal Delays

As noted above, DOE is liable for utilities' nuclear waste storage costs resulting from the missed NWPA disposal deadline. According to DOE, "for each additional year of delay, the Department estimates that there may be hundreds of millions of dollars of additional damages."[18] These mandatory payments would be a direct cost to the federal government, but they would stretch over several decades because utilities cannot recover damages until their extra storage costs are actually incurred. DOE projects that if disposal begins by 2020, $11 billion in liabilities will be incurred by 2056.[19]

If the Yucca Mountain site were abandoned without an alternative storage or disposal process in place, court judgments against DOE could rise far higher. The nuclear industry has raised the possibility that DOE could be found in complete default on its NWPA contracts and be ordered to refund all the nuclear waste fees that had been collected, in addition to paying utilities' extra at- reactor storage costs.[20] Through the end of FY2008, DOE had collected more than $28 billion in fees and interest payments – an amount that has been growing at about $1.5 billion per year.[21] In at least one of the nuclear utility cases before the Federal Court of Claims, a judge issued a show- cause order for why the DOE nuclear waste contracts should not be voided and all payments returned to utilities,[22] although that step was not included in the court's final decision.[23]

Licensing Complications for New Power Reactors

No new commercial reactors have been ordered in the United States since the 1970s, but concerns over potential carbon dioxide controls and high natural gas prices have prompted U.S. electric utilities to again consider the nuclear power option. License applications for 26 new reactors have been filed with NRC, and more are anticipated.[24] Further delays in the DOE nuclear waste program could pose an obstacle to licensing the proposed new reactors.

NRC established a policy in 1977 that it "would not continue to license reactors if it did not have reasonable confidence that the wastes can and will in due course be disposed of safely."[25] NRC then began a Waste Confidence proceeding that resulted in 1984 findings that there was "reasonable assurance" that a nuclear waste repository would be available by 2007-2009 and that waste could be safely stored at reactor sites for at least 30 years after reactors have shut down.[26]

After DOE's schedule for opening the Yucca Mountain repository slipped to 2010, NRC revised its Waste Confidence Decision in 1990 to find reasonable assurance that a repository "will be available within the first quarter of the twenty-first century."[27] With DOE now planning to open Yucca Mountain by 2020 at the earliest, NRC is proposing a further revision to find reasonable assurance that a repository will be available within 50-60 years after a reactor's licensed operating life and that spent fuel can be stored safely for at least 60 years after a reactor's licensed life.[28] Although the NRC's latest proposed revision would allow for decades of further slippage in the Yucca Mountain schedule, it is not clear that NRC's waste-related criteria for licensing new reactors would be satisfied if the Yucca Mountain project were canceled without an alternative plan in place.

Six states – California, Connecticut, Kentucky, New Jersey, West Virginia, and Wisconsin – have specific laws that link approval for new nuclear power plants to adequate waste disposal capacity. Kansas forbids cost recovery for "excess" nuclear power capacity if no "technology or means for disposal of high-level nuclear waste" is available.[29] The U.S. Supreme Court has held that state authority over nuclear power plant construction is limited to economic considerations rather than safety, which is solely under NRC jurisdiction.[30] No nuclear plants have been ordered since the various state restrictions were enacted, so their ability to meet the Supreme Court's criteria has yet to be tested.

The nuclear waste issue has also historically been a focal point for public opposition to nuclear power. Proposed new reactors that have no clear path for removing waste from their sites could face intensified public scrutiny, particularly at proposed sites that do not already have operating reactors.

Environmental Cleanup Penalties

For defense-related nuclear waste, which resulted from production of nuclear weapons and naval reactor fuel by DOE and its predecessor agencies, indefinite delays in developing a repository could also have legal consequences for DOE. Defense-related high-level radioactive waste resulted from decades of reprocessing spent fuel to extract plutonium for nuclear warheads or highly enriched uranium from spent naval reactor fuel. As noted above, DOE's inventory of defense high-level waste and unreprocessed spent fuel, plus waste from other DOE nuclear programs, totals the equivalent of 12,800 metric tons (the mass of spent fuel before reprocessing). This material is located primarily at Hanford, WA, Savannah River, SC, and the Idaho National Laboratory.

Congress has given states the authority to enforce waste management laws against federal agencies, including DOE. Without Yucca Mountain or an alternative repository plan, DOE would not have a permanent disposal site for waste now stored at its defense-related facilities. A lack of repository capacity, according to DOE, "could threaten the Department's ability to fulfill [regulatory] agreements with the states hosting those sites to remove the waste for permanent disposal."[31]

Long-Term Risk

The near-term environmental impact of further Yucca Mountain delays or abandonment would be minimal for at least 100 years, according to DOE's supplemental environmental impact statement (SEIS) for the repository program.[32] That assessment is consistent with the NRC Waste Confidence Decision cited above. As long as storage facilities at reactors and other sites are maintained and guarded through institutional controls, radioactive releases to the environment are expected to be small.

On-site storage of spent fuel will continue for many decades even if Yucca Mountain begins receiving waste shipments by 2020, as discussed in the baseline program section above. Moreover, some freshly discharged spent fuel will be stored on site as long as reactors are operating. Some environmental groups have argued that it would be safer to leave all nuclear waste for an extended period in hardened on-site storage facilities rather than begin sending it to a central facility as soon as possible, because allowing the waste's radioactivity to decay would reduce the consequences of transportation accidents or sabotage when the waste is ultimately moved.[33] Moreover, waste placed at a central interim storage facility would probably have to be moved a second time to a permanent repository, potentially further increasing transportation risks.

Beyond 100 years or so, the environmental risks of surface storage resulting from the lack of an underground repository become more uncertain. At some point in the future, maintenance and security of surface storage facilities would be expected to drop below adequate levels because of unforeseen circumstances. Whether that would occur after 500 years, 1,000 years, or 10,000 years is open to speculation. Federal nuclear waste policy would presumably continue to envision a permanent disposal method well before such a breakdown, but the risk would be expected to rise if delays continued indefinitely. The SEIS predicts that substantial amounts of radioactivity would reach the accessible environment within 10,000 years after the end of institutional controls on surface storage facilities, "with eventual catastrophic consequences for human health."[34]

NUCLEAR WASTE POLICY OPTIONS

Because NWPA specifies that only Yucca Mountain may be considered for a repository site and that a federal storage facility cannot open before the repository is licensed, the government's waste management options are sharply limited under current law. Without congressional action, alternatives to Yucca Mountain would consist primarily of indefinite on-site storage or licensing of new private storage sites.

New legislation would open up much broader possibilities, ranging from a search for a new repository site and federal interim storage to reprocessing and alternative disposal technologies.

Some – but probably not all – of the consequences of changing the current waste policy could also be mitigated through legislation. Any legislation dealing with nuclear waste siting is almost certain to prove extraordinarily controversial.

Institutional Changes

Almost since the beginning of the current nuclear waste program in 1982, DOE has regularly been accused of mismanagement and allowing political considerations to affect scientific decisions. Many proposals have been made by the nuclear industry and its critics alike to transfer the nuclear waste program to an independent organization that might be more efficient and less affected by politics. For example, a proposal in the 110th Congress (H.R. 6001, section 186) would have handed the DOE waste program to an independent High Level Waste Authority, headed by a presidentially appointed seven-member board. In implementing the nuclear waste program, the Waste Authority would have been authorized to consider all reasonable options, including alternative repository locations.

An independent waste agency could be a government agency, as in H.R. 6001, a government corporation, or a private-sector entity. Two studies conducted for DOE's Global Nuclear Energy Partnership recommended the establishment of a government corporation to manage nuclear waste, including spent fuel reprocessing. One of the studies, by a consortium led by the French firm Areva, called a government corporation the best option "because it allows the utilities to have some level of oversight while full government ownership keeps the cost of capital low."[35] A team led by EnergySolutions recommended that the government corporation have a board of directors drawn from the nuclear industry, with an independent oversight board "to assure that it meets its charter obligations."[36]

Licensing and regulation by NRC could be continued unchanged under any option. The existing funding system could also be transferred largely unchanged to a new government agency, but a new funding system would probably be needed for a private entity. Whether a private entity should take permanent title to all nuclear waste could also be an issue. The nuclear industry has long contended that nuclear waste payments by reactor owners should be available directly for nuclear waste disposal activities without the need for congressional appropriation. But even if the program's management were improved, it is far from clear whether any new waste management organization could avoid the political controversy that has persistently accompanied the DOE program.

Short of establishing an entirely new organization to run the waste program, it has been suggested that additional independent oversight could improve public confidence in DOE's decisions. This was a major reason cited for creating the Nuclear Waste Technical Review Board in 1987. Some have proposed that technical oversight by a non-federal agency would be more credible, such as the Environmental Evaluation Group (EEG) in New Mexico.[37] Congress in 1988 required DOE to sign a contract with a New Mexico university, the New Mexico Institute of Mining and Technology, to administer the EEG to provide independent review and evaluation of the Waste Isolation Pilot Plant (WIPP), a DOE repository for relatively low-radioactivity defense waste (P.L. 100-456, section 1433). The EEG closed in 2004 after DOE halted its funding,[38] and oversight activities are now carried out by the New Mexico Environment Department.[39]

Extended On-Site Storage

It appears unlikely, based on the history of the nuclear waste program, that any alternative storage or disposal sites could become operational earlier than the planned opening of Yucca Mountain in 2020. Therefore, any alternative to the Yucca Mountain repository would almost certainly result in longer on-site storage of nuclear waste than under the current baseline program. Essentially, extended on-site storage is the default option, with the only question being how long. On-site storage could be extended for decades under some policy changes, such as a restart of the repository site search or the pursuit of alternative disposal technologies. Waste might be moved more quickly if central interim surface storage facilities were developed (as discussed below), but designating such sites may be nearly as controversial as siting a repository.

On-site nuclear waste storage at reactor facilities takes place primarily in deep pools of water that are built into the reactor building. The water is necessary to provide cooling and radiation shielding for extremely radioactive spent fuel that is freshly discharged from the reactor. After its radioactivity has sufficiently decayed, usually after several years, spent fuel can be transferred to dry storage casks and stored outside the pools. Most spent fuel pools were not designed to hold all the spent fuel generated during a reactor's operating life. Therefore, as DOE's target date for taking spent fuel from reactor sites has slipped, nuclear reactor operators have had to expand their on-site dry storage capacity (and have sued DOE for compensation).

NRC considers extended on-site storage to be safe as long as storage facilities are adequately maintained and guarded, as discussed above. However, the National Academy of Sciences (NAS) determined in 2005 that spent fuel pools could be vulnerable to terrorist attacks, particularly as spent fuel has been stored more densely in the pools to increase their capacity. NAS found that an attack could drain the cooling water from a spent fuel pool and cause the spent fuel's zirconium cladding to overheat and catch fire, releasing "large quantities of radioactive materials to the environment."[40] The Energy and Water Development Appropriations Act for FY2006 (P.L. 109-103) included $21 million for NRC to assess the vulnerabilities found by NAS at each reactor site.

Keeping nuclear waste at reactor sites and other existing facilities has long been a major goal of Yucca Mountain opponents. Numerous bills have been introduced over the years to require DOE to take over all responsibility for storing spent fuel at reactor sites, including ownership of the waste and on-site storage facilities (such as S. 784 in the 110th Congress). Such an on-site DOE takeover is intended to reduce utilities' costs, and resulting federal liabilities, for DOE's failure to remove the spent fuel. However, states with nuclear reactors oppose indefinite on-site storage, and utilities and state regulators have opposed using the Nuclear Waste Fund to pay for on-site storage (as proposed by S. 784) rather than permanent disposal or central interim storage.

Federal Central Interim Storage

DOE does not believe it has the authority under current law to develop a central interim nuclear waste storage facility other than the "monitored retrievable storage" facility authorized by NWPA,[41] and the 1987 NWPA Amendments prohibit such an MRS facility from opening until Yucca Mountain is licensed. Moreover, construction of an MRS cannot begin until NRC grants a construction permit for the repository; the MRS is limited to 15,000 metric tons of spent fuel; and the MRS cannot be located in Nevada (NWPA sections 145 and 148). Numerous legislative efforts have been mounted since the mid-1990s to establish central interim storage capacity without the MRS restrictions, but without success. No matter how they have been structured, such proposals have consistently faced overwhelming concerns that any "interim" storage facility would undercut political support for a permanent repository and therefore become a "de facto" permanent disposal site.

Central interim nuclear waste storage facilities would use dry cask technology that is similar to that currently in place at reactor sites. Sealed waste canisters would be placed in individual above-ground concrete casks or bunkers for radiation shielding and for cooling by natural air circulation. Because the systems are modular, they can be constructed relatively quickly. And because the waste is not expected to remain in storage after active maintenance of the facility has ceased, a wide variety of sites are likely to be considered geologically suitable. However, public concern about large quantities of highly radioactive waste stored for an extended period of time, and perhaps indefinitely, has proven to be a major obstacle to central storage proposals.

DOE had proposed to build an MRS facility near Oak Ridge, TN, as a central receiving point for small waste shipments from individual plant sites east of the Rocky Mountains. Spent fuel was to be repackaged if necessary at the MRS facility for consolidated long-distance shipments to the planned Western repository.[42] The Oak Ridge selection was specifically nullified by the 1987 NWPA amendments, which established a new siting procedure along with the restrictions listed above. The 1987 Amendments also established an alternative, voluntary siting procedure for the MRS and other nuclear waste facilities. Under Title IV, a presidentially appointed "nuclear waste negotiator" was authorized to reach agreements with any states or Indian tribes to host nuclear waste facilities under any "reasonable and appropriate" terms. Such agreements could not take effect without being enacted into law, however.

By the early 1990s, finding a voluntary site for a central storage facility appeared to be DOE's best chance for meeting NWPA's 1998 waste acceptance deadline. DOE began providing feasibility study grants to potential volunteers, mostly Indian tribes. Potential agreements with Indian tribes proved highly objectionable to the states in which the tribes were located, and Congress blocked the grant funding in October 1993 (P.L. 103-126). The authority for the nuclear waste negotiator expired on January 21, 1995, without any proposed siting agreements having been reached.

The next major legislative push for an alternative to the MRS took place after it became clear that DOE would be unable to meet the NWPA disposal deadline. In the 104th Congress, nuclear power supporters developed legislation to authorize DOE to open an interim surface storage facility at the Yucca Mountain site by 1998, well before the then-anticipated opening of the underground repository in 2010 (H.R. 1020). The State of Nevada and nuclear power opponents contended that waste should not be transported to Yucca Mountain before the repository was licensed, because if the repository ultimately did not receive a license, the waste would have to be moved again, increasing potential transportation risks and costs. The bill was approved by the Commerce Committee (H.Rept. 104-254) but was not enacted. Similar bills were passed by the House and Senate in the 1 05th Congress (H.R. 1270, S. 104), but President Clinton threatened a veto and a conference was not held. A final try in the 106th Congress (S. 1287) drew a presidential veto that was narrowly sustained in the Senate.

After the proposals to develop interim storage capacity at Yucca Mountain were rejected, language was included in several appropriations bills and reports to require DOE to store commercial spent fuel at unspecified federal sites. The House Appropriations Committee included language in its report on the FY2006 Energy and Water Development Appropriations Bill to require DOE "to begin the movement of spent fuel to centralized interim storage at one or more DOE sites within fiscal year 2006" (H.Rept. 109-86), although the Senate did not go along with the idea. The Senate Appropriations Committee included an extensive provision in its version of the FY2007 Energy and Water bill (H.R. 5427, section 313) to authorize the Secretary of Energy to designate interim storage sites for spent nuclear fuel. The proposal, which was not enacted, would have required the Secretary to designate a storage site in each state with a nuclear power plant, after consultation with the governor, or to designate regional storage facilities.

A more limited central storage proposal was aimed solely at nine decommissioned reactor sites. Because the decommissioned sites have no ongoing nuclear activities except spent fuel storage, the removal of spent fuel would allow all nuclear-related maintenance and security at those locations to cease, producing significant operational cost savings, according to the nuclear industry. The House Appropriations Committee included report language with the FY2008 Energy and Water bill requiring DOE to "develop a plan to take custody of spent fuel currently stored at decommissioned reactor sites" (H.Rept. 110-185). The resulting DOE report concluded that all 2,800 metric tons of spent fuel at the nine decommissioned sites could be shipped to a federal central storage facility by 2018, but that DOE had no statutory authority to implement such a plan.[43]

DOE has taken spent fuel for storage at its facilities in the past in special cases, such as the damaged core from the 1979 Three Mile Island accident and from the unique Fort Saint Vrain gas-cooled reactor in Colorado. The Three Mile Island core material was shipped to DOE's Idaho National Laboratory for research. DOE is storing the Fort Saint Vrain spent fuel pursuant to a cooperative agreement signed with the reactor supplier and local utility before the demonstration reactor was built.[44] In addition, DOE stores highly enriched, U.S.-origin spent fuel from foreign research reactors because of its potential use in nuclear weapons. Some have contended that those precedents indicate that DOE has sufficient general authority under the Atomic Energy Act to store larger amounts of commercial spent fuel. However, DOE contends that its broad authority under the Atomic Energy Act is restricted to narrow circumstances under the more recently enacted and specific waste management provisions of NWPA.[45]

Private Central Storage

Although DOE does not believe it has authority under current law to construct a federal central interim storage facility for commercial nuclear waste, NRC regularly licenses private-sector interim storage facilities under the Atomic Energy Act.[46] Such "independent spent fuel storage installations" typically are licensed for on-site storage at reactor sites, but they can also include central storage facilities.

After a nearly nine-year licensing process, NRC issued a license for a private central storage facility on February 21, 2006, that was intended to receive waste from commercial reactor sites.[47] The facility was to be developed by a nuclear utility consortium called Private Fuel Storage (PFS) on the reservation of the Skull Valley Band of the Goshute Indians in Utah. The 20-year license, renewable for an additional 20 years, allows up to 40,000 metric tons of spent fuel to be stored in 4,000 dry casks pending shipment by DOE to a permanent repository. PFS will not take title to the spent fuel, so waste is to be returned to the utilities that own it if DOE cannot take it away before the PFS license expires.[48]

On September 7, 2006, the Department of the Interior issued two decisions blocking the PFS project. The Bureau of Indian Affairs disapproved a proposed lease of tribal trust lands to PFS, concluding there was too much risk that the waste could remain at the site indefinitely, among other objections.[49] The Bureau of Land Management rejected the necessary rights-of-way to transport waste to the facility, concluding that a proposed rail line would be incompatible with the Cedar Mountain Wilderness Area and that existing roads would be inadequate.[50] Contending that the Interior Department was motivated by political pressure from the State of Utah, which strongly opposed the facility, the Skull Valley Band of Goshutes and PFS filed a federal lawsuit July 17, 2007, to overturn the decisions.[51]

The PFS project was intended to provide a waste storage option for nuclear plants that might have trouble gaining approval for on-site storage facilities or decommissioned reactors that want to remove remaining spent fuel from their sites. If the PFS facility were considered potentially useful as part of a revised spent fuel strategy, the new Administration could revisit the Interior Department's administrative decisions that are blocking the project. However, if those decisions were reversed, the project would still need to overcome a challenge to the NRC license filed by the State of Utah.[52] Another consideration for this option is that, because the waste would have to be returned after 40 years, and utilities would be paying for the service, the PFS facility might not significantly reduce DOE's liabilities for delays in spent fuel acceptance.

Spent Fuel Reprocessing and Recycling

The major alternative to direct disposal of spent fuel (the "once through" fuel cycle) is the "closed" fuel cycle, in which spent fuel is reprocessed into new fuel. The closed fuel cycle could reduce the volume and long-term radioactivity of nuclear waste and potentially postpone the need for permanent disposal. However, a National Academy of Sciences study of reprocessing technologies found that "none of the S&T [separations and transmutation] system concepts reviewed eliminates the need for a geologic repository."[53] Recycling spent fuel could also greatly increase the amount of energy extracted from a given supply of uranium. However, the closed fuel cycle is generally considered to be substantially more expensive than the once-through cycle.[54] Moreover, the separation of plutonium from spent fuel has long been a subject of national policy debates because of its potential role in nuclear weapons proliferation.

Fuel for U.S. nuclear reactors currently consists of uranium in which the fissile isotope U-235 has been increased (enriched) to 3-5%, with the remainder being the non-fissile isotope U-238. During the fuel's several-year irradiation period in the reactor, most of the U-235 splits, or fissions, releasing energy. Some of the U-238 is transmuted into fissile isotopes of plutonium, some of which also fissions. In reprocessing, the uranium and plutonium are chemically separated to be made into new fuel, while the lighter elements resulting from the fission process, called fission products, are stored for disposal.

New fuel made from reprocessed uranium and plutonium can be recycled in existing commercial light water reactors, which is being done in other countries, primarily France. After being recycled once, however, the buildup of undesirable plutonium isotopes makes further recycling in today's commercial reactors problematic. Without multiple recycling, the plutonium and other long-lived isotopes cannot be fully fissioned or transmuted into shorter-lived radioactive isotopes, and the benefits for waste disposal would therefore be modest.

For multiple recycling of spent fuel, advanced reactors would be necessary. DOE has evaluated a wide variety of options as part of its Global Nuclear Energy Partnership (GNEP) program. These include initial recycling in existing light and heavy water reactors, and subsequent recycling in high-burnup gas-cooled reactors, reactors fueled by thorium and plutonium, and "fast" reactors (in which neutrons are not slowed by water or other materials).[55] A reprocessing and recycling system with sufficient capacity could eventually treat existing spent fuel inventories along with newly generated spent fuel.

For waste disposal, the goal of such a recycling system would be to send only the fission products and other short-lived radioisotopes to a permanent repository and feed all the uranium, plutonium, and other long-lived radioisotopes back into a reactor after each cycle. If that could be accomplished, the nuclear waste in a repository would decay to insignificant levels within about 1,000 years and eliminate longer-term uncertainty about the repository's performance. Spent fuel recycling could also save space in an underground repository by reducing the near-term heat load, which is the primary limit on repository capacity.[56] To address nuclear nonproliferation concerns, the GNEP program is conducting research on reprocessing technology that would not separate plutonium in a pure enough form for direct use in nuclear weapons.

A potential nearer-term benefit of a reprocessing strategy would be to provide an alternative destination for spent fuel currently stored at reactor sites if Yucca Mountain were to be abandoned. Because DOE is still conducting R&D on a variety of possible reprocessing technologies, however, a U.S. reprocessing facility would probably not open earlier than the current Yucca Mountain target date.

Earlier waste shipments might be possible under proposals that have been made for foreign reprocessing of U.S. spent fuel. Several foreign reprocessing plants are currently in operation. The Senate Energy and Natural Resources Committee included a provision in a nuclear waste bill in the 104th Congress (S. 1271) that would have authorized DOE to take title to spent fuel and ship it to a reprocessing plant in England. However, the provision proved highly contentious and was dropped from the final bill passed by the Senate (S. 1936). In a 2008 report for GNEP, a consortium led by the French nuclear firm Areva recommended that U.S. spent fuel be reprocessed overseas from 2010 to 2019 before the startup of a U.S. reprocessing plant after 2020.[57] The use of inactive defense-related reprocessing facilities at DOE's Savannah River Site in South Carolina has also been suggested for U.S. commercial spent fuel.[58]

The amount of spent fuel that could be shipped to reprocessing plants would be another consideration. Existing reprocessing plants in France and England are designed to handle about 800 metric tons of spent fuel per year. Therefore, at least three plants of that size would need to be constructed in the United States (assuming minimal foreign reprocessing) to handle the 2,000 metric tons of spent fuel discharged annually from U.S. reactors. About four plants would be needed to exceed the planned shipment rate to Yucca Mountain.

Many decades would be required to implement a reprocessing and recycling strategy. For example, the Areva consortium projected that a steady-state recycling system would not be fully in place until about 2070, even if the currently planned 63,000 metric tons of spent fuel were emplaced in Yucca Mountain rather than being reprocessed. The first U.S. reprocessing plant would become operational after 2020.[59] Proposals by three other GNEP consortia included similar time frames. (For more discussion of reprocessing policy, see CRS Report CRS Report RL34579, *Advanced Nuclear Power and Fuel Cycle Technologies: Outlook and Policy Options*, by Mark Holt).

Non-Repository Options

The inherent difficulty of siting a permanent geologic repository for high-level nuclear waste has led to a variety of proposals over the past few decades for non-repository disposal options. NWPA section 222 authorizes DOE to conduct research on such disposal alternatives. The most seriously analyzed ideas involve launching waste into space or burying it in the deep seabed. Some plausible concepts for implementing these ideas have been developed, but a great deal of development work would still be required to determine their likely feasibility.

Congress established a DOE Office of Subseabed Disposal Research in the Nuclear Waste Policy Amendments Act of 1987 (P.L. 100-203). The office was required to organize a Subseabed Consortium among leading research institutions to develop a research plan for identifying subseabed disposal sites, developing conceptual designs for subseabed disposal systems, and assessing potential environmental impacts. However, few resources were provided for the subseabed office before it was abolished in 1996 by P.L. 104-66.[60]

Previous research on subseabed disposal was conducted by the Nuclear Energy Agency (NEA) of the Organization for Economic Cooperation and Development. The United States participated in the effort through the DOE Subseabed Disposal Project, on which about $125 million was spent from 1974-1986.[61] The NEA program studied the emplacement of nuclear waste canisters in ocean sediments with gravity-driven penetrators or in drilled holes. NEA concluded in 1988 that the sediments would probably contain the waste well enough to keep the maximum dose to humans – occurring after about 100,000 years – "many orders of magnitude below present standards" and pose "insignificant risk to the deep sea environment." However, NEA also concluded that more research would be needed to confirm the safety of the subseabed disposal concepts.[62]

Subseabed disposal is currently prohibited under the 1996 Protocol to the 1972 London Dumping Convention, which was signed by the United States on March 31, 1998, and entered into force March 24, 2006, but has not been ratified by the Senate. The Protocol amended the definition of "dumping" to include "any storage of wastes or other matter in the seabed and the subsoil thereof from vessels, aircraft, platforms or other man-made structures at sea."[63] Previously it had been unclear whether the Convention prohibited subseabed disposal. Annex 1 of the Protocol requires parties to the agreement to complete a scientific study of sea disposal of radioactive material other than high-level waste by 2019 and every 25 years thereafter.

Disposal of nuclear waste in outer space has also been studied by DOE and its predecessor agencies. In a 1974 draft environmental statement on nuclear waste management, the Atomic Energy Commission (AEC) reviewed government studies of such concepts as "solar system escape, solar impact, high-earth orbit, and a solar orbit other than that of the planets." The report concluded that space disposal "does not seem an attractive alternative to the geological development program."[64] Major concerns include launch costs, launch safety, and the potential for future waste re-entry into Earth's atmosphere. Proposed alternatives to conventional rocket- based launch systems, such as laser propulsion and electromagnetic rail guns, might have safety and cost advantages, but a major federal commitment would be needed to determine their feasibility.[65]

Other disposal concepts studied by DOE and its predecessors include waste emplacement in polar ice sheets, deep boreholes, and deep well injection of liquid waste. AEC's draft environmental statement dismissed those alternatives as not viable,[66] and they have since received relatively little attention.

New Repository Site

Even if nuclear waste is placed in extended surface storage and is reprocessed to remove the longest-lived radioactive isotopes, a permanent disposal method almost certainly would still be required. Barring the non-repository options discussed above, that would mean that the abandonment of Yucca Mountain for any reason would eventually require a search for another repository site.

The history of site selection efforts under NWPA indicates that a new repository site search would be slow-moving and extremely controversial. Vast areas of the United States would again be under consideration, after having been eliminated by the 1987 congressional designation of Yucca Mountain as the sole candidate site. Every decision made by whatever entity were to be placed in charge of the site search would probably face intense opposition, especially as the search began to narrow. Designing a selection process that could overcome such pressures would be a major challenge.

NWPA was intended to set up a fair and technically sound process for selecting among numerous potential repository sites that DOE and its predecessor agencies had been considering. Without such a legislative mandate, DOE's previous efforts to find a waste site appeared unlikely to overcome the controversy that had arisen at every potential location.[67] However, the explicit waste siting process created by NWPA lasted only about five years before being paralyzed by renewed controversy.

Under NWPA as originally enacted, the Secretary of Energy was required to establish guidelines that DOE would follow in nominating at least five suitable sites, of which three were to be recommended to the President for detailed study, or "characterization" by January 1, 1985. Sites that DOE had been considering included salt domes along the Gulf Coast, bedded salt in the Great Plains and Midwest, volcanic tuff in the West, and basalt in the Pacific Northwest. Energy Secretary John S. Herrington recommended Hanford, WA; Deaf Smith County, TX, and Yucca Mountain for site characterization on May 27, 1986.[68] After completing the characterization of the three sites, the Secretary was to recommend one of them to the President for the nation's first permanent nuclear waste repository. The President was required to submit his choice to Congress by March 31, 1987.

To address concerns about whether a single site or region should take all of the nation's high-level nuclear waste, NWPA limited the first repository to 70,000 metric tons until a second repository was opened. A separate track was established for locating a second repository site. By July 1, 1989, the Secretary of Energy was to nominate five sites for a second repository, including at least three sites that had not been among the five sites nominated for the first repository, and recommend three of them to the President. The recommended sites were to be located, "to the extent practicable," in different geologic media. The President was to recommend a second repository site to Congress by March 31, 1990, from any of the sites previously characterized.

Unlike the process for the first repository, which started with specific candidate sites that were already under consideration, the site search for the second repository was conducted more systematically. DOE began by focusing on major formations of granite and other crystalline rock, which had not been included in the first repository effort, in 17 states in the upper Midwest and Atlantic coast. In consultation with states, DOE developed a screening methodology to rank candidate bodies of rock for their potential suitability as a repository.[69] DOE released preliminary rankings that identified 12 promising rock bodies in seven states in January 1986.[70]

DOE's identification of potential sites for the second repository drew intense opposition from the affected states. The three potential host states for the first repository also raised strong objections, which intensified when Secretary Herrington announced on May 28, 1986, that work on the second repository would be indefinitely postponed. Herrington said the decision was based on lower growth projections for nuclear power that delayed the need for a second repository, but officials from the first repository candidate states in the West contended that the Reagan Administration had responded to political pressure from the Eastern candidate states and had unraveled a key regional compromise in NWPA.[71] Opposition from Tennessee to DOE's proposed MRS site near Oak Ridge added to the controversy. The Senate Appropriations Committee made note of the deteriorating situation:

> Intense and widespread criticism, controversial programmatic decisions by the Secretary of Energy, and a proliferation of substantial litigation have taken a toll on progress toward the goals of the program.[72]

In addition to the controversy over site selection, it had become apparent that NWPA's timelines for characterizing the candidate sites and the anticipated cost of the characterization effort were unrealistic. With the future of the nuclear waste program in doubt, the 100th Congress decided to reopen NWPA for fundamental revision. The resulting NWPA Amendments Act of 1987 cancelled the second repository program, nullified DOE's selection of Oak Ridge for an MRS facility, and statutorily designated Yucca Mountain as the sole candidate site for a repository. Supporters of the legislation contended that characterizing only one site rather than three would be faster and save money, and noted that Yucca Mountain had been the most highly rated of the three candidates by DOE.[73] Some lawmakers, however, contended that the statutory designation of Yucca Mountain was made primarily for political reasons.[74]

The NWPA Amendments Act also provided for annual payments as an inducement to states for hosting nuclear waste facilities. States could receive up to $20 million per year for hosting a repository and $10 million for an MRS site if they agreed not to exercise their right under the law to disapprove those facilities. However, Nevada expressed no interest in the payments and, as noted previously, exercised its "state veto" in 2002. DOE did not conduct an MRS site search under the NWPA Amendments, relying instead on the Nuclear Waste Negotiator to find a voluntary site, as discussed earlier.

Although naming a single site for characterization was intended to speed up the development of a nuclear waste repository, the process actually took another 15 years after the 1987 Amendments, plus another five years to complete the license application to NRC. Supporters of the waste program contend that chronic underfunding by Congress was a major reason for the slow progress, while opponents primarily blamed DOE management problems. The State of Nevada was also able to slow the repository by denying state permits for various characterization activities and through successful lawsuits, such as the challenge to EPA's environmental standards. Nevada filed a 1,500-page petition with NRC in December 2008 to intervene in the Yucca Mountain license proceeding, raising dozens of safety, environmental, and other contentions.[75]

The history of U.S. efforts to site a nuclear waste repository illustrates the difficulty in successfully addressing local, state, and regional objections to such facilities. The United States did not succeed with the administrative process started by the Atomic Energy Commission, with the site-ranking system used for the NWPA first repository selection, the broad screening process used for the second repository, the benefits offered under the NWPA Amendments, or the voluntary selection process by the Nuclear Waste Negotiator. If Yucca Mountain is abandoned, that would arguably spell failure for the statutory designation method as well.

Just because those approaches were unsuccessful in the past does not mean they could not work in the future with program design modifications, better management, and changed circumstances. For example, it has been recently suggested that a negotiated benefits agreement with Nevada might now be feasible, given the current economic downturn.[76] During the debate on the 1987 Amendments, Representative Morris Udall, Chairman of the House Interior Committee, contended that the original NWPA selection process would have worked had it been implemented properly:

> We created a principled process for finding the safest, most sensible places to bury these dangerous wastes. We were confident that while no State wanted a nuclear waste repository, the States ultimately chosen would accept the outcome because the selection process would have been fair and technically credible.
>
> Today, just 5 years later, this great program is in ruins. To help a few office seekers in the last election, the administration killed the eastern repository program, shattering the delicate regional balance at the heart of the 1982 act. Since then the Western States have felt they are being treated unfairly, and they no longer trust the technical integrity of the Department of Energy's siting decisions.[77]

Others have expressed doubt that a purely scientific and objective selection process is possible, given the inherent difficulties in making extremely long-term projections of repository behavior. The Director of the Office of Civilian Radioactive Waste Management recently described the siting of nuclear waste facilities as a "technically informed political decision."[78]

DOE's long but ultimately successful struggle to open a deep geologic repository for mid-level waste – the WIPP facility near Carlsbad, NM – indicates that siting of nuclear waste facilities is not necessarily impossible. State and local officials had invited AEC to consider the deep salt beds in the economically depressed area in the early 1970s for a high-level waste repository. After a great deal of statewide controversy, although with consistent local support, Congress authorized WIPP in 1979 to hold defense-related transuranic waste (P.L. 96-1 64).[79]

Transuranic (TRU) waste is not considered to be as hazardous as spent fuel and high-level waste, but it nevertheless requires long-term isolation in a geologic repository. TRU waste consists of relatively low-radioactivity material contaminated with more than a minimum concentration of long-lived plutonium.

DOE's efforts to implement the 1979 WIPP authorization were hampered by concerns by state officials that spent fuel and high-level waste would eventually be disposed of along with the transuranic waste.[80] After a dozen years of controversy over the project's implementation, Congress in 1992 enacted the Waste Isolation Pilot Plant Land Withdrawal Act (P.L. 102-579), detailing the regulations and procedures that DOE would have to follow to open the facility and banning high-level waste and spent fuel. Slow progress prompted Congress to amend the WIPP Land Withdrawal Act in 1996 to exempt WIPP waste from some land disposal restrictions and provide $20 million for New Mexico bypass roads for waste shipments (P.L. 104-201). The first waste was shipped to the repository in March 1999, nearly 20 years after the facility was authorized.[81]

It has recently been suggested that WIPP again be considered as a site for high-level waste disposal. Spent nuclear fuel could be more technically problematic, because the physical flow of the salt within a period of years will close in on stored waste and eliminate the option to retrieve the waste after 100 years or so, as could be done at Yucca Mountain.[82] Such "salt creep" occurs more quickly at higher temperatures, which could result from the disposal of high-level waste and spent fuel. A potential advantage of salt creep is that it can provide a natural seal around the waste.[83] Nevertheless, the State of New Mexico continues to strongly oppose any disposal of high-level waste at WIPP.[84]

CONCLUDING DISCUSSION

Significant scientific uncertainty – if not clear technical unsuitability – has arisen at every potential high-level nuclear waste repository site evaluated by the federal government. Such doubts have fed the public controversy that inevitably accompanies the announcement of such sites. As a result, the federal government has not succeeded in opening any central facilities for permanent disposal or interim storage of spent nuclear fuel and high-level waste.

The controversial nature of siting nuclear waste facilities increases the likelihood that alternatives to the proposed Yucca Mountain repository would leave waste at existing storage sites longer than under the current program schedule. Major consequences under current law could include increased liability by the federal government for utility storage costs, and fines and penalties for missing cleanup deadlines at defense-related nuclear facilities. Although NRC has determined that waste can be stored safely at reactor sites for many decades, the licensing of new plants could be affected by the lack of a definite disposal plan. Extremely long disposal delays would also increase the risk that adequate maintenance and security at storage sites would end before the waste could be removed.

Central interim storage of nuclear waste has regularly been suggested as the quickest way to begin moving waste from existing storage sites. However, without a plan for permanent disposal, the development of interim sites could be especially controversial. Reprocessing of spent fuel has long been proposed as a way to reduce the hazards of nuclear waste by removing plutonium and other long-lived radioactive material. While such a technological approach could make it easier to site a permanent repository, the separation of plutonium raises significant opposition because of its potential use in nuclear weapons and effects on U.S. nonproliferation policy. DOE is researching reprocessing techniques that could reduce the separation of pure plutonium, but their effectiveness and potential high cost continues to be a subject of controversy.

The 1987 designation of Yucca Mountain as the nation's sole candidate site for a national high- level nuclear waste repository was a calculated risk that the site could be developed successfully. There is no backup plan in place. Yucca Mountain opponents contend that, as a result, the federal government has stuck with the site no matter what technical problems have been discovered. But if Yucca Mountain is determined to have significant problems, an alternative course will have little existing policy framework to build upon.

End Notes

[1] Obama for America, "Barack Obama and Joe Biden: New Energy for America," campaign issue statement, 2008, http://www.barackobama.com/pdf/factsheet_energy_speech_080308.pdf.

[2] U.S. Department of Energy, Office of Civilian Radioactive Waste Management, *Total System Life Cycle Cost Report*, DOE/RW-0591, Washington, DC, July 2008, p. 20, http://www.ocrwm.doe.gov/about/budget/pdf/ TSLCC_2007_8_05_08.pdf.

[3] U.S. Department of Energy, Office of Civilian Radioactive Waste Management, *Report to the President and the Congress by the Secretary of Energy on the Need for a Second Repository*, DOE/RW-0595, Washington, DC, December 2008, p. 6, http://www.rw.doe.gov/info_library/program_docs/Second_Repository_ Rpt_120908.pdf.

[4] DOE, *Life Cycle Cost Report*, op. cit., p. A-3.

[5] DOE, *Need for a Second Repository*, op. cit., p. 1.

[6] Department of Energy, Office of Civilian Radioactive Waste Management, *Monthly Summary of Program Financial & Budget Information*, as of September 1, 2008, p. 7.

[7] U.S. Department of Energy, Office of Civilian Radioactive Waste Management, *Total System Life Cycle Cost Report*, DOE/RW-0591, Washington, DC, July 2008, p. B-2.

[8] Christopher A. Kouts, Office of Civilian Radioactive Waste Management, "Yucca Mountain Program Status Update," Presentation to Environmental Protection Agency Workshop on Energy and Environmental Sustainability in a Carbon Constrained Future, New York, NY, September 11, 2008, p. 9, http://www.epa.gov/region2/energyworkshop/ workshop_presentations/session2/nuclear_session/panel1_nuclear_waste_disposal.pdf.

[9] 10 C.F.R. § 2.107.

[10] Nuclear Regulatory Commission, *Performance Budget Fiscal Year 2009*, NUREG-1100 Volume 24, February 2008, p. 2, http://www.nrc.gov/reading-rm/doc-collections/nuregs/staff/sr1100/v24/

[11] Erica Werner, "Reid Won't Allow Energy Secretary Who Supports Yucca Waste Dump," *Associated Press*, December 4, 2008, http://www.rgj.com.

[12] Senator Harry Reid, "Statement on the nomination of Dr. Steven Chu to be Secretary of Energy," press release, December 15, 2008, http://reid.senate.gov/newsroom/pr_121508_energysecnom.cfm.

[13] Lawrence Berkeley National Laboratory, "Growing energy: Berkeley Lab's Steve Chu on what termite guts have to do with global warming," press release, September 30, 2005, http://berkeley.edu/news/media/ releases/2005/10/03_chu.shtml.

[14] DOE National Laboratory Directors, *A Sustainable Energy Future: The Essential Role of Nuclear Energy*, August 2008, p. 1, http://www.ne.doe.gov/pdfFiles/rpt_SustainableEnergyFuture_Aug2008.pdf.

[15] Nuclear Regulatory Commission, "Public Health and Environmental Radiation Protection Standards for Yucca Mountain, Nevada," 73 *Federal Register* 61256, October 15, 2008.

[16] *State of Nevada v. U.S. Environmental Protection Agency* (U.S. Court of Appeals for the District of Columbia Circuit 2008).

[17] For more on this issue, see CRS Report RL34698, *EPA's Final Health and Safety Standard for Yucca Mountain*, by Bonnie C. Gitlin.

[18] Department of Energy, Office of Civilian Radioactive Waste Management, *Report to Congress on the Demonstration of the Interim Storage of Spent Nuclear Fuel from Decommissioned Nuclear Power Reactor Sites*, DOE/RW-0596, Washington, DC, December 2008, p. 6, http://www.rw.doe.gov/info_library /program_docs/ ES_Interim_Storage_Report_120108.pdf.

[19] Kouts, op.cit., p. 9.

[20] U.S. Congress, Senate Committee on Energy and Natural Resources, *Nuclear Waste Litigation*, To examine the impacts of federal court decisions on breach of federal nuclear waste contracts, 106th Cong., 2nd sess., September 28, 2000, S.Hrg. 106-918 (Washington: GPO, 2001), p. 46.

[21] Department of Energy, Office of Civilian Radioactive Waste Management, *Monthly Summary of Program Financial & Budget Information*, as of September 1, 2008, p. 7.

[22] Jeff Beattie, "Federal Judge Suggests Voiding Utilities' Yucca Mountain Contracts," *Energy Daily*, April 29, 2005, p. 1.

[23] *Sacramento Municipal Utility District v. United States*, (Court of Federal Claims 2006).

[24] Nuclear Regulatory Commission, "Combined License Applications for New Reactors," http://www.nrc.gov/reactors/ new-reactors/col.html.

[25] Nuclear Regulatory Commission, 42 *Federal Register* 34391, July 5, 1977.

[26] Nuclear Regulatory Commission, 49 *Federal Register* 34658, August 31, 1984.

[27] Nuclear Regulatory Commission, 55 *Federal Register* 38472, September 18, 1990.

[28] Nuclear Regulatory Commission, "Waste Confidence Decision Update," 73 *Federal Register* 59551, October 9, 2008.

[29] David L. Lovell, Wisconsin Legislative Council Staff, *State Statutes Limiting the Construction of Nuclear Power Plants*, October 5, 2006.

[30] *Pacific Gas & Electric Co. v. State Energy Resources Conservation and Development Commission*, 461 U.S. (190 1983).

[31] DOE, *Need for a Second Repository*, op. cit., p. 13.

[32] Department of Energy, Office of Civilian Radioactive Waste Management, *Final Supplemental Environmental Impact Statement for a Geologic Repository for the Disposal of Spent Nuclear Fuel and High-Level Radioactive Waste at Yucca Mountain, Nye County, Nevada*, DOE/EIS-0250F-S1, Washington, DC, June 2008, p. S-50, http://www.rw.doe.gov/ym_repository/seis/index.shtml.

[33] U.S. Congress, House Committee on Commerce, Subcommittee on Energy and Power, *The Nuclear Waste Policy Act of 1997*, hearing on H.R. 1270, 105th Cong., 1st sess., April 29, 1997, Serial No. 105-27 (Washington: GPO, 1997), p. 125.

[34] DOE, *Final Supplemental Environmental Impact Statement*, op. cit., p. S-51.

[35] International Nuclear Recycling Alliance, *Integrated U.S. Used Fuel Strategy*, May 1, 2008, p. 10.

[36] EnergySolutions, *GNEP Deployment Studies: Overall Summary Report*, Richland, WA, May 19, 2008, p. 2-2.

[37] Allison M. Macfarlane, Rodney C. Ewing, et al., *Uncertainty Underground: Yucca Mountain and the Nation's High- Level Nuclear Waste* (Cambridge, MA: MIT Press, 2006), p. 407.

[38] John Fleck, "WIPP Oversight Bureau Planned," *Albuquerque Journal*, June 19, 2004.

[39] http://www.nmenv.state.nm.us/doe_oversight/wipp.htm

[40] National Academy of Sciences Board on Radioactive Waste Management, *Safety and Security of Commercial Spent Nuclear Fuel Storage: Public Report*, Washington, DC, 2005, p. 6.

[41] DOE, *Report to Congress on Interim Storage*, op. cit., p. 14.

[42] Department of Energy, Office of Civilian Radioactive Waste Management, *Monitored Retrievable Storage Submission to Congress*, DOE/RW-0035, Washington, DC, February 1986.

[43] DOE, *Report to Congress on Interim Storage*, op. cit., p. 14.

[44] Department of Energy, "DOE Holds License for Colorado Spent Fuel Facility," press release, June 28, 1999, http://newsdesk.inl.gov/press_releases/1999/DOE_Holds_Licen.htm.

[45] DOE, *Report to Congress on Interim Storage*, op. cit., p. 6.

[46] 42 U.S.C. § 2011 et seq., 10 CFR Part 72.

[47] Nuclear Regulatory Commission, *License for Independent Storage of Spent Nuclear Fuel and High-Level Radioactive Waste SNM-2513*, February 21, 2006.

[48] Private Fuel Storage, LLC, *Frequently Asked Questions: Financial Accountability*, http://www.privatefuelstorage.com/faqs/faqs.html.

[49] Bureau of Indian Affairs, *Record of Decision for the Construction and Operation of an Independent Spent Fuel Storage Installation (ISFSI) on the Reservation of the Skull Valley Band of Goshute Indians (Band) in Tooele County, Utah*, September 7, 2006.

[50] Bureau of Land Management, *Record of Decision Addressing Right-of-Way Applications U 76985 and U 76986 to Transport Spent Nuclear Fuel to the Reservation of the Skull Valley Band of Goshute Indians*, September 7, 2006.

[51] *Skull Valley Band of Goshute Indians and Private Fuel Storage, LLC, v. James E. Cason et al.* (U.S. District Court for the District of Utah, Central Division 2007).

[52] Todd D. Lovinger, "Utah Challenges License Issuance to PFS," *LLW Forum News Flash*, March 12, 2006.

[53] National Academy of Sciences, National Research Council, *Nuclear Wastes: Technologies for Separations and Transmutation*, Washington, DC, August 1995, p. 17.

[54] Peter R. Orszag, *Costs of Reprocessing Versus Directly Disposing of Spent Nuclear Fuel*, Congressional Budget Office, Statement Before the Senate Committee on Energy and Natural Resources, Washington, DC, November 17, 2007, http://www.cbo.gov/ftpdocs/88xx/doc8808/11-14-NuclearFuel.pdf.

[55] Department of Energy, Office of Nuclear Energy, *Draft Global Nuclear Energy Partnership Programmatic Environmental Impact Statement*, DOE/EIS-0396, Washington, DC, October 2008, http://www.gnep.energy.gov/ peis.html.

[56] Electric Power Research Institute, *Projected Waste Packages Resulting From Alternative Spent-Fuel Separation Processes*, EPRI NP-7262 Project 3030 Final Report, Palo Alto, CA, April 1991, pp. 5-3.

[57] International Nuclear Recycling Alliance, *Presentation for GNEP Deployment Studies*, April 2008, p. 6, http://www.gnep.energy.gov/pdfs/INRA%20Presentation.pdf.

[58] David Kramer, "Report by SRS Contractor Appears to Advocate Reprocessing at Site," *Inside Energy/with Federal Lands*, January 8, 1996, p. 8.

[59] International Nuclear Recycling Alliance, *op. cit.*, p. 43.

[60] Steven Nadis, "The Sub-Seabed Solution," *The Atlantic Monthly Digital Edition*, October 1996.

[61] Office of Technology Assessment, *Staff Paper on the Subseabed Disposal of High-Level Radioactive Waste*, Washington, DC, May 1986, p. 3.

[62] Organization for Economic Cooperation and Development, Nuclear Energy Agency, *Feasibility of Disposal of High- Level Radioactive Waste into the Seabed, Overview of Research and Conclusions*, Volume 1, Paris, 1988, p. 60.

[63] *1996 Protocol to Convention on Prevention of Marine Pollution by Dumping of Wastes*, Treaty Doc. 110-5, September 4, 2007.

[64] Atomic Energy Commission, *Draft Environmental Statement on Management of Commercial High Level and Transuranium-Contaminated Radioactive Waste*, WASH-1539, September 1974, pp. 5.3-6.

[65] Jonathan Coopersmith, "Nuclear Waste in Space?," *The Space Review*, August 22, 2005, http://www.thespacereview.com/article/437/1.

[66] Atomic Energy Commission, op. cit., p. 5.3.

[67] Luther J. Carter, *Nuclear Imperatives and Public Trust: Dealing with Radioactive Waste* (Washington, DC: Resources for the Future, 1987), p. 198.

[68] Department of Energy, *Recommendation by the Secretary of Energy Regarding the Suitability of the Yucca Mountain Site*, February 2002, p. 4, http://www.ocrwm.doe.gov/ym_repository/sr/sar.pdf.

[69] Department of Energy, Office of Civilian Radioactive Waste Management, *Draft Mission Plan for the Civilian Radioactive Waste Management Program*, DOE/RW-0005 DRAFT Volume 1, Washington, DC, April 1984, pp. 3-A-23.

[70] Carter, op. cit., p. 410.

[71] Mary Louise Wagner, "DOE Decision to Halt Second Repository Program Could Derail Entire Waste Act," *NuclearFuel*, June 2, 1986, p. 7.

[72] U.S. Congress, Senate Committee on Appropriations, *Energy and Water Development Appropriation Bill, 1987*, Report to accompany H.R. 5162, 99th Cong., 2nd sess., September 15, 1986, S.Rept. 99-441 (Washington: GPO, 1986), p. 157.

[73] Department of Energy, Office of Civilian Radioactive Waste Management, *A Multiattribute Utility Analysis of Sites Nominated for Characterization for the First Radioactive-Waste Repository—A Decision-Aiding Methodology*, DOE/RW-0074, Washington, DC, May 1986, Chapter 5.

[74] Sen. Quentin Burdick, "Nuclear Waste Provisions," Remarks in the Senate, *Congressional Record*, vol. 133, part 26 (December 21, 1987), p. 37697.

[75] State of Nevada's Petition to Intervene as a Full Party in the Matter of Docket No. 63-00 1 (High Level Waste Repository), before the Nuclear Regulatory Commission, December 19, 2008. http://www.state.nv.us/nucwaste/ news2008/pdf/nv08 1219nrc.pdf

[76] Elaine Hiruo, "Funding Prospects Look Bleak for Yucca Project," *NuclearFuel*, January 12, 2009, p. 11.

[77] Rep. Morris Udall, House Debate, *Congressional Record*, vol. 133, part 26 (December 21, 1987), p. 37068.

[78] Edward F. Sproat III, Director, DOE Office of Civilian Radioactive Waste Management, speech to the Center for Strategic and International Studies, November 6, 2008.

[79] Carter, op. cit., p. 177.

[80] Carter, op. cit., p. 188.

[81] Shawn Terry, "Waste Isolation Pilot Plant Opens Doors," *Inside Energy/with Federal Lands*, March 29, 1999, p. 1.

[82] Rick Michal, "James Conca: On WIPP and Other Things Nuclear," *Nuclear News*, February 2008, p. 44.

[83] D.J. Clayton, "Effects of Heat Generation on Nuclear Waste Disposal in Salt," American Geophysical Union Fall Meeting, abstract #H53A-1010, 2008, http://adsabs.harvard.edu/abs/2008AGUFM.H53A1010C.

[84] "New Mexico Bars High-Level Waste From Carlsbad Salt Caverns," *Environment News Service*, November 4, 2004.

In: Nuclear Waste: Disposal and Liability Issues
Editor: Ylenia E. Farrugia

ISBN: 978-1-61761-590-0
© 2011 Nova Science Publishers, Inc.

Chapter 4

THE YUCCA MOUNTAIN LITIGATION: LIABILITY UNDER THE NUCLEAR WASTE POLICY ACT (NWPA) OF 1982[*]

Todd Garvey

SUMMARY

Over 25 years ago, Congress addressed growing concerns regarding nuclear waste management by calling for federal collection of spent nuclear fuel (SNF) for safe, permanent disposal. To this end, the Department of Energy (DOE) was authorized by the Nuclear Waste Policy Act (NWPA) to enter into contracts with nuclear power providers to gather and dispose of their SNF in exchange for payments by the providers into the statutorily established Nuclear Waste Fund (NWF). Congress subsequently named Yucca Mountain in the state of Nevada as the sole candidate site for the permanent underground geological storage of collected SNF. Congress also mandated that federal disposal of SNF begin no later than January 31, 1998. Over 10 years ago, DOE breached these contracts by failing to begin the acceptance and disposal of SNF by the statutory deadline established in the NWPA. As a result, nuclear utilities have spent hundreds of millions of dollars on temporary storage for toxic SNF that DOE was contractually and statutorily required to collect for disposal. The breach has triggered a prolonged series of suits by nuclear power providers, many of which continue unresolved to this day.

At least 72 breach of contract claims have been filed against DOE since 1998, resulting in the awarding of approximately $1.2 billion in damage awards and settlements thus far. Many of these awards, however, remain on appeal in the U.S. Court of Appeals for the Federal Circuit and are not yet final. Estimates for the total potential liability incurred by DOE as a result of the Yucca Mountain litigation range as high as $50 billion. Moreover, after decades of political, legal, administrative, and environmental delays, the Obama Administration's

---

[*] This is an edited, reformatted and augmented edition of a United States Congressional Research Service publication, Report R40996, dated March 8, 2010.

FY2011 proposed budget eliminates all funding for the Yucca Mountain project, seeks to close the Office of Civilian Radioactive Waste Management, and reemphasizes an intention to pursue other alternatives for the disposal of SNF by establishing the Blue Ribbon Commission on America's Nuclear Future. Accordingly, contract damages will continue to build as delays in the disposal of SNF continue.

DOE's liability for breach of contract was first established in 1996 by the U.S. Court of Appeals for the District of Columbia in *Indiana Michigan Power Co. v. U.S.* After DOE hesitated to act on its legal obligations, citing the absence of a completed SNF storage facility, the court issued a writ of mandamus mandating that DOE "proceed with contractual remedies in a manner consistent with NWPA's command that it undertake an unconditional obligation to begin disposal of SNF by January 31, 1998." The mandamus, issued in *Northern States Power Co. v. U.S.*, essentially prohibited DOE from deflecting liability by arguing that the lack of an existing storage facility constituted an "unavoidable delay."

In 2006, the U.S. Court of Federal Claims (CFC) held that the D.C. Circuit mandamus order in *Northern States* was void for lack of jurisdiction and could not preclude DOE from raising the "unavoidable delay" defense in the former's court. The case was appealed to the Federal Circuit, where the court, *en banc*, overturned the CFC decision and affirmed the D.C. Circuit's jurisdiction in both *Indiana Michigan* and *Northern States*. Accordingly, DOE continues to be prohibited from raising the "unavoidable delay" defense in future litigation.

This chapter will present a brief overview of the NWPA and its subsequent amendments, provide a survey of key issues that have emerged from the protracted waste storage litigation, describe the jurisdictional conflict between the D.C. Circuit and the U.S. Court of Federal Claims, and consider the potential for future liability arising from delays relating to the storage and disposal of nuclear waste.

INTRODUCTION

Over 25 years ago, Congress addressed growing concerns regarding nuclear waste management by calling for federal collection of spent nuclear fuel (SNF) for safe, permanent disposal. To this end, the Department of Energy (DOE) was authorized by the Nuclear Waste Policy Act (NWPA) to enter into contracts with nuclear power providers to gather and dispose of their SNF[1] in exchange for payments by the providers into the statutorily established Nuclear Waste Fund (NWF). Congress subsequently named Yucca Mountain in the state of Nevada as the sole candidate site for the permanent underground geological storage of collected SNF. Congress also mandated that federal disposal of SNF begin no later than January 31, 1998. Over 10 years ago, DOE breached these contracts by failing to begin the acceptance and disposal of SNF by the statutory deadline established in the NWPA. As a result, nuclear utilities have spent hundreds of millions of dollars on temporary storage for toxic SNF that DOE was contractually and statutorily required to collect for disposal.[2] The breach has triggered a prolonged series of suits by nuclear power providers, many of which continue unresolved to this day.

At least 72 breach of contract[3] claims have been filed against DOE since 1998, resulting in approximately $1.2 billion in damage awards and settlements thus far.[4] Many of these awards, however, remain in appeals with the U.S. Court of Appeals for the Federal Circuit and are not yet final. Estimates for the total potential liability incurred by DOE as a result of the Yucca Mountain litigation range as high as $50 billion.[5] Moreover, after decades of political, legal, administrative, and environmental delays, the Obama Administration's FY2011 proposed budget eliminates all funding for the Yucca Mountain project, seeks to close the Office of Civilian Radioactive Waste Management,[6] and reemphasizes an intention to pursue other alternatives for the disposal of SNF by establishing the Blue Ribbon Commission on America's Nuclear Future. Accordingly, contract damages will continue to build as delays in the disposal of SNF continue.[7]

This chapter analyzes the more than 14 years of ongoing litigation over the government's obligations to collect and dispose of SNF under the NWPA.[8] Part I will provide a brief overview of the NWPA and its subsequent amendments. Part II will provide a survey of key issues that have emerged from the protracted litigation and describe the jurisdictional conflict between the U.S. Court of Appeals for the District of Columbia Circuit (D.C. Circuit) and the U.S. Court of Federal Claims. Part III will describe the Administration's plan to develop alternatives to nuclear waste storage at Yucca Mountain and consider the potential costs of further delay in establishing a permanent repository for SNF.

PART I: THE ROAD TO LITIGATION

The Nuclear Waste Policy Act of 1982

Responding to the serious hazards of nuclear waste, Congress passed the Nuclear Waste Policy Act of 1982 in an effort to centralize the long-term management of nuclear waste by making the federal government responsible for collecting, transporting, storing and disposing of the nation's SNF.[9] In order to achieve this goal, the NWPA established a statutory system for selecting a site for a geologic repository for the permanent disposal of nuclear waste.[10] DOE was authorized by the statute to carry out the disposal program and develop the permanent nuclear waste repository. Commercial nuclear power owners and operators would fund a large portion of the program through significant annual contributions, or fees, to the newly established Nuclear Waste Fund (NWF).[11]

To carry out the statutory scheme created by the NWPA, DOE was also authorized to enter into contracts with nuclear facilities to allow the department to take possession of nuclear waste and ensure its storage and disposal in the prospective permanent repository. [12] Section 302 of the NWPA sets out the critical statutory deadline established in the NWPA and forms the main basis for litigation. This provision mandates:

(A) Following commencement of operation of a repository, the Secretary shall take title to the high-level radioactive waste or spent nuclear fuel involved as expeditiously as practicable upon the request of the generator or owner of such waste or spent fuel; and

(B) In return for payment of fees established by this section, the Secretary, *beginning not later than January 31, 1998,* will dispose of the high-level radioactive waste or spent nuclear fuel involved as provided in this subtitle.[13]

In an effort to streamline the collection and disposal process, DOE elected to create a single "Standard Contract for Disposal of Spent Nuclear Fuel and/or High Level Radioactive

Waste" (Standard Contract) for use with all nuclear power providers. DOE chose to develop the Standard Contract through the formal notice-and-comment rulemaking process. The final contract, published in the Federal Register, somewhat modified the language of the NWPA and provides:

> The services to be provided by DOE under this contract shall begin, after commencement of facility operations, not later than January 31, 1998 and shall continue until such time as all SNF ... has been disposed of.[14]

Although the NWPA did not expressly mandate that all nuclear utility providers enter into an agreement with DOE for the disposal of nuclear waste, the utilities were required to enter into the Standard Contract as a condition of renewing or obtaining the required operating license from the Nuclear Regulatory Commission (NRC).[15] All operating nuclear facilities, therefore, became parties to the Standard Contract.

By 1987, pursuant to its obligations under the NWPA, DOE had identified three potential sites for the permanent repository: Yucca Mountain; Hanford, WA; and Deaf Smith County, TX. In 1987, Congress amended the NWPA to name Yucca Mountain as the sole candidate site for the permanent repository.[16] The amendments, strongly lobbied for by the congressional delegations from Washington and Texas, did not, however, end DOE selection and approval process which continued as outlined under the NWPA.

Breach of the Standard Contract

By 1993, DOE had made little progress in preparing to take possession of SNF, and the Yucca Mountain facility was at least a decade or more away from completion. Concerned as to whether DOE would be able to meet its contractual obligations by the end of January 1998, the utilities, which had been paying into the NWF for 11 years,[17] requested in writing that DOE address its responsibilities under the NWPA and update the signatories of the Standard Contract on DOE's overall preparedness. DOE initially responded to this request with an informal letter, stating that DOE's interpretation of the Standard Contract was that the department's contractual obligations were not triggered until the nation's permanent repository was complete. [18]

In response to this interpretive dispute, DOE sought comments from the public on the department's statutory obligations under the NWPA and the Standard Contract. After further review, DOE issued a "Final Interpretation of Nuclear Waste Acceptance Issues" which formally pronounced the department's position that it had no "legal obligation under either the [NWPA] or the Standard Contract to begin disposal of SNF by January 31, 1998, in the absence of a repository or interim storage facility."[19] Pursuant to this interpretation, the department added that it would not begin accepting nuclear waste from nuclear utilities by the date specified in the act, nor did it have authority under the NWPA to provide interim storage for spent nuclear fuel.[20] In the alternative, the DOE notice stated that were section 302 to create an unconditional obligation on the part of DOE to begin disposing of nuclear waste by January 31, 1998, redress should be governed by the "unavoidable delay" provisions of the Standard Contract which expressly states that "no party shall be liable for damages in the case of unavoidable delay."[21]

Nuclear utility companies, having paid billions into the NWF since 1982[22] in addition to the millions spent for on-site temporary storage, turned to the federal courts to review DOE's interpretation of its own obligations under the NWPA and the Standard Contract.

PART II: LITIGATION

Issues relating to the NWPA have been consistently litigated for the last 14 years, and will continue to be litigated into the immediate future. Many difficult legal questions have arisen during this time period due to the somewhat peculiar relationship between the NWPA and the Standard Contract and the courts' attempts to distinguish between statutory and contractual duties. Although DOE argued early on that the department had no obligations absent a completed permanent repository, the courts have ruled that DOE had a statutory obligation to begin collecting SNF by no later than January 31, 1998.[23] As that statutory obligation was also converted into a contractual obligation through the Standard Contract, the courts have also determined that DOE's delay in collecting the nuclear utilities' SNF has placed the federal government in partial breach of contract.[24] Additionally, overturning a divergent decision by the U.S. Court of Federal Claims, the Federal Circuit has affirmed a D.C. Circuit order that prohibits DOE from concluding that the lack of a permanent repository excuses DOE from liability for the delay in acceptance of SNF.

As of February 2010, at least 72 lawsuits had been filed against DOE related to the department's failure to commence the collection and disposal of SNF. Of the filed lawsuits, 10 have been settled, six were withdrawn, four reached final judgment, and 52 remain pending.[25] According to the Congressional Budget Office (CBO), the government's current liability—based on settlements, final judgments, and entered judgments under appeal—stands at $1.3 billion.[26] The following section will highlight key court decisions that have emerged from the ongoing contractual dispute between DOE and the nuclear power utilities.

DOE's Statutory Obligation to begin Accepting SNF

The first NWPA-related claim against DOE was filed in the U.S. Court of Appeals for the District of Columbia Circuit in 1996.[27] Although DOE had not yet breached the contract, as performance was not required before January 31, 1998, Indiana Michigan Power Company sought a preemptive judicial review of the department's determination that it had no obligation to begin accepting SNF until the completion of the Yucca Mountain facility.

In *Indiana Michigan Power Co. v. Department of Energy*, the D.C. Circuit, applying the *Chevron*[28] analysis for reviewing an agency's statutory interpretation, invalidated DOE's interpretation as contrary to the plain meaning of the NWPA.[29] The court reasoned that section 302(A) and section 302(B) represented independent statutory obligations. While the obligation to "take title to" nuclear waste in section 302(A) may have been conditioned on the construction of a repository, the obligation to "dispose" of nuclear waste under section 302(B) contained no such limitation.[30] Indeed, DOE's duty to commence disposal of nuclear waste, held the court, was to begin "not later than January 31, 1998 without qualification or condition."[31] The argument put forth by DOE, and rejected by the court, was that section

302(A) and section 302(B) "must be read together," since taking title to SNF cannot be separated from disposing of SNF.[32] In construing DOE's "disposal" obligation broadly, the court noted that "it is not unusual, particularly in the nuclear area, to recognize a division between ownership of materials and other obligations relating to such materials."[33] The court concluded that the NWPA and Standard Contract had created a "reciprocal" and binding contractual relationship between DOE and the nuclear utilities, whereby DOE would dispose of the utilities' nuclear waste in return for the payment of fees into the NWF.[34]

DOE did not immediately take action in response to the D.C. Circuit's holding in *Indiana Michigan*. Instead, the department informed the nuclear utilities involved that it would be unable to comply with the January 31, 1998, deadline and was not prepared to begin accepting spent nuclear fuel for disposal.[35] DOE asserted that it was waiting for the results of the Yucca Mountain Project Viability Assessment before proceeding, but predicted that the Yucca Mountain facility could potentially be opened by 2010.[36]

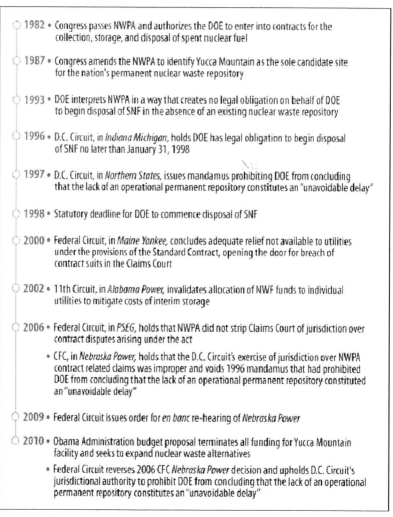

Source: Congressional Research Service.

Figure 1. Litigation Timeline

Prohibiting the "Unavoidable Delay" Defense

In addition to informing the nuclear utilities that it would be unable to comply with the January 31, 1998, deadline, DOE also asserted that the department was not responsible for any monetary damages incurred by the utilities as a result of DOE's delay.[37] The department had determined that the lack of a permanent repository at Yucca Mountain constituted an "unavoidable delay" under article IX of the Standard Contract.[38] The "unavoidable delay" provision of the Standard Contract provides:

> Neither the Government nor the purchaser shall be liable under this contract for damages caused by failure to perform its obligations hereunder, if such failure arises out of the causes beyond the control and without the fault or negligence of the party failing to perform.[39]

As such, argued DOE, the terms of the Standard Contract relieved the department from any obligation to "provide a financial remedy for the delay."[40]

The nuclear utilities responded to DOE's communications in 1997 by asking the D.C. Circuit to issue a writ of mandamus, compelling DOE to adhere to the court's earlier decision in *Indiana Michigan* and begin accepting nuclear waste for disposal. In *Northern States Power Co. v. U.S.*, the court refused to grant the "drastic" and broad relief the utilities asked for, holding that the terms of the Standard Contract provided for another "potentially adequate remedy."[41] Before the court would consider compelling DOE to act, the utilities would first have to pursue the administrative remedies available under the Standard Contract for delayed performance.[42]

However, the court was unwilling to accept DOE's interpretation of its own delays as "unavoidable" under the Standard Contract. The court reiterated, in rejecting DOE's argument that a lack of an operational repository qualified as an unavoidable delay, that DOE's obligation to begin disposal of SNF by January 31, 1998, existed regardless of the existence of an operational storage facility.[43] DOE's "unavoidable delay" defense, noted the court, represented a simple "recycling [of] the arguments [previously] rejected by this court."[44] Based on DOE's "repeated attempts to excuse its delay on the grounds that it lacks an operational repository," the D.C. Circuit, in a significant exercise of authority, issued a writ of mandamus prohibiting DOE from concluding that the lack of an operational permanent repository constituted an "unavoidable delay" under the Standard Contract.[45] The court ordered DOE to "proceed with contractual remedies in a manner consistent with NWPA's command that it undertake an unconditional obligation to begin disposal of the SNF by January 31, 1998."[46]

In a preview of the jurisdictional dispute that would develop a decade later, DOE filed a petition for rehearing in response to the *Northern States* mandamus. DOE challenged the D.C. Circuit's exercise of authority by asserting that the court "lacked jurisdiction to construe the unavoidable delays clause of the Standard Contract," as such an interpretation of a government contract was squarely within the jurisdiction of the Court of Federal Claims under the Tucker Act.[47] The D.C. Circuit denied the motion for rehearing, holding that the court had not adjudicated a contractual dispute, but rather issued the mandamus in an effort to enforce a statutory duty.[48] Accepting the D.C. Circuit's reasoning, DOE interpreted the *Northern States* mandamus as prohibiting the department from raising the unavoidable delay clause as a defense in future litigation.[49]

Litigation Continues: Remedies, Offsets, and Damages

After establishing DOE's statutory obligations under the NWPA in the D.C. Circuit, many nuclear utilities awaited the expiration of the January 31, 1998, deadline before seeking monetary damages by filing their claims in the U.S. Court of Federal Claims (CFC).[50] Under the Tucker Act, the CFC has jurisdiction over monetary claims against the United States "founded either upon the Constitution, or any Act of Congress or any regulation of an executive department, or upon any express or implied contract with the United States."[51] Decisions of the CFC are appealed to the Federal Circuit.

In considering the cases, the CFC initially had to answer the threshold question of whether the nuclear utilities were required to exhaust available administrative remedies under the Standard Contract prior to seeking judicial relief. Generally, if administrative remedies can provide adequate relief for a claim, the plaintiff must first exhaust those remedies before seeking redress in another court.[52] Judges on the CFC came to opposite conclusions as to whether the Standard Contract could provide adequate relief to the nuclear utilities, and the issue was left for the Federal Circuit to settle on appeal.[53]

Remedies under Standard Contract Inadequate

In an important 2000 case, entitled *Maine Yankee Atomic Power Co. v. U.S.,* the Federal Circuit concluded that adequate relief was not available to the nuclear utilities under the Standard Contract, a conclusion that would allow breach of contract claims against DOE to go forward in the CFC.[54] DOE, with the "unavoidable delay" clause unavailable, argued that the "avoidable delays" clause of the contract provided the plaintiffs with an avenue for adequate administrative relief.[55] The "avoidable delay" provision of the Standard Contract requires that:

> In the event of any delay in the delivery, acceptance, or transport ... caused by circumstances within the reasonable control of either [party] ... the charges and schedules specified by this contract will be equitably adjusted to reflect any estimated additional costs incurred by the party not responsible for or contributing to the delay.[56]

The court disagreed, holding that the "avoidable delay" provision applied only to routine delays occurring after the parties had begun performance of their obligations under the contract, not to breaches of a "critical and central obligation of the contract," such as a failure to begin performance by the statutory deadline.[57] The court added that relief in the form of a "charge or schedule adjustment," as provided under the Standard Contract, was wholly inadequate to compensate the nuclear utilities for damages they had sustained in storing spent nuclear fuel that had been covered by the contract.[58] As a result of the *Maine Yankee* decision, signatories to the Standard Contract were now free to seek monetary damages against DOE, by filing their breach of contract claims in the CFC, without first exhausting DOE administrative process.

NWF Offset Invalid

Following the *Indiana Michigan Power* and *Maine Yankee* decisions, and the realization that a large number of breach of contract claims were being filed in the CFC, DOE attempted to curtail its potential contract liability by modifying contract terms with individual nuclear utilities. Under the proposed modification, DOE was willing to return a portion of payments made by a utility into the NWF, and suspend any future payments if the utility was willing to relinquish all future claims against DOE.[59] The department entered into one such agreement with Exelon Generation Company in 2002. Other utilities that had also contributed to the NWF, however, challenged this arrangement as an invalid use of NWF funds.

The 11th Circuit, in *Alabama Power Co. v. U.S.*, invalidated the contractual modification reached between DOE and Exelon Generation Company.[60] The agreed upon "offset," the court held, was "tantamount to an expenditure of funds" from the NWF.[61] Under the NWPA, NWF funds were to be used only for the "permanent disposal" of nuclear waste.[62] DOE could not, therefore, allocate NWF funds to individual nuclear utilities to pay for what the court classified as on-site "interim storage." Were DOE allowed to use NWF funds to offset the costs of the department's failure to dispose of SNF, it would be analogous to allowing DOE to "pay for its own breach out of a fund paid for by the utilities."[63] Any arrangement in which the utilities were made to "bear the costs of the [department's] breach" was invalid.[64] Pursuant to the court's stringent interpretation of the statutory purposes of the NWF, DOE is likely prohibited from using NWF funds for any use other than the development and construction of a permanent repository.[65]

Calculating Damages

Although DOE had acknowledged its partial breach of the Standard Contract in most cases by 2005,[66] significant litigation has been required to determine the level of damages individual nuclear utilities can legally recover as a result of DOE's breach. Generally speaking, when one party to a contract materially breaches the contract, the non-breaching party has the option to sue for damages under either a "full breach" or "partial breach" theory.[67] A successful claim for full breach discharges the contractual obligations of both parties and allows the non-breacher to sue for all past, present, and future damages.[68] A claim for partial breach, on the other hand, preserves the ongoing contractual relationship between the parties—meaning both parties are still obligated to perform under the terms of the contract.[69] Additionally, a party suing for partial breach may only recover the costs of mitigating the other party's breach that were incurred between the time the party became aware of a potential breach and the date of trial.[70] A party suing for partial breach may not, therefore, recover future damages. Fundamentally, in electing to pursue a claim under a partial or full breach theory, the non-breaching party is choosing between continuing the contract, in the hope that the breaching party will eventually perform, or ending the contract in its entirety.

The nuclear utilities have pursued their breach of contract claims under a partial breach theory.[71] Although a party may typically elect whether to sue for partial or full breach in response to a material breach, the CFC and the Federal Circuit have repeatedly and consistently expressed doubt as to whether a full breach claim seeking to discharge the existing contractual obligations would even be available to the nuclear utilities, noting that the utilities have been "compelled" to sue for partial breach by the statutory obligations underlying the Standard Contract.[72] In *Indiana Michigan Power Co. v. U.S.*, the court stated in dicta that were a nuclear utility to bring an action for total breach "DOE would [be] discharged from further responsibility under the [Standard] contract, a situation apparently not desired by [the utilities] *and foreclosed by statute.*"[73] The courts have noted three incongruous consequences that could result from a court's decision to discharge the parties' obligation to perform under the Standard Contract. First, Nuclear Regulatory Commission operating permits for all nuclear utilities are currently contingent on entering into the Standard Contract with DOE.[74] As a result, if the contract is discharged, the utility may lose its operating license. Second, the NWPA makes DOE the exclusive collector of SNF, meaning the utilities may not seek alternative means of disposing of their SNF.[75] Third, the NWPA places a statutory duty on the utilities that generate SNF to pay for the waste's disposal. Discharging the utilities contractual obligation to make payments into the NWF would run counter to this statutory duty.[76] Accordingly, the Federal Circuit has repeatedly affirmed the notion that nuclear utilities are foreclosed from suing for a full breach.[77]

Even if permitted, it is not clear that the nuclear utilities would wish to pursue a claim for full breach. In 2006, in response to an order by the court to show why the CFC should not simply void the Standard Contract, more than 30 nuclear utilities, through amicus briefs, voiced opposition to the court's proposal.[78] Absent a contract, the utilities would be exposed to "substantial regulatory risks," and likely bear the burden and responsibility of permanently disposing of their own SNF.[79] Although available damages could potentially be higher than what the utilities have been recovering through their numerous claims for partial breach, under a claim for full breach, the utilities would lose the benefit, no matter how remote, of the government collecting and disposing of their SNF.[80]

For these reasons, the nuclear utilities have sought to pursue, and courts have been hesitant to depart from, a partial breach scenario.[81] As a result, the nuclear utilities continue to have the obligation to pay into the NWF and DOE continues to have the obligation to collect and dispose of SNF. As the Federal Circuit has stated, the utilities have had "no choice but to hold the government to the terms of the Standard Contract while suing for partial breach."[82]

In August of 2008, the Federal Circuit further clarified the method for calculating damages in NWPA breach of contract suits by establishing the rate at which DOE was expected to accept SNF under the Standard Contract.[83] The anticipated rate of acceptance was essential to calculating the total amount of SNF DOE was contractually obligated to accept from the nuclear utilities from the 1998 deadline forward. DOE argued for a lower rate established under a report issued in 1991, as opposed to the initial rate of acceptance established in a 1987 DOE scheduling report.[84] The Federal Circuit, however, rejected this argument, holding instead that damages would be calculated in relation to the higher 1987 acceptance rate, as that rate most closely reflected the intent and expectations of the parties at the time of the contract.[85] The 1991 rate, held the court, was most likely the result of a "litigation strategy," put forth to "minimize DOE's exposure for its impending breach, rather than as a realistic, good faith projection for waste acceptance."[86]

Nuclear utilities have thus been successful in recovering all reasonable and foreseeable expenses incurred in mitigation of DOE's breach.[87] Generally, these damages consist of costs associated with developing, implementing, and maintaining on-site interim SNF storage.[88] Damages are limited, however, to the costs incurred from the date at which the utility became aware of DOE's potential breach, a realization often occurring well before the January 31, 1998, deadline, to the date of trial. Nuclear utilities are free, however, to re-file future claims as new mitigation damages are incurred.[89]

Jurisdictional Dispute Develops in *Nebraska Public Power District v. United States*

From 1998 forward, the CFC had been entertaining breach of contract suits filed by the nuclear utilities against DOE without any significant discussion of jurisdiction. Then, in 2005, the court, for the first time, dismissed a NWPA breach of contract suit for lack of subject matter jurisdiction.[90] The court reasoned that the Standard Contract, created through the formal administrative process, qualified as a final agency action under the jurisdiction of the U.S. Court of Appeals as established pursuant to section 119 of the NWPA. Section 119 of the NWPA grants the U.S. courts of appeals

> original and exclusive jurisdiction over any civil action ... for review of any final decision or action of the Secretary, the President, or the Commission under this subtitle.[91]

The dismissal was appealed to the Federal Circuit for review of the jurisdictional question.

In *PSEG Nuclear v. U.S.*, the Federal Circuit reversed the lower court's decision, holding that the NWPA had not stripped the CFC of jurisdiction over contract disputes.[92] The court based its holding on the fact that § 119 only acted to preclude CFC jurisdiction in instances of official agency action taken under the NWPA.[93] The utilities' claims were for breach of contract and did not challenge any "agency action taken under the agency's statutory mandate," but rather were concerned with "whether DOE breached its contractual obligations, and if so, to what damages, if any, PSEG is entitled for the breach."[94] After *PSEG*, it was clear that the CFC had the authority to exercise jurisdiction over an NWPA-related breach of contract claim. However, because the court in *PSEG* limited itself only to whether the exercise of jurisdiction by the CFC was proper,[95] the larger question of whether the D.C. Circuit's previous exercise of jurisdiction over similar contract-related claims impermissibly infringed on the CFC's jurisdiction remained unresolved.

The Court of Federal Claims

Shortly after the *PSEG* decision, which ensured the CFC's jurisdiction over contract disputes arising under the NWPA, DOE asked the CFC to invalidate the D.C. Circuit's initial exercise of jurisdiction in *Indiana Michigan*. At oral argument in *Nebraska Public Power Dist. v. U.S.*, DOE expressed a desire to raise the "unavoidable delay" defense that the D.C. Circuit had specifically prohibited through the writ of mandamus in *Northern States*.[96] The CFC decided to entertain the question and asked the parties to brief the issue of whether the D.C. Circuit mandamus precluded DOE's assertion of the "unavoidable delay" defense in the CFC. On October 31, 2006, the court handed down a sweeping decision that voided the longstanding mandamus issued by the D.C. Circuit for lack of jurisdiction.[97]

In *Nebraska Public Power*, the CFC held that the D.C. Circuit had exceeded its jurisdiction in issuing the *Indiana Michigan* decision.[98] Since the mandamus prohibiting DOE's use of the "unavoidable delay" defense issued in *Northern States* was issued as a means of enforcing the ruling in *Indiana Michigan*, the mandamus, therefore, was also void and had no preclusive effects in the CFC. The court based its decision on the jurisdictional conclusions underlying *PSEG*, the limited scope of section 119 of the NWPA, and the absence of an effective waiver of sovereign immunity.

Defining the Jurisdiction of the CFC and U.S. Appellate Courts

Nebraska Public Power focused on whether the string of claims filed under the NWPA and the Standard Contract should be classified as a review of formal agency action within the direct purview of the U.S. Appellate Courts, or as a straightforward breach of contract claim within the exclusive jurisdiction of the CFC (subject to appeal to the Federal Circuit). The opinion made clear the CFC's position that the claims relating to the January 31, 1998, statutory deadline qualified as contract claims within the CFC's exclusive jurisdiction.[99] In considering the jurisdictional role of the two courts, the CFC adopted and applied much of the reasoning behind *PSEG*, asserting that the case had "rejected many of the key jurisdictional concepts that underlie the relevant D.C. Circuit cases."[100] Although *PSEG* focused only on whether the CFC could exercise jurisdiction over the contract claims, the court in *Nebraska Public Power* went further to establish that jurisdiction as exclusive in an attempt to resolve the two competing claims to jurisdiction over cases related to the Standard Contract.[101]

The Scope of Section 119 of the NWPA

In issuing the *Northern States* mandamus, the D.C. Circuit had invoked section 119, which granted the U.S. Appellate Courts exclusive jurisdiction over final agency action under Title I of the NWPA, as the basis for its exercise of jurisdiction. However, the Federal Circuit, reviewing the exercise of jurisdiction by the CFC, had limited the scope of section 119, based on the provision's plain language, to only those claims relating to the establishment of a permanent repository for spent nuclear fuel.[102] In *Nebraska Public Power*, the CFC adopted the reasoning in *PSEG*, and applied it to the D.C. Circuit's initial exercise of jurisdiction in *Indiana Michigan*. The resulting conclusion was that *Indiana Michigan* involved "interpretations of contract provisions that have nothing to do with the creation of repositories of spent nuclear fuel," and therefore "plainly exceeded" the grant of jurisdiction to the D.C. Circuit under section 119.[103]

Contrary to the D.C. Circuit's argument that the *Northern States* mandamus was issued pursuant to a breach of a statutory and regulatory obligation, the court added that the "essential character" of the actions brought by the nuclear utilities was contractual and therefore exclusively within the jurisdiction of the CFC.[104] The mere fact that DOE developed the Standard Contract through formal administrative rulemaking procedures was not sufficient to alter the nature of the claim from an action based on contract to an action based on statutory or regulatory interpretation.[105] In classifying the claims in *Indiana Michigan* and *Northern States* as contractual, the court emphasized the utilities' reliance on the Standard Contract, the asserted claim for breach of contract, and the request for monetary damages.[106] As the "mandamus dispute in *Northern States* could be conceived as entirely contained within the terms of the contract" rather than a "regulation asserted to be in conflict with the NWPA," the D.C. Circuit had engaged in an interpretation of the Standard Contract that intruded on the CFC's exclusive jurisdiction.[107]

Waiver of Sovereign Immunity under Section 702 of the APA

The CFC also held that the D.C. Circuit's decisions in *Indiana Michigan* and *Northern States* were not supported by a waiver of sovereign immunity.[108] Even if section 119 had granted the D.C. Circuit jurisdiction over the NWPA contract claims, the grant of jurisdiction was not accompanied by any waiver of sovereign immunity that would allow the case to go forward. Federal courts do not infer waivers of sovereign immunity lightly, requiring that any such waiver be "unequivocally expressed" by Congress.[109] The mere grant of jurisdiction to a court, such as the grant found in section 119, is not sufficient to constitute a waiver of sovereign immunity.[110] The required express waiver is generally characterized by a "specification of the remedy or relief that may be awarded against the U.S."[111] The court could find no express waiver anywhere in the NWPA.

With no express waiver in the NWPA, the D.C. Circuit had proceeded in *Indiana Michigan* as if the waiver derived from section 702 of the Administrative Procedure Act (APA). Section 702 acts as a general waiver of sovereign immunity for claims against the U.S. that are based on agency action.[112] The CFC determined that any reliance on section 702 was misplaced, as the APA general waiver applies only where there is "no other adequate remedy in a court."[113] Although the D.C. Circuit had taken the position that the CFC was unable to accord adequate relief to a plaintiff seeking equitable relief,[114] the Federal Circuit concluded that the section 702 waiver was inapplicable under these circumstances because the nuclear utilities had an adequate remedy in the CFC under the Tucker Act.[115] The Federal Circuit, citing the U.S. Supreme Court, rejected the notion that the limitation on the available remedies made relief in the CFC "inadequate."[116] Any other conclusion, reasoned the court, would allow plaintiffs to circumvent the jurisdiction of the CFC simply by attaching a prayer for equitable relief to what was essentially a damages suit. With an alternate and adequate remedy available in the CFC, the necessary trigger for section 702 had not been met. The court held, therefore, that absent a waiver of sovereign immunity under either section 119 of the NWPA or section 702 of the APA, the D.C. Circuit had improperly granted relief against the United States in *Indiana Michigan*.[117]

The court concluded by holding that the D.C. Circuit's decision in *Indiana Michigan* exceeded the court's jurisdiction without the support of a valid waiver of sovereign immunity and was therefore void.[118] The mandamus issued in *Northern States*, which was predicated on the decision in *Indiana Michigan*, was, therefore, also void and could not preclude DOE from raising the unavoidable delay defense.[119] The court closed by ordering the parties to brief the issue of whether DOE's failure to commence disposal of SNF by the established deadline was excused by the "unavoidable delay" clause of the Standard Contract.[120]

The Federal Circuit

Nebraska Power appealed the CFC's decision to the Federal Circuit and the case was argued in December of 2007. It was not until June 4, 2009, that the Federal Circuit answered, not with an opinion, but with an order for *en banc* rehearing before the entire Federal Circuit.[121] The order for *en banc* hearing included a request that the parties file supplemental briefs addressing whether the mandamus issued by the D.C. Circuit in *Northern States* precludes DOE from pleading the "unavoidable delay" defense to breach of contract claims currently pending before the CFC.[122] "If so," asked the court, "does the order exceed the jurisdiction of the District of Columbia Circuit?"[123]

On January 17, 2010, the Federal Circuit issued an 11-1 decision upholding the D.C. Circuit's exercise of jurisdiction in *Indiana Michigan* and *Northern States*, thereby affirming the D.C. Circuit mandamus prohibiting DOE's use of the "unavoidable delay" defense. [124] The decision rejected all of the CFC's major jurisdictional determinations. The court held that (1) § 119 of the NWPA had properly granted the D.C. Circuit jurisdiction over statutory claims arising under the act; (2) sovereign immunity was validly waived under the APA; and (3) the D.C. Circuit had not "improperly intruded" on the CFC's exclusive jurisdiction over contract interpretation. [125]

Jurisdiction under § 119

On appeal, the Federal Circuit interpreted the scope of § 119 of the NWPA more broadly than had the CFC. Whereas the CFC determined that the provision only granted the federal appellate courts review of claims arising from Title I of the act—the title pertaining to the siting of a permanent repository—the Federal Circuit held that § 119 also granted federal appellate courts jurisdiction over claims arising from the statutory deadline found in Title III. [126] The court looked to the legislative history of the NWPA to support its conclusion, noting that it was clear that the statutory deadline's "physical separation from the judicial review provision in section 119 [was] pure happenstance and in no way indicate[d] a congressional intent that review under the different subchapters be governed by different standards." [127] Accordingly, claims relating to DOE's failure to begin the acceptance of SNF by the statutory deadline of January 31, 1998, were included within the D.C. Circuit's jurisdiction under § 119 of the NWPA.

Waiver of Sovereign Immunity under the APA

The Federal Circuit further held that the APA did indeed constitute a valid waiver of sovereign immunity for claims arising from the statutory deadline of the NWPA. [128] In disagreeing with the CFC's interpretation of § 704 of the APA, the court noted that the provision created two distinct categories of agency action that were subject to judicial review. The APA waived sovereign immunity and granted judicial review only to "agency action made reviewable by statute" *and* "final agency action for which there is no other adequate remedy in a court." [129] The court referred to the first category of action as "special statutory review," or agency action made reviewable by a "specific review-authorizing statute." [130] The court referred to the second category of action as "nonstatutory review." [131] There the APA acts as a waiver of sovereign immunity for a limited class of cases where no review of agency action has been granted by statute, but where absent review, the plaintiff can find "no other adequate remedy at law." The court, distinguishing between the two categories, reasoned that the limitation that there be "no other adequate remedy" applied only to non-statutory review of agency action. [132] The court concluded that because § 119 of the NWPA made DOE action specifically reviewable by the federal appellate courts, the fact that another adequate remedy may have been available in the CFC did not make the waiver of sovereign immunity invalid. [133]

CFC Exclusive Jurisdiction over Contract Interpretation

Finally, the Federal Circuit held that the D.C. Circuit's mandamus in *Northern States* did not encroach upon the CFC's exclusive jurisdiction over the adjudication and interpretation of contract rights. The court characterized the D.C. Circuit's action as an implementation of DOE's statutory duties under the NWPA rather than an interpretation of the language of the Standard Contract.[134] By prohibiting DOE's use of the "unavoidable delay" defense, the D.C. Circuit was utilizing the mandamus as a means to enforce DOE's statutory obligations as established in *Indiana Michigan*. The Federal Circuit concurred with the D.C. Circuit's view that it had "merely prohibited DOE from implementing an interpretation that would place it in violation of its duty under the NWPA to assume an unconditional obligation to begin disposal by January 31, 1998. The statutory duty ... is independent of any rights under the contract."[135] In short, the Federal Circuit concluded that in issuing its mandamus, the D.C. Circuit had been interpreting the NWPA and not the Standard Contract.

In overturning the CFC's decision, the Federal Circuit all but extinguished DOE's attempt to limit damages through the "unavoidable delay" clause of the Standard Contract.[136] As a result, litigation under the Standard Contract will continue, as it had prior to the CFC's decision in *Nebraska Public Power,* with a focus on measuring recoverable damages rather than liability.

PART III: FUTURE PROSPECTS

Yucca Mountain and the Obama Administration

Both the President and the Secretary of Energy have publicly stated that Yucca Mountain does not represent a viable option for the permanent storage of SNF.[137] In accordance with that view, and following years of decreases in funding for the Yucca Mountain project,[138] the Obama Administration recently decided to terminate the Yucca Mountain program and instead seek to develop nuclear waste disposal alternatives.[139] The Administration's FY2011 budget proposal eliminates all funding for the Yucca Mountain program and eliminates the Office of Civilian Radioactive Waste Management (OCRWM). Pursuant to the President's budget proposal, the administration of the NWF, and responsibility for DOE's ongoing obligations under the Standard Contract, are to be shifted to the Office of Nuclear Energy.[140] Not entirely unexpected, the FY2011 budget proposal came on the heels of a 2010 budget appropriation that had included only enough funds, approximately $197 million, to finance the ongoing Nuclear Regulatory Commission licensing process and to "explore alternatives for nuclear waste disposal."[141]

At least two Members of Congress have expressed concern over the legality of the Administration's decision to eliminate the statutorily established OCRWM.[142] The OCRWM had been specifically created by the NWPA for the purpose of "carrying out the functions of the Secretary" under the act.[143] In response to these concerns, DOE has suggested that the 1977 Department of Energy Organization Act grants the Secretary of Energy "broad authority to create, eliminate, and merge organizations" within DOE.[144] Generally speaking, Congress has the authority to structure the administrative bureaucracy. Thus, absent specific statutory authority, the President has no legal power to direct how statutorily defined functions and powers of agencies are to be utilized, allocated, or abandoned.[145] In this instance, the Secretary of Energy has been granted statutory authority to "establish, alter, consolidate or discontinue, such organizational units or components within the Department as he may deem to be necessary or appropriate."[146] The Administration's proposal—which Congress, through its appropriation power, is free to either follow or disregard—is to "terminate" the OCRWM and transfer the office's responsibilities to the Office of Nuclear Energy.[147] Given the Secretary's statutorily granted authority, it is likely that such a transfer would be a valid consolidation of DOE offices. However, any statutory duties or obligations that were placed in OCRWM must continue to be carried out by the Office of Nuclear Energy.[148]

Shortly before releasing the FY2011 budget proposal, the President asked DOE to establish a Blue Ribbon Commission on America's Nuclear Future (Commission) to explore, study, and evaluate alternatives to the Yucca Mountain facility for the permanent storage of SNF.[149] The 15- member commission, appointed by the Secretary of Energy, consists of distinguished scientists, academics, industry representatives, labor representatives, and former elected officials. The commission's goal is to "provide recommendations for developing a safe, long-term solution to managing the nation's used nuclear fuel and nuclear waste."[150] The Commission will not, however, be considering specific sites for a future repository.[151] Co-chaired by former Congressman Lee Hamilton and former National Security Advisor Brent Scowcroft, the commission is charged with producing an interim report within 18 months and a final report within 24 months. Although not expressly prohibited from considering Yucca Mountain as a potential solution to the nation's nuclear waste problems,[152] Secretary Chu and the White House have conveyed that the commission should focus only on "alternatives" to Yucca Mountain. Accordingly, Co-chairman Hamilton asserted in the commission's first press conference that "Secretary Chu has made it quite clear that nuclear waste storage at Yucca Mountain is not an option."[153]

The Obama Administration has also announced its intent to withdraw the Yucca Mountain license application from NRC consideration.[154] The application, requesting approval to construct the permanent repository, was initially submitted by DOE in June of 2008.[155] DOE formally filed its motion asking the Atomic Safety and Licensing Board (Board) to dismiss the application "with prejudice" on March 3, 2010.[156] A common legal term, an application that is withdrawn "with prejudice" is generally barred from being re-filed in the future. However, whether or not an application, motion, or claim, is dismissed with prejudice is a decision made by the NRC, and not by the requesting party.[157] DOE specifically asked the Board to dismiss the application with prejudice because the agency "does not intend ever to refile an application to construct a permanent geologic repository for spent nuclear fuel and high-level radioactive waste at Yucca Mountain."[158] As the Yucca Mountain facility cannot be built without a construction authorization from the NRC, many commentators consider a successful withdrawal of the application as marking the formal termination of any potential repository at Yucca Mountain.[159]

Regardless of whether the Administration chooses completely to abandon the Yucca Mountain project, new legislative action will be required to establish a permanent repository capable of storing the nation's SNF.[160] Under the 1987 amendments to the NWPA, Yucca Mountain is the only authorized candidate site for a permanent SNF repository.[161] Therefore, if Congress or the President chooses to pursue an alternative site, the NWPA will have to be amended to allow for such a selection. If, on the other hand, the choice is made to proceed with the Yucca Mountain project, Congress may face a decision on amending the NWPA to lift the statutory limit on the facility's nuclear waste storage capacity. The current statutory cap of 70,000 metric tons is insufficient to hold existing amounts of SNF.[162]

Although problems related to the storage of SNF remain unresolved, the Obama Administration has recently pronounced a commitment to invest in domestic nuclear power. In his State of the Union address, the President advocated for creating new "clean energy jobs" by "building a new generation of safe, clean nuclear power plants in this country."[163] In a step toward implementing that vision, President Obama announced on February 16, 2010, the government approval of an $8.3 billion conditional loan guarantee to help finance the construction of two new nuclear reactors in the state of Georgia.[164] The proposed reactors would be the first to begin construction in the United States in more than 30 years.

Future Contract Liability

The total costs to taxpayers for delays associated with the Yucca Mountain project are difficult to project, especially given the uncertainty regarding the future of the facility or any alternative permanent repository for SNF. However, absent a significant change in the direction of NWPA related litigation, DOE predicts that damages stemming from breach of contract claims will measure close to $12.3 billion if the department is able to begin accepting SNF by 2020—an unlikely occurrence given the Administration's decision to terminate the Yucca Mountain project. [165] Approximately $500 million in additional legal damages will continue to build with each year that DOE is unable to begin accepting SNF.[166] The nuclear utilities, on the other hand, estimate DOE's total potential liability at approximately $50 billion.[167] In addition, to date the Department of Justice, which has handled DOE defense, has spent over $150 million on litigation-related expenses. The nuclear utilities reportedly incur $5 million to $7 million in litigation costs in each individual case.[168]

In an attempt to curtail damages, DOE has sought to reach settlement agreements with a number of nuclear utilities. As of September 2009, the government had entered into agreements with nuclear utilities that operate 36 of the 118 nuclear facilities covered by the Standard Contract.[169] Under the settlements, contract parties submit annual reimbursement claims to DOE for any delay-related nuclear waste storage costs that they incurred during that year. As the settlement agreements cover continuing damages, the affected nuclear utilities are able to submit annual claims directly to DOE rather than re-litigating ongoing damages in the federal courts. As of the end of 2008, DOE had paid over $400 million pursuant to these settlements.[170]

States Respond and a Shift toward Statutory Claims

The decision to terminate the Yucca Mountain project will likely trigger new legal battles in addition to the continuing breach of contract litigation. This next round of litigation, however, will likely be brought pursuant to the many arguable statutory duties included within the NWPA, rather than those existing under the Standard Contract. Additionally, concerned plaintiffs can be expected to attempt to persuade the courts to order DOE to take affirmative action rather than request relief in the form of monetary damages.[171] Any potential plaintiff, however, will have to meet the Court's strict justiciability requirements before the claim can proceed.[172]

South Carolina Governor Mark Sanford, for example, announced at a press conference on February 16, 2010, that he had asked his attorney general to "pursue every legal action possible" to block the Administration from abandoning the Yucca Mountain facility.[173] South Carolina plans to carry out its legal recourse by engaging in "consultation and collaborative discussions with attorneys general in similarly situated states, utility executives, nuclear industry legal experts, former DOE officials, and state and local officials."[174] Any such legal action would likely take the form of either a petition for an injunction to stop the elimination of the facility,[175] a petition for a writ of mandamus compelling the Secretary of Energy to take action,[176] or an attempt to intervene before the NRC to stop the withdrawal of the Yucca Mountain licensing application.[177] Indeed, shortly thereafter, South Carolina simultaneously filed a petition with the NRC for leave to intervene in the construction authorization proceeding, as well as a statutory claim with the U.S. Court of Appeals for the 4th Circuit asking the court to take action to block the withdrawal of the Yucca Mountain application.[178] Both filings assert that a "with prejudice" dismissal of the Yucca Mountain licensing application would constitute a violation of both DOE's statutory obligation to submit the application and NRC's statutory obligation to consider and rule on the application.[179]

Additionally, Aiken County, SC, filed a statutory claim against DOE on February 19, 2010, in an effort to stop DOE from withdrawing the Yucca Mountain license application.[180] Aiken County is home to the Savannah River Site, currently a DOE defense-related nuclear waste storage site. The county has expressed concern that terminating the Yucca Mountain facility could eventually lead to the Savannah River Site becoming a permanent repository.[181] The complaint, filed in the D.C. Circuit, specifically asks the court to enjoin both DOE from withdrawing the application, and the NRC from allowing the withdrawal.[182] In addition, the county has asked for a writ of mandamus directing DOE to fulfill its statutory obligations under the NWPA, arguing, as the state of South Carolina did in its 4th Circuit filing, that the statutory scheme of the NWPA creates a mandatory obligation on behalf of the Secretary to submit the application, as well as a mandatory obligation on behalf of the NRC to review the application.[183] Any withdrawal, the county argues, would be in violation of the site selection provisions of the NWPA.

The state of Washington also filed a petition for leave to intervene in the NRC construction authorization proceeding in an effort to prevent DOE from withdrawing the Yucca Mountain application.[184] DOE's Hanford Nuclear Reservation, located in southeast Washington, is currently home to approximately 53 million gallons of defense-related nuclear waste—a majority of which was to be disposed of in the future Yucca Mountain repository.[185] A group of concerned citizens living in close proximity to the Hanford site have also threatened to sue over the Administration's decision to terminate the Yucca Mountain project.[186]

Other states are considering legislation that would effectively withhold utility payments into the NWF.[187] The Minnesota legislature is currently considering a bill that would place half of the approximately $14 million that the state contributes to the NWF each year into an escrow account.[188] The remaining funds would go to a state commission on nuclear waste storage. A dozen other states are reportedly considering similar legislative action.[189] At the federal level, a number of bills have been introduced in the 111th Congress that would suspend or alter mandatory utility payments made into the NWF or expand the purposes for which NWF funds could be used.[190]

CONCLUSION

Litigation related to the NWPA will undoubtedly continue. Whether defending breach of contract claims brought pursuant to the Standard Contract, or actions seeking equitable relief pursuant to the NWPA, the federal government will continue to incur substantial legal costs in connection with its delay in disposing of the nation's SNF. In response to the impending litigation, the Department of Justice (DOJ) has requested $11.4 million in the FY20 11 budget specifically for the purpose of defending against NWPA related suits.[191] DOJ is seeking to add 10 new attorneys to its Civil Division in preparation for the 25 trials the department expects to litigate in FY2011.[192] As the government makes preparations for future legal disputes, both litigation expenses and damages awards will continue to build as there seems to be no prospect for a completed facility capable of storing SNF anywhere on the horizon.

End Notes

[1] Spent nuclear fuel consists of radioactive fuel rods, containing uranium and plutonium, that have been permanently withdrawn from a nuclear reactor because they can no longer efficiently sustain a nuclear chain reaction. See CRS Report RL33461, *Civilian Nuclear Waste Disposal*, by Mark Holt, at 8.

[2] U.S. nuclear power providers individually spend these funds to store radioactive SNF at the bottom large pools or in "dry casks" located outside of the facility. Steve Hargreaves, *Nuclear Waste: Coming to a Town Near You?*, CNNMoney.com, November 4, 2009, *available at* http://www.money.cnn.com. *See also*, CRS Report R40202, *Nuclear Waste Disposal: Alternatives to Yucca Mountain*, by Mark Holt.

[3] Each one of these claims included a Fifth Amendment takings claim in addition to the breach of contract claim. The takings claims, however, were dismissed early in the litigation. *See e.g.,* Consumers Energy Co. v. U.S., 84 Fed. Cl. 152 (2008).

[4] The $1.2 billion consists of approximately $400 million in out-of-court settlements and approximately $800 million in damages awarded by the Court of Federal Claims. Of the $1.2 billion, the federal government has paid only $565 million in settlements and damages. The remaining judgments are in the appeals process and are not yet final. *See*, Compilation of Office of General Counsel Materials Provided to the President-Elect's DOE Transition Team, at 46, *available at* http://www.management.energy.gov/documents; Statement of Kim Cawley, Chief, Natural and Physical Resources Costs Estimates Unit, Congressional Budget Office Before the House Committee on the Budget, July 16, 2009 (hereinafter *CBO Testimony*).

[5] Marcia Coyle, *Nuclear Dispute Fallout*, The National Law Journal, September 14, 2009.

[6] The NWPA created the Office of Civilian and Radioactive Waste Management to carry out the DOE's obligations to manage and dispose of high-level radioactive waste and SNF. 42 U.S.C. § 10224.

[7] See, *CBO Testimony,* at 1 ("The Department of Energy has not yet disposed of any civilian nuclear waste and currently has no identifiable plan for handling that responsibility.").

[8] This chapter does not discuss the significant amount of environmental litigation relating to the licensing of the Yucca Mountain facility by the Nuclear Regulatory Commission.

[9] P.L. 97-425, *codified at* 42 U.S.C. §§ 10101 *et seq.*

[10] *Id.* at §§ 111-125.

[11] *Id.* at § 302.

[12] *Id.* at § 302(a).

[13] *Id.* at §302(a)(5) (emphasis added).

[14] 10 C.F.R. § 961.11.

[15] 42 U.S.C. § 10222(b)(1)(A).

[16] 42 U.S.C. § 10172.

[17] Fees by nuclear providers into the NWF have been estimated at $750 million annually. *CBO Testimony*, at 3.

[18] *See*, Indiana Michigan Power Co. v. U.S., 88 F.3d 1272, 1274 (D.C. Cir. 1996).

[19] 60 Fed. Reg. 2 1,793-94 (May 3, 1995).

[20] *Id.* at 21,794.

[21] *Id.* at 21,797.

[22] As of December 31, 2009, the NWF had an existing balance of $22.5 billion. Utilities have contributed approximately $17 billion in fees which have accumulated $14 billion in interest. Expenditures from the fund

amount to \$7.4 billion. OCRWM Financial Summary of Program Financial & Budget Information, *available at* http://www.ocrwm.doe.gov.

[23] Indiana Michigan Power Co. v. U.S., 88 F.3d 1272, 1277 (D.C. Cir. 1996).

[24] *See, e.g.*, Pacific Gas & Elec. Co. v. U.S., 536 F.3d 1282, 1289 (Fed. Cir. 2008).

[25] *CBO Testimony*, at 6-7.

[26] *Id.*

[27] *Indiana Michigan Power*, 88 F.3d 1272.

[28] Under the *Chevron* doctrine, a court will defer to an agency's interpretation of an ambiguous statute where the agency's "answer is based on a permissible construction of the statute." Chevron U.S.A. Inc. v. Natural Resources Defense Council, 467 U.S. 837 (1984).

[29] *Id.* at 1274.

[30] *Id.* at 1276.

[31] *Id.*

[32] *Id.* ("DOE next argues that subsections (A) and (B) of 302(a)(5) are not independent provisions, but rather must be read together.").

[33] *Id.*

[34] *Id.* at 1277 ("Thus we hold that section 302(a)(5)(B) creates an obligation in DOE, reciprocal to the utilities' obligation to pay, to start disposing of the SNF no later than January 31, 1998.").

[35] *See*, Northern States Power Co. v. U.S., 128 F.3d 754, 757 (D.C. Cir. 1997).

[36] *Id.*

[37] *Id.*

[38] 10 C.F.R. § 961.11.

[39] *Id.* The provision continues: "In the event circumstances beyond the reasonable control of the Purchaser or DOE— such as acts of God, or of the public enemy, acts of Government in either its sovereign or contractual capacity, fires, floods, epidemics, quarantine restrictions ... cause delay in scheduled delivery acceptance or transport of SNF ... the parties will readjust their schedules, as appropriate, to accommodate such delay."

[40] *Northern States*, 128 F.3d at 757.

[41] *Id.* at 758,761. The remedy that was considered "potentially adequate" in Northern States was later deemed "inadequate" in Maine Yankee Atomic Power Co. v. U.S., 225 F.3d 1336 (Fed. Cir. 2000).

[42] The remedy available under the contract allows for an equitable adjustment of charges and schedules. 10 C.F.R. 961.11.

[43] *Northern States*, 128 F.3d at 760.

[44] *Id.*

[45] *Id.*

[46] *Id.*

[47] Northern States Power Co. v. United States, 1998 U.S. App. LEXIS 12919 (D.C. Cir. May 5, 1998); Tucker Act, 28 U.S.C. § 1491(a).

[48] *Id.* ("The Tucker Act does not prevent us from exercising jurisdiction over an action to enforce compliance with the NWPA.").

[49] *See, e.g.*, Yankee Atomic Electric Company v. U.S., 42 Fed. Cl. 223 (1998) ("As a result, DOE maintains that it is prohibited from arguing that its failure to begin SNF disposal services is an unavoidable, non-compensable delay under Article IX.A of the Standard Contract.").

[50] The D.C. Circuit, though retaining jurisdiction over review of final agency actions, rejected the notion that the U.S. Courts of Appeals had jurisdiction over breach of contract claims under the NWPA, holding that the "Court of Federal Claims, not this court, is the proper forum for adjudicating contract disputes." Wisconsin Elec. Power v. U.S. Dep't of Energy, 211 F.3d 646, 647 (D.C. Cir. 2000).

[51] 28 U.S.C. § 1491.

[52] *See*, McKart v. U.S. 395 U.S. 185, 193 (1969) ("No one is entitled to judicial relief ... until the prescribed administrative remedy has been exhausted.").

[53] *See*, Yankee Atomic Elec. Co. v. U.S., 42 Fed. Cl. 223 (1998) (holding available administrative relief was not adequate); Northern States Power Co. v. U.S. 224 F.3d 1361 (Fed. Cl. 2000) (holding available administrative relief was adequate).

[54] 225 F.3d 1336 (Fed. Cir. 2000).

[55] *Id.* at 1341-1342.

[56] Standard Contract, 10 C.F.R. § 961.11.

[57] Maine Yankee Atomic Power Co. v. U.S., 225 F.3d 1336, 1341-42 (Fed. Cir. 2000).

[58] *Id.* at 1342.

[59] *See*, Alabama Power Co. v. U.S., 307 F.3d 1300, 1306 (11th Cir. 2002).

[60] *Id.* at 1315. The case was brought in the Eleventh Circuit, rather than the CFC, because the issue was a statutory question on the permissible use of NWF funds under the NWPA and not a breach of contract claim.

[61] *Id.* at 1312.

[62] *Id.* at 1313 ("An expenditure on interim storage is not an act of 'disposal.'").

[63] *Id.* at 1314.

[64] *Id.*

[65] This prohibition would arguably include utilizing NWF funds as part of any alternative solution to a permanent repository or any judicial order for restitution of NWF fees.

[66] *See, e.g.*, System Fuels Inc. v. U.S., 66 Fed. Cl. 722, 730 (2005) ("The government admitted on February 10, 2005 that 'DOE's delay in beginning acceptance of SNF ... constitutes a partial breach of the Standard Contract.'")

[67] Restatement (Second) of Contracts § 236 cmt. b ("If the injured party elects to or is required to await the balance of the other party's performance under the contract, his claim is said instead to be one for damages for partial breach."); Restatement (Second) of Contracts § 243 cmt. a.

[68] Restatement (Second) of Contracts § 236.

[69] *Id. See also,* E. Alan, Farnsworth, Contracts § 8.15 (3d ed. 1999) ("Damages are calculated on the assumption that both parties will continue to perform in spite of the breach.").

[70] Indiana Michigan Power Co. v. U.S., 422 F.3d 1369, 1374 (Fed. Cir. 2005) (holding that a partial breach plaintiff can recover damages incurred from the point at which the "party has reason to know that performance by the other party will not be forthcoming" to the date of trial.).

[71] *See, e.g.* Pacific Gas & Elec. Co. v. U.S., 536 F.3d 1282 (Fed. Cir. 2008) ("A series of cases has established that DOE has partially breached the contract by failing to begin its performance.")

[72] *Indiana Michigan Power*, 422 F.3d 1369, 1374 (Fed. Cir. 2005).

[73] *Id.* (emphasis added).

[74] *Id.*

[75] *Id.*

[76] Roedler v. DOE, 255 F.3d 1347, 1353 (Fed. Cir. 2001).

[77] Pacific Gas & Elec. Co. v. U.S., 70 Fed. Cl. 766, 774 (2006) ("[I]n the circumstances of this case, where the regulatory framework of the NWPA ... precludes plaintiff from suing for total breach of the contract ..."); Yankee Atomic Elec. Co. v. U.S., 536 F.3d 1268, 1280 (Fed. Cir. 2008) ("As this court has already acknowledged, the NWPA and the terms of the Standard Contract foreclose any claim for total breach.").

[78] Brief for Florida Power and Light Co. et al. as Amici Curiae, Sacramento Mun. Util. Dist. v. U.S. 65 Fed. Cl. 180 (2005).

[79] *Id.* at 11.

[80] "[T]he amici do not seek to be restored to their pre-Standard Contract position. Rather, their consistent position throughout the SNF litigation has been that they want—and need—DOE to perform its obligations under the Standard Contract." *Id.* at 9.

[81] At least one CFC judge has expressed concern over the manner in which the litigation has been progressing. Sacramento Mun. Util. Dist. v. U.S. 70 Fed. Cl. 332, 357 (2006) ("The prospect of continuing to issue rolling damage awards ad infinitum for interim storage costs, however, falls far short of resolving the 'national problem' that Congress identified in 1982 ...").

[82] *Indiana Michigan Power*, 422 F.3d at 1374.

[83] Pacific Gas & Elec. Co. v. U.S., 536 F.3d 1282 (Fed. Cir. 2008).

[84] The initial predicted rate of acceptance was 1200 metric tons of uranium (MTU) per year in 1998, 2000 MTU/year by 2003, and 2650 MTU/year by 2004. The proposed 1991 rate of acceptance schedule reduced those numbers to 300 MTU/year in 1998, 875 MTU/year in 2001, and 1800 MTU/year by 2010. *Id.*

[85] *Id.* at 129 1-92.

[86] *Id.*

[87] As a general rule, to recover damages the utilities must show that "(1) the damages were reasonably foreseeable ... at the time of contracting; (2) the breach is a substantial causal factor in the damages; and (3) the damages are shown with reasonable certainty." *Indiana Michigan Power*, 422 F.3d at 1373.

[88] On-site interim storage commonly requires "re-racking" or the construction of "dry casks." For further information on interim storage see CRS Report R40202, *Nuclear Waste Disposal: Alternatives to Yucca Mountain*, by Mark Holt.

[89] *Indiana Michigan Power*, 422 F.3d at 1377 ("When a party sues for partial breach, it retains its rights to sue for damages for its remaining rights to performance.").

[90] Florida Power and Light Co. v. U.S., 64 Fed. Cl. 37 (2005).

[91] P.L. 97-425 § 119.

[92] 465 F.3d 1343 (Fed. Cir. 2006).

[93] *Id.* at 1349-1351.

[94] *Id.* at 1350.

[95] *Id.* ("The difference in the parties' positions amounts to whether the courts of appeals continue to have jurisdiction to decide the propriety of agency actions ... because this issue need not be resolved in this appeal, we merely agree ... that the NWPA does not strip the court of its Tucker Act jurisdiction.").

[96] 73 Fed. Cl. 650 (2006).

[97] *Id.*

[98] *Id.*

[99] *Id.* at 664 ("in describing where the [Federal Circuit's] jurisdiction begins, the federal circuit *sub silentio* described where the D.C. Circuit's jurisdiction ends, *to wit*, that the latter court's jurisdiction does not extend beyond reviewing agency actions under Title III that relate to the creation of the repository.").

[100] *Id.* at 662.

[101] *Id.* at 664-665 ("The decisions in *Indiana Michigan* and *Northern States* bounded across the [jurisdictional] line, thereby intruding on this court's jurisdiction.").

[102] *Id.* at 664-666.

[103] *Id.* at 664.

[104] *Id.* at 665.

[105] *Id.* at 662-663 ("The fact that DOE chose to use 'administrative rulemaking' in developing the Standard Contract and in putting forth its interpretations thereof did not confer jurisdiction on the D.C. Circuit to resolve what are, in effect, contract claims.").

[106] *Id.* at 665.

[107] *Id.* at 666.

[108] Under the doctrine of sovereign immunity, "the United States is immune from suit save to the extent it consents to be sued." Murray v. Hoboken Land & Improvement Co., 59 U.S. 272, 283-84 (1855).

[109] *Nebraska Power*, 73 Fed. Cl. at 666.

[110] *Id.*

[111] *Id.*

[112] 5 U.S.C. § 702 ("A person suffering legal wrong because of agency action, or adversely affected or aggrieved by agency action within the meaning of a relevant statute, is entitled to judicial review thereof ... The United States may be named as a defendant in any such action, and a judgment or decree may be entered against the United States.").

[113] *Nebraska Power*, 73 Fed. Cl. at 666 (*citing* 5 U.S.C. § 704).

[114] Courts have construed the Tucker Act as waiving sovereign immunity only for claims for damages. The CFC, therefore, cannot grant a plaintiff equitable relief in these circumstances. *See, e.g.*, Richardson v. Morris, 409 U.S. 464- 65 (1973).

[115] *Nebraska Power*, at 672 ("[A]n adequate remedy was and is available in this court.").

[116] *Id.* at 669. The Federal Circuit has held that the U.S. Supreme Court did "not enunciate a broad rule that the Court of Federal Claims cannot supply an adequate remedy in any case seeking injunctive relief." Consol. Edison Co. of N.Y. v. U.S., 247 F.3d 1378, 1383 (Fed. Cir. 2001).

[117] *Id.* at 672-73.

[118] *Id.* at 673 ("[T]he court is left with the firm conviction that, in issuing the subject mandamus, the D.C. Circuit operated in excess of its jurisdiction and, specifically, without an appropriate waiver of sovereign immunity.").

[119] *Id.*

[120] *Id.* at 674.

[121] Nebraska Public Power Dist. v. U.S., 2009 U.S. App. LEXIS 12668 (Fed. Cir 2009).

[122] *Id.*

[123] *Id.*

[124] Nebraska Public Power Dist. v. U.S., 2010 U.S. App. LEXIS 643 (Fed. Cir 2010).

[125] *Id.* at 18-19.

[126] *Id.* at 20-31. The court added, that even were the scope of § 119 ambiguous, "[w]here there is a question whether judicial review was meant to be in district courts or courts of appeals, that ambiguity is resolved in favor of court of appeals review." *Id.* at 24.

[127] *Id.* at 22 (citing General Electric Uranium Mgmt. Corp. v. U.S., 764 F.2d 896, 903 (D.C. Cir. 1985)).

[128] *Id.* at 31-41.

[129] 5 U.S.C. § 704.

[130] *Nebraska Public Power*, 2010 U.S. App. Lexis at 33 ("the most natural reading of [§704] is that it relates to two categories of agency action.").

[131] *Id.*

[132] *Id.* ("[T]he 'adequate remedy at law' proviso applies only to nonstatutory review and not to special statutory review, such as the review at issue in this case.").

[133] *Id.*

[134] *Id.* at 53 ("The mandamus order was issued pursuant to the D.C. Circuit's authority to construe the NWPA and to direct DOE to comply with its obligations under the statute. The order did not address any issue of contract breach.").

[135] *Id.* at 43.

[136] Although the Federal Circuit court's decision is subject to appeal to the U.S. Supreme Court, it would seem unlikely that the Court would grant certiorari. First, the Supreme Court generally looks for cases where different U.S. appellate courts have disagreed on a point of law. Here, both the Federal Circuit and the D.C. Circuit concur on the jurisdictional question. Second, the Federal Circuit voted overwhelmingly, 11-1, to

The Yucca Mountain Litigation: Liability under the Nuclear Waste Policy...   133

reverse the CFC. Finally, DOE petitioned the Supreme Court to review the D.C. Circuit's exercise of jurisdiction in *Northern States* in 1997 and was denied.

[137] Statement of Steven Chu, Secretary, Department of Energy, Before the Senate Committee on the Budget, March 11, 2009 ("[B]oth the President and I have made clear that Yucca Mountain is not a workable option.").

[138] Funding for the Yucca Mountain facility has steadily decreased from $572 million in FY2005, to $288 million in FY2009, to $197 million in FY2010, to potentially zero in FY2011. *Available at* http://www.ocrwm.doe.gov.

[139] President's FY 2011 Budget Proposal at 173-177.

[140] *Id.* at 176.

[141] Statement of Steven Chu, Secretary, Department of Energy, Before the Senate Committee on Appropriations Subcommittee on Energy and Water Development, and Related Agencies, May 19 2009. Secretary Chu had requested $25 million in FY2011 to "wrap up" the Yucca Mountain project and preserve "critical knowledge and data." *See*, Stephen Power, *Chu, Orszag at Odds Over Yucca Funding*, Wall St. J., Jan. 14, 2010.

[142] *See*, Letter from Rep. Ralph Hall and Rep. Paul Broun, to Steven Chu, Secretary of Energy, February 3, 2010.

[143] 42 U.S.C. § 10224 ("There hereby is established within the Department of Energy an Office of Civilian Radioactive Waste Management.").

[144] Janice Valverde, *Two House Republicans Challenge Decision to End Yucca Mountain Funding, Close Office*, BNA Daily Report for Executives, Feb. 9, 2010.

[145] *See e.g.,* Kendall v. U.S. ex. rel Stokes, 37 U.S. (12 Pet.) 524 (1838)(holding that the President has no authority to direct the Post Master's performance of his statutory duty).

[146] 42 U.S.C. § 7253.

[147] President's FY 2011 Budget Proposal at 176. ("The Administration has ... decided to terminate the Office of Civilian Radioactive Waste Management.").

[148] Such duties include annually preparing and submitting to Congress a "comprehensive report on the activities and expenditures of the office." 42 U.S.C. 10224.

[149] Memorandum from President Barack Obama, to Steven Chu, Secretary of Energy, *Blue Ribbon Commission on America's Nuclear Future*, Jan. 29, 2010.

[150] DOE Press Release, *Secretary Chu Announces Blue Ribbon Commission on America's Nuclear Future*, Jan. 29, 2010. *Available at* http://www.doe.gov. According to Secretary Chu, the Commission will be looking at "different types of disposal options." Janice Valverde, *Administration to Withdraw License Bid for Yucca Mountain, Eliminates Funding*, BNA Daily Report for Executives, Feb. 2, 2010.

[151] DOE itself is currently prohibited by statute from considering specific sites other than Yucca Mountain. 42 U.S.C. § 10172 ("The Secretary shall terminate all site specific activities ... at all candidate sites, other than the Yucca Mountain site, within 90 days after the enactment of the Nuclear Waste Policy Amendments Act of 1987.").

[152] The initial House-passed bill approving the Administration's FY2010 proposed budget included language mandating that any review of nuclear waste disposal alternatives include Yucca Mountain as a potential option. However, the final DOE appropriations bill only contained language mandating that DOE "consider all alternatives for nuclear waste disposal." P.L. 111-85 (2009).

[153] Steve Tetreault, *Federal Panel to Examine Nuclear Waste Storage*, Las Vegas Review-Journal, Jan. 30, 2010.

[154] President's FY 2011 Budget Proposal at 176 ("[I]n 2010, the [DOE] will discontinue its application to the U.S. Nuclear Regulatory Commission for a license to construct a high-level waste geologic repository at Yucca Mountain ...").

[155] The NRC reportedly spent $58 million in FY2009 to review the Yucca Mountain license. *See*, Janice Valverde, *Administration to Withdraw License Bid for Yucca Mountain, Eliminates Funding*, BNA Daily Report for Executives, Feb. 2, 2010.

[156] U. S. Department of Energy's Motion to Withdraw, *In the Matter of U.S. Department of Energy*, ASLBP No. 09-892-HLW-CAB04, March 3, 2010.

[157] 10 C.F.R. § 2.107 ("The Commission may ... on receiving a request for withdrawal of an application, deny the application or dismiss it with prejudice.").

[158] U.S. Department of Energy's Motion to Withdraw, *In the Matter of U.S. Department of Energy*, ASLBP No. 09-892-HLW-CAB04, March 3, 2010.

[159] *See*, 42. U.S.C. § 10134; Shannon Dininny, *Wash. To Intervene in Yucca Mountain Case*, Seattle Times, March 1 2010.

[160] Additionally, GAO predicts that the government will incur disposal costs in the tens of billions of dollars whether the administration pursues Yucca Mountain, interim centralized storage followed by permanent disposal, or continues to bear the expenses of on-site storage. GAO Report 10-48, *Nuclear Waste Management: Key Attributes, Challenges, and Costs for the Yucca Mountain Repository and Two Potential Alternatives*, Nov. 2009.

[161] 42. U.S.C. § 10172 ("The Secretary shall terminate all site specific activities ... at all candidate sites, other than the Yucca Mountain site, within 90 days after December 22, 1987."); 42 U.S.C. § 10172(a) ("The Secretary may not conduct site-specific activities with respect to a second repository unless Congress has specifically authorized and appropriated funds for such activities.").

[162] 42 U.S.C. § 10 134(d). *See, Report to the President and the Congress By the Secretary of Energy on the Need for a Second Repository*, Dec. 2008, *available at* http://www.ocrwm.doe.gov.

[163] Remarks by the President in State of the Union Address, Jan. 27, 2010. *Available at* http://www.whitehouse.gov.

[164] Matthew Wald, *In bid to Revive Nuclear Power, U.S. Is Backing New Reactors*, N.Y. Times, Feb. 17, 2010.

[165] *CBO Testimony*, at 7.

[166] *Id.*

[167] *Id.*

[168] *Id.* With at least 72 lawsuits filed against DOE, one could estimate that the nuclear utilities as a whole have expended over $400 million in litigation costs.

[169] *See*, CRS Report RL 33461, Civilian Nuclear Waste Disposal, by Mark Holt, at 3.

[170] *Id.*

[171] Federal courts have authority to grant equitable relief against the federal government under the APA. *See*, 5 U.S.C. §702-706.

[172] Given the nature of the dispute between the DOE and the nuclear utilities, outside plaintiffs may have trouble satisfying constitutional standing requirements. The Court has identified three essential elements to standing: (1)The plaintiff must have suffered an "injury in fact," i.e., a legal injury that is concrete, actual or imminent, and not conjectural or hypothetical; (2) the plaintiff must show that the injury is "fairly traceable" to the challenged conduct; and (3) the injury must be able to be redressed by a favorable decision. Lujan v. Defenders of Wildlife, 504 U.S. 555, 560-6 1 (1992).

[173] Steve Tetreault, *South Carolina Governor Protests Yucca Termination*, Las Vegas Review-Journal, Feb. 16, 2010.

[174] *Id.*

[175] Whether to issue an injunction is a discretionary decision based on a balancing of interests. The court will weigh: (1) the plaintiffs' likelihood of success on the merits; (2) whether the plaintiffs would suffer irreparable harm absent an injunction; (3) whether the injunction would substantially injure other parties; and (4) whether the injunction would further the public interest. *See, e.g.*, Ark. Dairy Coop. Ass'n v. U.S., 573 F.3d 815, 821 (D.C. Cir. 2009).

[176] The D.C. Circuit has stated that "the remedy of mandamus is a drastic one, to be invoked only in extraordinary situations." A mandamus requires a showing that "(1) the plaintiff has a clear right to relief; (2) the defendant has a clear duty to act; and (3) there is no other adequate remedy available to plaintiff." *Northern States*, 128 F.3d at 758. In denying Northern States first petition for a mandamus directing the DOE to begin acceptance of SNF, the D.C. Circuit held that Northern States had a clear right to relief, DOE had a clear duty to act, but that Northern States had another potentially adequate remedy under the Standard Contract. *Id.* at 759.

[177] *See*, 10 C.F.R. § 2.309.

[178] Statement by Attorney General Henry McMaster Regarding Yucca Mountain, February 24, 2010, *available at* http://www.scattorneygeneral.org; Petition for Review, South Carolina v. DOE, No. 10-1229 (Feb. 26, 2010).

[179] See, 42 U.S.C. §10134(b) ("[T]he Secretary shall submit to the Commission an application for a construction authorization ..."); 42 U.S.C. § 10134(d)("The Commission shall consider an application for a construction authorization for all or part of a repository in accordance with the laws applicable to such applications, except that the Commission shall issue a final decision ...").

[180] *See*, Petition for Declaratory and Injunctive Relief and Write of Mandamus, In Re Aiken County, No. 10-1050 (D.C. Cir. 2010).

[181] *Id.* at 14. Whether the county has standing to bring its claim will likely be an issue for the D.C. Circuit to consider given the speculative nature of the county's injury. Additionally, it is important to note that while the Supreme Court has relaxed standing requirements when states seek to bring *parens pat riae* suits in an effort to protect their citizens general health and welfare, *See*, Bradford Mank, *Should States Have Greater Standing Rights than Ordinary Citizens?: Massachusetts v. EPA's New Standing Test for States*, 49 Wm. & Mary L. Rev. 1701 (2008), the doctrine has not been extended to other political subdivisions. Roseville v. Norton, 219 F. Supp. 2d 130 (D.D.C. 2002). In the immediate case, the county is alleging an injury to the county's own property, rather than a more general injury to its citizens. Petition for Declaratory and Injunctive Relief and Writ of Mandamus, In Re Aiken County, No. 10-1050 (D.C. Cir. 2010).

[182] *Id.* at 4. The U.S. courts of appeals have original jurisdiction over challenges to agency action under the NWPA. *See*, 42 U.S.C. §10139.

[183] *Id.* at 10-11.

[184] Shannon Dininny, *Wash. To Intervene in Yucca Mountain Case*, Seattle Times, March 1 2010.

[185] State of Washington's Petition for Leave to Intervene and Request for Hearing, *In the Matter of U.S. Department of Energy*, ASLBP NO. 09-892-HLW-CAB04, March 3, 2010.

[186] *See*, George Lobsenz, *First Lawsuit Filed Over Yucca Mountain Termination*, The Energy Daily, Feb. 19, 2010.

[187] In a related response, the Nuclear Energy Institute, which advocates on behalf of the nuclear energy industry, has asked the Secretary of Energy to suspend all required payments into the NWF. The Secretary has the authority to "propose an adjustment to the [NWF] fee." 42 U.S.C. § 10223.

[188] H.R. 2440, 86th Leg. (Minn. 2010).

[189] Charley Shaw, *Nukes in 2010*: Tussle with Feds Joins the Minnesota Legislative Agenda, *The Legal Ledger*, Jan. 22, 2010.

[190] *See, e.g.*, S. 861, 111th Cong. (2010); H.R. 3385, 111th Cong. (2010).

[191] Department of Justice FY 2011 Budget Request for General Legal Activities, Civil Division. *Available at* http://www.justice.gov.

[192] *Id.*

In: Nuclear Waste: Disposal and Liability Issues
Editor: Ylenia E. Farrugia

ISBN: 978-1-61761-590-0
© 2011 Nova Science Publishers, Inc.

Chapter 5

THE FEDERAL GOVERNMENT'S RESPONSIBILITIES AND LIABILITIES UNDER THE NUCLEAR WASTE POLICY ACT[*]

Kim Gawley

Mr. Chairman, Congressman Ryan, and Members of the Committee, I am pleased to appear before you today to discuss the federal government's responsibilities and liabilities under the Nuclear Waste Policy Act of 1982 (NWPA). Since I last testified on this subject in 2007, there have been a number of important developments that I would like to highlight in my testimony:

- The Administration has announced that it intends to terminate the Yucca Mountain project and explore other alternatives for disposing of nuclear waste. Despite that change in policy, however, the federal government remains responsible for permanently disposing of spent nuclear fuel generated by civilian facilities, which pay fees for that service. Regardless of how the government meets that responsibility, discharging those liabilities will require significant federal spending over many decades.
- The Department of Energy (DOE) has not yet disposed of any civilian nuclear waste and currently has no identifiable plan for handling that responsibility. Nevertheless, the operators of nuclear utilities continue to pay fees—of about $750 million annually—to cover the costs of disposing of the nuclear waste they generate. Over the past 25 years, those firms have paid a total of $16.3 billion for waste disposal services that they have not yet begun to receive.
- The federal government is more than 10 years behind schedule in its contractual obligations to remove and dispose of such waste, and the government has paid nuclear utilities $565 million in compensation for costs incurred because of its failure

---

[*] These remarks were delivered as testimony of Kim Cawley before the House of Representatives Committee on the Budget, given on July 16, 2009.

to meet that schedule. DOE currently estimates that liabilities to electric utilities for such damages will total more than $12 billion if the department begins to accept nuclear waste by 2020. How the Administration's decision to terminate the Yucca Mountain project will affect the federal government's liabilities is unclear, but the estimate will climb if the department's schedule slips beyond 2020. Regardless of whether or when the government opens a repository, such payments (which come from the Department of the Treasury's Judgment Fund) will probably continue for several decades.

- The Nuclear Regulatory Commission (NRC) has now extended the operating licenses of more than half of the nation's nuclear power plants for another 20 years beyond the span of their initial operating licenses. Meanwhile, the amount of existing waste may already exceed the amount authorized to be disposed of at the repository envisioned under NWPA. Ultimately, a change in law will be required to authorize DOE to permanently dispose of all of the waste anticipated to be generated by existing nuclear power plants at a site other than Yucca Mountain. Without such a change and steps toward that end, taxpayers will continue to pay utilities—through settlements and claims awards—to keep storing substantial amounts of waste.

THE FEDERAL GOVERNMENT'S RESPONSIBILITIES UNDER THE NUCLEAR WASTE POLICY ACT

The Nuclear Waste Policy Act established statutory responsibility for federal actions to take possession of and permanently dispose of spent nuclear fuel generated at civilian nuclear reactors, as well as to dispose of radioactive waste resulting from federal activities in manufacturing nuclear weapons. Under current law, the only solution that the government is authorized to pursue involves permanent disposal of waste at a geologic repository, and Yucca Mountain in Nevada is the only place where such a repository may be located.

Under NWPA, the federal government, through DOE, faces substantial costs to establish a repository for the nation's nuclear waste. It has also incurred contractual obligations to remove waste from civilian nuclear facilities. Under the legislation, the federal government will have to spend tens of billions of dollars over many decades to fulfill its obligations to dispose of waste from the current generation of civilian nuclear reactors. The government will also be responsible for waste from any new facilities built in the future. However, because of statutory constraints on the amount of waste that the repository envisioned under NWPA can store, waste from any such new facilities cannot be accommodated without a change to the law.

NWPA authorized DOE to build a geologic repository to permanently store up to 70,000 metric tons of spent nuclear fuel generated by civilian nuclear power plants and high-level radioactive waste generated by federal facilities. The total amount of commercial and defense-related waste that has already been generated may exceed that capacity.

FINANCING THE COSTS OF DISPOSING OF NUCLEAR WASTE

The Nuclear Waste Policy Act also addressed how the disposal of spent nuclear fuel and defense-related waste was to be paid for. Under NWPA, the costs are to be borne by the parties that generate it, and the law authorizes DOE to levy fees on the nuclear power industry to cover the costs for the waste it generates. The law also authorizes appropriations from the Treasury's general fund to pay for disposing of high-level radioactive waste generated by the nation's defense programs.

Financing the Costs Associated with Civilian Nuclear Waste

Starting in 1983, NWPA authorized DOE to charge electric utilities fees to cover the costs of disposing of the nuclear waste they generate. Utilities today pay annual fees at a rate of 1 mil (0.1 cent) per kilowatt-hour of electricity generated and sold by nuclear power plants. The fees, which are recorded in the budget as offsetting receipts (a credit against direct spending), are deposited into the Treasury's Nuclear Waste Fund. Amounts in that fund are available for spending only to the extent provided in annual appropriation acts. Under NWPA, DOE is required to periodically review and, if necessary, adjust the level of fees to ensure that the fund has sufficient resources to pay for disposing of the utility industry's nuclear waste. The department has not increased that annual charge since 1983.

In addition to the ongoing yearly fees, NWPA established one-time fees to cover the costs of disposing of waste that was generated before the law was enacted. DOE provided utilities with several options for paying that one-time charge, but several utilities have not yet paid the fee, and a significant amount remains uncollected.

NWPA authorized appropriations from the Nuclear Waste Fund to cover the costs of the civilian nuclear waste program and also permitted DOE to borrow from the Treasury (subject to approval in advance in appropriation acts) if balances in the fund were insufficient to cover the program's immediate costs. (The law stipulated that amounts borrowed from the Treasury be repaid from future fee collections.) In addition, the law authorized the Secretary of the Treasury to invest the fund's unspent balances in nonmarketable Treasury securities, which are credited with interest.

From 1983 through the end of fiscal year 2008, $29.1 billion was credited to the fund (see Table 1). That amount includes fees paid by the nuclear industry totaling $16.3 billion, as well as $12.8 billion from intragovernmental transfers of interest earnings. Cumulative expenditures from the fund during that period totaled about $7.1 billion, mostly for analyses related to the waste disposal program and for appropriations to DOE for initial design work on the Yucca Mountain facility. The NRC and other federal entities also received modest appropriations from the fund for work related to the program, leaving an unspent balance of $22.0 billion at the end of fiscal year 2008. The Congressional Budget Office (CBO) estimates that in 2009, another $2.0 billion will be credited to the fund—nearly $800 million from fees and the rest from interest. Expenditures in 2009 will total $0.2 billion, bringing the fund's end-of-year balance to $23.8 billion, CBO estimates.

If all of today's 104 licensed nuclear reactors continue to generate electricity, future annual receipts from industry fees are likely to average between $750 million and $800 million for at least the next decade. Most U.S. nuclear power plants began operating in the mid-1970s or during the 1980s under 40-year licenses. The NRC has approved 20-year extensions to the licenses of more than half of the plants in operation today, and it anticipates that many of the others will apply for such extensions. When those plants reach the end of their license extensions (or their economically useful lives) and cease operations—probably in the 2030s and 2040s—they will no longer pay fees to the Nuclear Waste Fund to dispose of their waste.

Receipts from the one-time fees that remain unpaid and become due once the federal repository is opened currently amount to about $3.2 billion, DOE estimates.[1] Interest accrues on the balances due from those one-time fees until the utilities pay them to the government; therefore, eventual deposits of such fees will probably be significantly greater than the current balances due. Also accruing and adding significantly to the fund's balances are credits of interest on the fund's unspent dollars. Those amounts are intragovernmental transfers and do not create net receipts to the federal government, but they do add to the resources that are authorized to be used for the waste disposal program.

Financing the Costs Associated with Defense-Related Nuclear Waste

In addition to the amounts appropriated from the fees and interest credited to the Nuclear Waste Fund, the Congress has made annual appropriations to the nuclear waste program to cover the costs that DOE estimates are related to the disposal of nuclear waste generated by federal defense programs. In 2008, DOE determined that about one-fifth of the total costs of the waste disposal program was attributable to that endeavor and that this share of the program's total costs should be paid for with appropriations from the general fund of the Treasury.[2] Since 1993, the Congress has provided about $3.7 billion from the general fund for such costs.

Table 1. Federal Cash Flows for Nuclear Waste Disposal (Billions of dollars)

	Cumulative Totals, 1983 Through 2008	CBO's Estimates, 2009
Nuclear Waste Fund (for civilian nuclear waste)		
Deposits		
Annual fees	14.8	0.8
One-time fees	1.5	0
Subtotal	16.3	0.8
Interest credited [a]	12.8	1.2
Total	**29.1**	**2.0**
Disbursements	7.1	0.2
End-of-Year Balance	22.0	23.8
General Fund (for defense-related activities)		
Appropriations	3.6	0.1

Sources: Congressional Budget Office and Department of Energy.

Note: Amounts are in nominal dollars.

a. Components may not add up to totals because of rounding.

Estimates of Total Life-Cycle Costs

In 2008, DOE published an estimate of the total costs—including those for transportation and project management—associated with the planned underground nuclear waste disposal facility. In DOE's estimation, the project would cost about $96 billion in 2007 dollars over an operating period of more than 100 years.[3]

DOE also reported on the adequacy of the annual fee charged for nuclear waste disposal.[4] In its study, DOE evaluated several scenarios in which the costs attributable to civilian nuclear waste ranged from 70 percent to 85 percent of total costs. In nearly all cases, DOE determined that the annual fee, along with accrued interest, was likely to generate sufficient balances to cover the estimated costs. The agency also noted, however, that under certain conditions, a future increase in the fee might become necessary.

Judgments about whether the fee is adequate are highly sensitive to estimates of certain key variables, such as the costs for the envisioned method of disposal and inflation. Such determinations are also sensitive to estimates of the interest credited to the fund—estimates that are a function of interest rates and fund balances, which in turn depend on projections of appropriated spending from the fund. In light of the Administration's policy to terminate the Yucca Mountain project and pursue an alternative means of waste disposal, there is no current basis to judge the adequacy of the fee to cover future costs because the method of disposal and its life-cycle costs are unknown.

FEDERAL CONTRACTUAL OBLIGATIONS AND LIABILITIES FOR NUCLEAR WASTE

Under contracts signed with electric utilities pursuant to the Nuclear Waste Policy Act, DOE was scheduled to start removing waste from storage sites at individual power plants for transport to a federal storage or disposal facility by 1998. After the federal government missed its 1998 contractual deadline to start collecting waste, electric utilities began—successfully—to sue the government for resulting damages. In seeking to resolve the initial lawsuits, DOE anticipated that it would pay court-awarded damages to individual utilities from amounts appropriated from the Nuclear Waste Fund or by issuing credits to those utilities (to reduce their future payments to the fund) in the amount of the damages that had been awarded.

In 2002, however, the U.S. Court of Appeals for the Eleventh Circuit held that DOE could not use the Nuclear Waste Fund to pay the damages resulting from the government's partial breach of its contracts.[5] According to the court, payment of the costs of interim storage incurred by the utilities because of the partial breach was not within the uses of the fund that were permitted under NWPA. Also, the court pointed out, because the department would inevitably raise future fees to compensate for any such payments, the injured utilities would be the ones to ultimately bear the costs of the partial breach of the contracts if they were paid from the fund. In addition, utilities that did not litigate their claims would end up paying larger fees to cover the costs of damage claims made by other utilities. Agreeing with the parties that brought the lawsuit, the court stated that making utilities contribute to a fund that disproportionately paid the storage costs of other utilities would raise a serious constitutional question about whether the action constituted a "taking." Following the court's decision, the government subsequently paid damages to the utilities from the Treasury's Judgment Fund.

The Judgment Fund

The Judgment Fund is a permanent, indefinite appropriation from the Treasury that is available to pay final judgments and awards against the United States that cannot legally be paid from any other existing appropriation.[6] (The fund has no fiscal year limitations, and there is no need for the Congress to appropriate money to replenish it.) The fund provides the authority for the government to pay for most court judgments and settlement agreements entered into by the Department of Justice to resolve actual or imminent lawsuits against the federal government. Generally, agencies are not required to reimburse the Judgment Fund for payments made on their behalf unless the Congress appropriates money specifically for that purpose.

Judgments Awarded and Paid to Utilities under the Nuclear Waste Policy Act

Under the Department of Justice's settlements with electric utilities, utilities have been reimbursed for the actual costs they incurred because of DOE's partial breach of its contracts. Such costs are unique to each nuclear power plant and depend partly on the age and operating status of the plant and the size and configuration of the plant's available space for nuclear waste storage.

According to the Department of Justice, as of May 2009 electric utilities had filed 71 lawsuits seeking compensation for costs they incurred because the federal government could not begin to accept nuclear waste for disposal in 1998. Of those lawsuits, 10 have been settled, 6 were voluntarily withdrawn, and 4 have been litigated to a final judgment that cannot be appealed. Of the 51 pending cases, 13 have been decided, but some are under appeal. In total, if those decisions stand, the federal government's liabilities under judgments and settlements currently total $1.3 billion. That amount includes $565 million that has already been paid to five electric utilities pursuant to settlements (including a payment of $35 million to the federally owned Tennessee Valley Authority.)[7] Because judicial claims for damages are made retrospectively, many more cases can be expected in the coming decades as utilities seek to recover their ongoing costs for storing nuclear waste long after they expected it to be removed and sent to a permanent disposal site.

Future Settlements under the Nuclear Waste Policy Act

Litigation is ongoing regarding how to calculate damages for DOE's partial breach of its contractual commitments. The department currently estimates that if it begins to accept waste in 2020, taxpayers' total liabilities to electric utilities will total $12.3 billion (in today's dollars).[8] Further, DOE anticipates that payments from the Judgment Fund will span a number of decades after 2020.

DOE's estimate of future damages is uncertain and is predicated on the department's views of the types of additional business and storage expenses that the courts will determine are appropriate and reasonable and should be paid by the department. Those determinations will depend on such factors as the estimated rate at which DOE would have removed waste from a particular facility if the department had been able to accept waste in 1998. If utilities successfully argue that the waste-acceptance rate used for the purpose of calculating damages should exceed the rate used in DOE's projections of liabilities, costs will probably surpass $12.3 billion.

Similarly, costs may be greater if the courts take a broader view of the expenses for which utilities should be compensated. Although the federal government is responsible for the permanent disposal of nuclear waste, individual utilities are responsible for storing the waste until it can be delivered to a permanent storage facility. Because the characteristics of utilities' sites vary, the determination of incremental expenses incurred at particular sites must be made on a case-by-case basis and will ultimately depend on the courts' views, which could differ from DOE's.

DOE has previously estimated that liabilities will increase—by roughly $500 million annually—if the schedule for completing the planned repository slips further and waste continues to accumulate at utilities' storage sites.[9] And even once the department begins to accept waste, it will face a backlog that, at best, will take more than 20 years to eliminate. As long as the department remains behind schedule, taxpayers will continue to incur liabilities.

Finally, it is not clear how the Administration's decision to terminate the Yucca Mountain repository will affect the federal government's liabilities to electric utilities. If DOE is found at some point to have fully breached its contractual commitments, the federal government's liabilities could increase considerably.

THE OUTLOOK FOR THE FEDERAL GOVERNMENT'S LIABILITIES

Ultimately, a change in law will be required to authorize DOE to permanently dispose of all of the waste anticipated to be generated by existing nuclear facilities at a site other than Yucca Mountain. Otherwise, taxpayers will continue to pay utilities, through settlements and claims awards, to keep storing substantial amounts of waste.

The Nuclear Waste Policy Act sets the storage capacity of the Yucca Mountain site at no more than 70,000 metric tons. DOE estimates that it is responsible for disposing of nearly that many tons of existing spent nuclear fuel and high-level waste. The nation's existing nuclear power plants are producing another 2,000 metric tons of waste per year. In other words, the total volume of waste may already exceed the statutory capacity of the repository envisioned under NWPA.

Moreover, the NRC has received 26 applications for licenses to build new nuclear power plants in the next few years. If constructed, each of those plants would produce around 20 metric tons of waste per year, or about 1,000 metric tons over a 40- to 60-year operating period. Such plants would also pay fees to the Nuclear Waste Fund, and their waste would become a federal liability because, under NWPA, nuclear plants are required to sign waste disposal agreements with DOE. Without additional storage capacity, the cost of storing that waste would probably become an additional liability of the Judgment Fund.

In any case, even if legislation is enacted to authorize DOE to pursue a repository at an alternative site with sufficient capacity to store all anticipated nuclear waste, federal liabilities will remain substantial, and payments from the Judgment Fund to compensate utilities for storing waste will continue for many years.

End Notes

[1] Data supplied to the Congressional Budget Office in July 2009 by the Department of Energy's Office of Civilian Radioactive Waste Management.

[2] Department of Energy, Office of Civilian Radioactive Waste Management, *Analysis of the Total System Life Cycle Cost of the Civilian Radioactive Waste Management Program,* DOE/RW-0591 (July 2008).

[3] Ibid.

[4] Department of Energy, Office of Civilian Radioactive Waste Management, *Fiscal Year 2007 Civilian Radioactive Waste Management Fee Adequacy Assessment Report,* DOE-RW-0593 (July 2008).

[5] *Alabama Power Co.* v. *United States,* 307 F.3d 1300 (2002).

[6] In 2008, several thousand individual payments from the Judgment Fund amounted to nearly $0.8 billion; over the past 10 years, such payments have averaged around $1.2 billion annually. Most of the payments are made to settle claims related to federal employment, torts, property loss, discrimination, medical malpractice, and contract disputes.

[7] Information supplied to CBO in July 2009 by the Department of Justice.

[8] Information provided to CBO in July 2009 by the Department of Energy's Office of Civilian Radioactive Waste Management.

[9] Statement of Edward F. Sproat III, Director, Office of Civilian Radioactive Waste Management, Department of Energy, before the Subcommittee on Energy and Water Development of the House Committee on Appropriations (March 28, 2007).

INDEX

A

adjustment, 118, 130, 134
affirmative action, 127
affirming, 124
agencies, 4, 14, 29, 54, 55, 92, 94, 102, 103, 125, 142
annual rate, 61, 64
appropriations, 8, 9, 15, 16, 18, 20, 31, 39, 82, 89, 98, 133, 139, 140
aquifers, 33
arbitration, 5
arithmetic, 14
assessment, 37, 40, 48, 94
attachment, 22
Attorney General, 134
average costs, 78

B

background, 11, 28, 82, 87
barriers, 18, 35, 37, 82, 83
boreholes, 41, 102
breakdown, 55, 95
Bureau of Land Management, 13, 22, 33, 99, 108
bureaucracy, 125
business model, 56

C

campaigns, 73, 74
cancer, 13, 30
candidates, 104
carbon, 27, 35, 93
carbon dioxide, 93
carbon emissions, 27, 35
certification, 9, 20
challenges, vii, 8, 25, 26, 28, 34, 36, 37, 39, 45, 50, 52, 54, 57, 58, 59, 83, 84, 134
civil action, 121
cladding, 11, 97
clean energy, 127

climate, 27, 35
climate change, 27
closure, 16, 38, 49, 53, 55, 83, 84
community, 33, 34, 48, 50, 52, 54
compatibility, 71, 75
compensation, vii, 5, 83, 97, 137, 142
complexity, 46
compliance, 7, 13, 14, 18, 37, 39, 130
conference, 16, 98, 126, 128
configuration, 50, 142
conflict, 112, 113, 122
Congressional Budget Office, 5, 22, 33, 49, 67, 82, 83, 108, 115, 129, 139, 140, 144
consensus, 4, 34, 45, 72, 92
consent, 17, 48
consolidation, 43, 53, 126
Constitution, 118
consulting, 41, 57, 58
contamination, 10, 33
conviction, 132
cooling, 47, 96, 97
corrosion, 35, 52, 82
cost, 4, 16, 25, 26, 28, 29, 31, 33, 34, 36, 38, 39, 40, 41, 43, 44, 45, 46, 48, 49, 50, 51, 52, 53, 54, 55, 56, 57, 58, 59, 60, 62, 63, 64, 66, 70, 71, 72, 73, 74, 75, 76, 77, 78, 79, 82, 83, 84, 88, 89, 94, 96, 99, 102, 104, 107, 141, 144
cost saving, 99
Court of Appeals, 3, 5, 7, 8, 14, 22, 23, 83, 107, 111, 112, 113, 115, 121, 128, 141
criticism, 86, 87, 104
critics, 31, 95
crystalline, 104
current balance, 140
current limit, 85

D

damages, vii, 5, 18, 26, 93, 112, 113, 114, 117, 118, 119, 120, 121, 122, 123, 125, 127, 129, 131, 132, 138, 141, 142, 143
data collection, 43, 57, 58, 59, 65

146 Index

decay, 28, 34, 35, 82, 87, 95, 101
degradation, 49, 52
Department of Defense, 67, 68, 69
Department of Energy, vii, 1, 2, 3, 7, 21, 22, 25, 27, 54, 60, 80, 85, 86, 105, 107, 108, 109, 111, 112, 115, 125, 129, 133, 134, 137, 140, 144
Department of Justice, 5, 40, 55, 67, 127, 129, 135, 142, 144
Department of the Interior, 13, 33, 86, 99
deposits, 3, 140
destination, 26, 36, 101
directors, 91, 96
discharges, 10, 88, 119
discrimination, 144
disposition, 26, 27, 28, 30, 35, 42, 44, 49, 50, 54, 60
District of Columbia, 3, 8, 17, 22, 23, 107, 112, 113, 115, 123
drinking water, 27
dumping, 91, 102

E

economic downturn, 105
economic incentives, 48
election, 85, 105
electricity, 1, 31, 35, 46, 139
electromagnetic, 102
electronic systems, 16
employment, 144
England, 101
environmental conditions, 52, 55
environmental effects, 79
environmental impact, 82, 94, 102
environmental policy, 12
environmental protection, 18
Environmental Protection Agency, 1, 10, 23, 27, 34, 82, 91, 107
environmental standards, 13, 105
EPA, 1, 10, 13, 14, 18, 22, 23, 27, 34, 37, 82, 91, 104, 107, 134
exercise, 104, 117, 121, 122, 124, 133
expenditures, 78, 133, 139
expertise, 41, 56, 57, 59, 60, 66
experts, 25, 26, 27, 28, 29, 30, 36, 37, 39, 40, 41, 43, 46, 47, 48, 49, 50, 51, 52, 53, 55, 56, 57, 58, 59, 60, 66, 70, 84, 128
explosives, 87
exposure, 1, 13, 14, 23, 30, 47, 83, 91, 120

F

faith, 17, 120
federal courts, 115, 127
federal law, 13, 33, 100

Fifth Amendment, 129
Finland, 34
fission, 9, 10, 15, 100, 101
flexibility, 46, 54
forecasting, 83
fragments, 9
France, 33, 34, 100, 101
fuel management, 56, 88
full capacity, 61
funding, 1, 2, 3, 6, 8, 12, 15, 16, 19, 28, 31, 37, 39, 50, 54, 78, 85, 86, 87, 89, 90, 96, 98, 112, 113, 125

G

General Accounting Office, 21
geography, 56
geology, 8
Georgia, 127
groundwater, 10, 13, 14, 91
guidelines, 13, 18, 103
Gulf Coast, 103

H

hazardous substances, 25, 27
hazards, 12, 46, 48, 106, 113
height, 77
host, 26, 33, 45, 48, 98, 104
human behavior, 13

I

immunity, 122, 123, 124, 132
impacts, 48, 52, 108
incidence, 60
Independence, 19
Indians, 12, 22, 33, 48, 99, 108
inflation, 16, 141
insight, 57
inspections, 31
interest rates, 75, 141
international standards, 14
investors, 35
irradiation, 82, 100
isolation, 4, 9, 10, 35, 38, 82, 87, 92, 105
isotope, 10, 100
issues, vii, 1, 31, 32, 37, 39, 46, 59, 60, 72, 82, 91, 92, 112, 113

J

jurisdiction, 94, 112, 117, 118, 121, 122, 123, 124, 130, 131, 132, 133, 134
justification, 1, 2, 15, 91

Index

L

laboratory tests, 37
land disposal, 106
legality, 125
legislation, 2, 17, 37, 85, 86, 87, 92, 95, 98, 104, 128, 138, 144
legislative proposals, 8, 87
litigation, 26, 36, 40, 46, 51, 53, 104, 111, 112, 113, 117, 119, 120, 125, 127, 129, 131, 134
local community, 47
local government, 13

M

Maine, 17, 69, 118, 130
majority, 128
management, 16, 21, 25, 28, 29, 30, 34, 40, 41, 43, 44, 55, 56, 57, 58, 79, 84, 91, 96, 104, 105, 113, 129, 141
mandates, 113
manufacturing, 138
methodology, 6, 29, 40, 43, 45, 48, 53, 55, 57, 59, 70, 71, 72, 104
Mexico, 10, 67, 96, 106, 109
migration, 91
Monte Carlo method, 76

N

naming, 104
national policy, 27, 100
National Research Council, 4, 21, 22, 67, 68, 70, 83, 108
national security, 36
national strategy, 54
natural disasters, 27
natural gas, 93
natural resources, 33
neutrons, 10, 101
nuclear energy, 27, 35, 87, 134
nuclear power, vii, 1, 3, 4, 5, 7, 10, 11, 12, 16, 18, 28, 31, 35, 40, 47, 52, 65, 82, 83, 85, 86, 87, 88, 89, 92, 93, 94, 98, 104, 111, 112, 113, 114, 115, 127, 129, 138, 139, 140, 142, 143
nuclear program, 94
nuclear weapons, 9, 16, 27, 33, 86, 87, 94, 99, 100, 101, 106, 138
nuclei, 9, 10

O

Obama Administration, 1, 2, 3, 4, 85, 87, 89, 90, 91, 111, 113, 125, 126, 127

obstacles, 15, 86, 92
orbit, 102
Organization for Economic Cooperation and Development, 102, 109
oversight, 83, 96, 108
ownership, 96, 97, 116

P

Pacific, 67, 103, 108, 130, 131
parallel, 54
peer review, 71
penalties, 7, 35, 51, 76, 82, 106
performance, 4, 13, 29, 35, 37, 51, 58, 101, 115, 117, 118, 131, 133
permission, iv
permit, 97
planets, 102
plants, vii, 4, 18, 82, 85, 86, 87, 88, 89, 92, 94, 100, 101, 106, 138, 139, 140, 143
plutonium, 4, 9, 10, 15, 33, 35, 86, 87, 94, 100, 101, 105, 106, 129
policy makers, 54
policy options, 4, 92
political party, 91
pools, 10, 11, 31, 35, 43, 46, 52, 55, 61, 64, 74, 88, 96, 97, 129
power plants, vii, viii, 1, 3, 18, 127, 138, 141
prayer, 123
precedents, 99
predictability, 51
prejudice, 2, 3, 7, 126, 128, 133
preparedness, 114
present value, 26, 28, 29, 34, 38, 45, 49, 53, 55, 70, 71, 72, 75, 76, 77, 82
presidential veto, 98
probability, 11, 77
project, vii, 1, 6, 8, 12, 13, 15, 16, 18, 26, 38, 39, 85, 86, 87, 89, 90, 91, 93, 99, 100, 106, 112, 113, 125, 126, 127, 128, 133, 137, 138, 141
proliferation, 33, 41, 46, 87, 100, 104
property taxes, 46
public health, 30, 46, 83
public interest, 134
public support, 35

R

radiation, 1, 10, 13, 18, 23, 31, 35, 37, 39, 47, 82, 83, 91, 97
Radiation, 23, 66, 67, 68, 70, 107
radioactive isotopes, 4, 87, 100, 103

radioactive waste, vii, 1, 2, 3, 4, 5, 8, 9, 11, 16, 18, 20, 22, 39, 82, 85, 87, 88, 92, 94, 98, 113, 126, 129, 138, 139

radon, 10

ratepayers, 8, 36, 51

reading, 107, 132

reasoning, 117, 122

recommendations, 11, 12, 26, 126

recycling, 9, 15, 20, 21, 34, 92, 100, 101, 117

regulatory framework, 131

relief, 117, 118, 123, 127, 129, 130, 132, 134

repackaging, 42, 49, 52, 53, 64, 65, 71, 74

replacement, 52, 65, 74

reprocessing, 4, 9, 15, 18, 20, 21, 28, 33, 34, 36, 41, 42, 46, 49, 50, 54, 82, 86, 87, 94, 95, 96, 100, 101, 106

requirements, 12, 13, 18, 31, 37, 52, 65, 87, 127, 134

Reservation, Washington, 42

residues, 10, 35

resolution, 4, 21, 48, 90

resources, 22, 36, 37, 102, 139, 140

Richland, 33, 108

rights, 13, 17, 33, 38, 99, 125, 131

rods, 9, 10, 33, 129

Russia, 33

S

sabotage, 11, 52, 95

Sacramento Municipal Utility District, 108

salt domes, 103

screening, 104, 105

Secretary of the Treasury, 139

sediments, 102

Senate, 8, 15, 16, 19, 20, 21, 27, 83, 91, 98, 101, 102, 104, 108, 109, 133

settlements, viii, 5, 6, 40, 111, 112, 115, 127, 129, 138, 142, 143

simulation, 44, 45, 70, 71, 76, 83

software, 44, 71, 83

solar system, 102

space, 15, 31, 33, 92, 101, 102, 142

speculation, 95

state laws, 18

State of the Union address, 127

state regulators, 97

statute, 17, 113, 119, 124, 130, 132, 133

strategy, 2, 12, 18, 28, 31, 41, 46, 50, 54, 100, 101, 120

Supreme Court, 94, 123, 132, 134

Sweden, 34

Switzerland, 34

T

temperature, 9, 47

terrorism, 27

terrorist attacks, 11, 97

terrorists, 33, 52

thorium, 100

time frame, 37, 39, 44, 47, 58, 72, 88, 101

titanium, 35

Title I, 12, 98, 122, 124, 132

Title II, 124, 132

Title IV, 12, 98

Title V, 92

total costs, 40, 44, 50, 70, 71, 76, 77, 78, 127, 140, 141

toxicity, 4, 86

training, 62, 65

transport, 13, 15, 33, 48, 56, 99, 118, 130, 141

transportation, 21, 35, 43, 45, 48, 49, 51, 53, 57, 61, 62, 63, 64, 71, 73, 89, 95, 98, 141

trial, 72, 119, 120, 131

U

U.S. Geological Survey, 66, 68

U.S. Treasury, 5, 83

unforeseen circumstances, 95

uranium, 9, 10, 15, 22, 33, 94, 100, 101, 129, 131

V

veto, 4, 86, 90, 98, 104

vulnerability, 4, 11

W

waiver, 122, 123, 124, 132

waste disposal, vii, 1, 2, 3, 5, 7, 8, 9, 10, 11, 14, 15, 16, 18, 19, 20, 21, 26, 30, 71, 73, 94, 96, 100, 101, 106, 125, 133, 137, 139, 140, 141, 144

waste management, 2, 15, 16, 25, 28, 29, 31, 34, 40, 41, 43, 44, 45, 46, 49, 50, 52, 53, 54, 55, 56, 57, 58, 70, 72, 79, 86, 92, 94, 95, 96, 99, 102, 111, 112

waste treatment, 18, 19

weapons, 4, 33

White House, 126

withdrawal, 2, 3, 8, 16, 90, 126, 128, 133

Z

zirconium, 11, 97